M000251437

150 best
donut
best
recipes

fried or baked

George Geary

Robert
ROSE

150 Best Donut Recipes
Text copyright © 2012 George Geary
Cover, text design and technique photographs copyright © 2012 Robert Rose Inc.
Other photographs copyright © 2012 iStockphoto.com (see details below)

No part of this publication may be reproduced, stored in a retrieval system or transmitted, in any form or by any means, without the prior written consent of the publisher or a license from the Canadian Copyright Licensing Agency (Access Copyright). For an Access Copyright license, visit www.accesscopyright.ca or call toll-free: 1-800-893-5777.

For complete cataloguing information, see page 224.

Disclaimer
The recipes in this book have been carefully tested by our kitchen and our tasters. To the best of our knowledge, they are safe and nutritious for ordinary use and users. For those people with food or other allergies, or who have special food requirements or health issues, please read the suggested contents of each recipe carefully and determine whether or not they may create a problem for you. All recipes are used at the risk of the consumer.

We cannot be responsible for any hazards, loss or damage that may occur as a result of any recipe use.

For those with special needs, allergies, requirements or health problems, in the event of any doubt, please contact your medical adviser prior to the use of any recipe.

Design and production: Daniella Zanchetta/PageWave Graphics Inc.
Editor: Carol Sherman
Recipe Editor: Jennifer MacKenzie
Copy Editor: Karen Campbell-Sheviak
Techniques Photographer: David Shaughnessy
Techniques Stylist: Anne Fisher
Techniques Hand Model: Shannon Knopke

Donut photographs: Light As Air Donuts © iStockphoto.com/Floortje; Fresh Jelly Donuts © iStockphoto.com/Torsten Schon; Applesauce Donuts © iStockphoto.com/Ryan Carter; Mandarin Orange Donuts © iStockphoto.com/ShyMan; Perfect Chocolate–Glazed Donuts © iStockphoto.com/Michael Ballard; Blackout Donuts © iStockphoto.com/Duane Ellison Photography; White Chocolate Crème Donuts © iStockphoto.com/Paul Johnson; Chocolate Cake Donuts © iStockphoto.com/Kathy Dewar; Delicate Dainty Donut Bites with Chocolate Fudge Filling © iStockphoto.com/Teresa Kasprzycka; Boules de Berlin Donuts © iStockphoto.com/Tomo Jesenicnik; Rum-Glazed Donuts © iStockphoto.com/Jack Jelly; All Spiced-Up Bites © iStockphoto.com/Lauri Patterson; Hanukkah Sufganiyot Donuts © iStockphoto.com/Yula Zubritsky; Italian Crème–Filled Donuts © iStockphoto.com/Marek Mnich; French Crullers © iStockphoto.com/C. Gissemann; New Orleans Beignets © iStockphoto.com/Sandra O'Claire

Cover image: donut line © iStockphoto.com/YinYang. Cover recipes (left to right): Orange Yeast Donuts (page 14) with Milk Chocolate Glaze (page 201), Cinnamon Honey Donuts (page 38) and Key Lime Donuts (page 44) with Honey Glaze (page 200).

We acknowledge the financial support of the Government of Canada through the Book Publishing Industry Development Program (BPIDP) for our publishing activities.

Published by Robert Rose Inc.
120 Eglinton Avenue East, Suite 800, Toronto, Ontario, Canada M4P 1E2
Tel: (416) 322-6552 Fax: (416) 322-6936
www.robertrose.ca

Printed and bound in Canada

1 2 3 4 5 6 7 8 9 FP 20 19 18 17 16 15 14 13 12

Contents

● ●

Acknowledgments 4
Introduction 5
Equipment 6
Common Ingredients 9

Making Donuts Step-by-Step 13
Raised Donuts 33
Cake-Based Donuts 61
Baked Donuts 91
Holiday Donuts 119
One-Bite Donuts 141
Specialty Donuts 167
Icings, Glazes and Sugars 195
Fresh Fillings 207

Sources 217
Index 218

Acknowledgments

With each year passing I cherish my parents more and more. To my father for bringing donuts home as a special treat. Mom for making a son very proud. My two sisters for letting me eat more donuts growing up. Neil, my number one supporter, for never saying no when I am in a jam and doing anything and everything to help. I love you for that. Jonathan…If I had the position, I would make you my personal assistant! Sean for keeping my entire computer network going. Starbucks Corona for always having my drink ready and a smile. Erika at Holland America Line for believing in me, putting me on your "Dam" ship, and letting me share my love of food around the world many times over. Bob Dees, my publisher. Thank you for nine great books! Carol Sherman and Jennifer MacKenzie, the best editing and testing team around. I am still in awe of all you both do and in a timely manner. The entire staff at PageWave Graphics, but especially Daniella Zanchetta for making this book a work of art. And, finally, all of my students, and the cooking schools and directors across the globe, for welcoming me into their kitchens.

This book is dedicated to **Renate Edda Bonner**.
You are missed.

Introduction

●●

Donuts. **Just one** word and it explains why I am a pastry chef and author. I loved them as a kid and I enjoy a great donut today. While working on this book I went all over the U.S. locating the prime donut shops of the country. I ate so many great donuts. I saw a trend from coast to coast — gourmet donuts that are fresh and tasty. Now you can create your own.

As you flip through the recipes, you will find many favorites and some brand new flavors. The chapters in this book range from Raised Donuts and Baked Donuts to Specialty and Holiday ones. There's even a One-Bite Donut chapter!

If you've never made a yeast dough before try the Orange Yeast Donut (page 14). This is the recipe that started it all for me in culinary school. Yeast can sometimes be intimidating for the beginner, but with the simple instructions you will become a professional with one try. (There's even easy step-by-step photos for you to follow for many of the techniques.) Baked donuts are as simple as mixing up a cookie batter.

You don't need to get out the mixer and you will learn how to use a resealable bag as a pastry bag. When I was working on the baked donuts I found how simple and easy it was to create so many great flavors that would have been more difficult as a fried donut. In making the baked donuts, you won't have to heat up any oil — just turn on your oven and you are ready to go.

When I was researching donut stores in North America for this book, I kept finding the crazy flavor combination of maple and bacon. It was funny how so many places claimed it as their signature donut. The flavor was sweet and savory and smoky because of the bacon. It really was fantastic! I hope you open your taste buds to a new flavor and try my Maple Bacon Bars (page 184) in the Specialty chapter.

Also, look beyond breakfast time and try some of the mini-donuts for parties, showers or special events. A nice white cake donut with a simple sugar glaze sprinkled with an array of toppings may just fit the bill.

– **George Geary**

Equipment

To **make perfect** donuts at home you don't have to invest in expensive tools and equipment. I guarantee that you probably have most of the items in your kitchen already.

Fryers

What will I fry my donuts in? While working on recipes for this book, I found that a deep-fat fryer was not always the best choice. You do need something to fry in though. I looked for easy cleanup and equipment that was simple to use. Here are a few different choices for you and if you already have one of them, try that before purchasing something new.

Large stainless-steel pot: Use a pot that is at least 7 inches (18 cm) deep to allow for enough oil to fry the donuts and enough space above the oil to prevent spilling. One that is at least 8 inches (20 cm) in diameter will allow you to cook batches of donuts without crowding the pan.

Cast-iron pan: The oil for frying does maintain the temperature in cast iron better than in other items. A cast-iron pan is very heavy, which you already know if you have tried to pick one up when it's full of oil.

Wok: This was my favorite pan to use. It was deep enough to keep the oil hot for a long period of time. I could fry up to 10 donuts at a time and it is light to use. I used a 12-inch (30 cm) size. If using a wok, you may not be able to use the full 4 inches (10 cm) of oil called for in the recipes so just be sure there is enough depth to allow the donuts plenty of room

to float around as well as at least 3 inches (7.5 cm) space above the oil to prevent spills. Look for one with an attached second handle so you can pour the used oil out of the pan more easily when you are done.

Deep-fat fryer: These range in price, size and capacity of oil. Most come with a cover and you can store the fryer with the oil for use at a later date. They come with a dial for you to set to the temperature you want to achieve. I also used a second digital candy/deep-fry thermometer to monitor the heat of the oil. If you enjoy other fried foods such as french fries or fried chicken, a fryer would be a great addition to your appliances.

Stand mixer

Select a stand mixer that's sturdy and comes with a paddle and whip attachments. Professional quality is not essential, but a 6-quart KitchenAid® is a delight to use and takes care of most mixing needs. When mixing the yeast-raised and cake donut recipes here, a mixer is essential.

Food processor

Select a sturdy processor that is large enough to handle the volume of the recipes you use most often. I use an 11-cup Cuisinart® processor.

Donut pans

These are similar to a muffin pan with 6 large or 12 small ring-shaped indentations that look like a donut. I have only seen them with a nonstick coating and dark in color. I always prefer to use nonstick spray even with a nonstick coating to make it easy to release the finished baked donut. Let them cool in the pan on a wire rack for 5 minutes and then flip them over onto the rack to cool completely. If they stick, just use a plastic spatula to get under the donut.

Hand Tools

Try shopping at your local restaurant supply store for your hand tools. You don't have to own a restaurant to shop in most of these stores.

Rubber spatulas

A rubber spatula is the perfect tool for scraping a bowl clean. It also allows for the most thorough mixing of ingredients. The silicone spatulas are heatproof up to 800°F (427°C) and ultra-efficient because they can go from the mixing bowl to the stove top.

Whisks

You will notice that many times I use a whisk to incorporate the dry ingredients instead of sifting. I also like a balloon whisk to blend eggs and other liquids together. Purchase a medium-size whisk with a large balloon.

Liquid measuring cups

The most accurate way to measure liquid ingredients is with a glass measuring cup with a pouring spout. They are widely available in sizes ranging from 1 cup (250 mL) to 8 cups (2 L). Make sure you place the measuring cup on a solid surface and use eye level to see the height of the ingredients. Some brands have angled measuring cups with the markings on the inside so you don't have to bend down. The glass varieties can also be used in the microwave to heat water or melt butter.

Dry measuring cups

The most accurate way to measure dry ingredients is with metal nesting measuring cups. They usually come in sets of four to six cups in sizes ranging from 1/4 cup (60 mL) to 1 cup (250 mL). Spoon the dry ingredients into the appropriate cup and then level off by sliding the flat side of a knife or spatula across the top of the cup. The exceptions are brown sugar and shortening, which need to be packed firmly in the cup for correct measurement.

Measuring spoons

The most accurate measuring spoons are metal. A set of sturdy spoons ranging from 1/8 tsp (0.5 mL) to 1 tbsp (15 mL) is necessary for measuring small amounts of both liquid (such as vanilla extract) and dry ingredients.

Microplane® zester/grater

I always say in my cooking classes that if I had invented the Microplane I would be on a South Pacific island drinking umbrella drinks. A Microplane zester/grater with a handle is the best tool for quickly making zest from lemons or other citrus fruits. It's also great for hard cheeses and chocolate. When using the Microplane, hold the fruit in the palm of your hand, scraping the Microplane across the skin of the fruit and collecting the zest in the top of the zester. Make sure that you only zest the skin once because if you go over the zested skin you will be zesting the white pith, which is bitter.

Rolling pins

There are two main types of rolling pins: with or without handles. I rely on a traditional wooden pin. My favorites are the box or French tapered rolling pins. You use the palm of your hands instead of gripping the handles. The narrower rolling surface on many handled pins is not large enough to roll out your dough.

Pastry bag and tips

A pastry bag fitted with a tip allows you to pipe beautiful garnishes and decorations. It also creates an easy way to inject fillings into donuts.

Pastry bags

I like to use a pastry bag made from poly plastic in a 12- to 16-inch (30 to 40 cm) size. They clean up easily and last for many uses. To wash, take the tip out, wash with warm soapy water inside and out and rinse. Place over the neck of a bottle to air-dry.

Tips

Large French star tips: Perfect for creating beautiful looking filled donuts.

Bismarck tip: It is longer then the normal tip. It's about 2-inches (5 cm) long with a slanted point. It's perfect for filling jelly donuts. You will need to go to a specialty baking supply store or shop online for a Bismarck tip. For Sources, see page 217.

Thermometers

Digital instant-read thermometer: My favorite kind of thermometer. There are many types available these days. I prefer the type you can program to alarm at the exact temperature required and get a very accurate reading. The traditional, analog candy or frying thermometers, which require you to estimate the temperature, aren't as precise. Make sure the thermometer you use has a clip to attach the probe to the side of the pot you're frying in.

Donut cutters

Many cookie cutters can double as a donut cutter. I like using metal cutters because they provide a clean cut from the dough. Cutters come in different sizes and shapes. If you do not have the cutter that is called for in the recipe, you can use a smaller or larger size but you could get a slightly different yield and may have to adjust the frying time. I have a set of round cutters and use two of them — the smaller one for the center of the donut hole instead of the full cutter with the hole because I can use these cutters for other baking needs rather than buying a specialty donut cutter that has the center hole fixed inside the outer ring. You can use the two rounds or the special donut cutter any time "donut cutter" is called for. For recipes calling for "round cutter," "bar cutter" or "square cutter," these don't have the center hole so just use a regular circle, square or rectangle. You can also cut bar or square shapes with a knife or pizza cutter to the size specified.

Wooden chopsticks

I turn the frying donuts over with ease (see Step 11, page 17) with a set of wooden chopsticks. There is less splatter from the oil and you can turn the donuts faster as a few minutes can cause the donuts to burn. Make sure the chopsticks are made of bamboo or wood because plastic will melt.

Slotted spatula

Use a large, slotted spatula to lift the cooked donuts from the oil to allow as much oil as possible to drain from the donut while preventing the donut from breaking.

Common Ingredients

Most recipes in this book contain ingredients that are commonly found in a local supermarket. There are a few special ingredients that I like to use and have included sources for those on page 217.

Dairy Products
Liquid Milk Products

Milk: I prefer to use whole milk in all of the recipes. Lower-fat milk may alter the texture and taste of the final donut.

Cream: There are many different creams on the market under the names that include heavy, whipping, table etc. Make sure you use the liquid cream that you would whip to make whipped cream in all of the recipes here that call for "heavy or whipping (35%) cream." It is normally 35% milk fat (labeled M.F.), but its not always listed on the packaging.

Canned Milks

Evaporated milk: Canned unsweetened milk, from which 60% of the water has been removed. Be sure to purchase the full-fat version for these recipes rather than nonfat (skim) or 2% fat. Unopened cans can be stored at cool room temperature for up to 1 year. Once opened, it must be refrigerated and consumed within 5 to 7 days.

Sweetened condensed milk: Whole milk and sugar is heated until 60% of the water has evaporated. This milk has a sugar content of 40 to 45%. These cans should never been heated unopened in water. Labeling of sweetened condensed milk is different in every country. Make sure you use the exact amount called for in the recipe.

Cream Cheese

Cream cheese is a fresh cheese made from cow's milk and by USDA standards must contain 33% milk fat and no more than 55% moisture to be classified as such.

Light or lower-fat cream cheese has about half the calories of regular cream cheese. Whipped cream cheese, which is soft because it has air whipped into it, has slightly fewer calories. Nonfat cream cheese has no calories from fat and is best used on a bagel or sandwich, not for baking.

Use a name-brand cream cheese. Some of the store brands have added ascorbic gum acids and moisture, which diminish the texture and quality of the baked goods.

Eggs

The recipes in this book were tested using large eggs. Eggs are easier to separate when cold. After separating, allow eggs to come to room temperature before using. Leftover egg whites and yolks will keep for up to 2 days in a covered container in the refrigerator. Both can be frozen as well. Refrigerate eggs in the carton in which they came for up to a month.

If you don't have large eggs, beat the eggs and measure carefully to substitute as follows: One large egg equals about $\frac{1}{4}$ cup (60 mL).

Butter and Oils
Butter

I use unsalted butter throughout the book. Unsalted butter allows me to control the amount of salt in each recipe whereas regular butter that contains salt does not. I suggest that you use name-brand butter and not a store brand one because it may have added moisture.

Oils

I use canola oil to fry donuts. It holds the heat and also helps prevent the donuts from absorbing any aftertastes from the frying. I was able to keep canola oil in a cool, dark place for up to 2 months after the first frying of donuts, depending on the type of donut frying. See page 32 for more about oil and frying.

Flours and Grains
Flour

The sack of flour that you see on the store shelf is a recipe all by itself. Most bakeries have flour mills that create flour to their specifications. I try to always use the flours that are most readily available in major supermarkets.

Hard wheat flour is grown in spring and has a higher protein content than soft wheat, which is grown in winter. The protein in flour is the factor that determines the gluten content.

You may run across many different brands and types. Here are the main flours used in this book:

Whole wheat flour: Light brown in color, it should never be the only flour in your recipe. It is mainly used for breads and dense baked goods.

All-purpose flour: This flour is made from a combination of hard and soft wheats. It has less gluten-forming protein than hard or bread flour. Gluten is what gives the elasticity to your yeast-raised baked products. Unbleached all-purpose flour can be used interchangeably.

Cake flour: Milled from soft wheat with more moisture, it is perfect for pastries when you want less gluten for a more tender product. Cake flour is sometimes hard to find because it is often sold in a box that looks like a cake mix. Look for it close to the biscuit mix.

Nut flours (almond, pecan, hazelnut): These flours can be found in health food stores. You can also make your own with a food processor by adding 10% by volume of all-purpose flour to your toasted nuts. Process until flour-like.

Storing Flours

I place mine in my pantry in a sealed container and store away from the light. I do not use the freezer to store my flours because the added moisture from the freezer can create a different product. If you tend to get bugs in your flour, you're not baking enough!

Sugars

Sugar has many uses besides sweetening. As an ingredient in donut dough, it adds tenderness. It is a natural preservative that allows jelly and jams to have a long shelf life. Heat makes it turn brown, so it adds an attractive color to many baked goods and glazes.

Granulated Sugar

Granulated or white sugar is the more common form of sugar. When it is pulverized, which is easily done in a blender or food processor, it is called superfine sugar. Because superfine sugar melts so quickly, it is used for sweetened cold liquids and in delicate sweets and toppings. When it is crushed to an even finer powder with a bit of cornstarch added, it is called powdered sugar or confectioner's (icing) sugar, which is excellent for icings and glazes.

Brown Sugar

Light and dark brown sugars are created when white sugar is mixed with molasses. The light variety is light in taste, but both have some nutritional value from the molasses, while white sugar has none.

Unless a recipe specifies, you can use either light or dark. Because it is very moist and tends to clump, brown sugar should be packed tight in a measuring cup to get the exact amount required.

Store brown sugar in an airtight container. If the sugar becomes too hard, restore its moisture by placing an apple slice in the container, by warming the sugar in a low oven with a few drops of water for 20 minutes, or by microwaving it at medium (50%) power 20 seconds at a time until softened.

Liquid Sugars

Liquid sugars come in a variety of different flavors and can be used to add sweetness to baked goods and also to glaze tops of donuts. Store in a cool, dry place for the best shelf life.

Honey is made by bees from flower nectar and is a natural sugar, but that doesn't mean it has fewer calories. It actually has a few more. Because it is sweeter, use less honey if substituting it for other liquid sweeteners.

Molasses is made from sugarcane or sugar beet syrup and is available in three varieties: light (fancy), dark (cooking) and blackstrap. Light molasses is typically used as table syrup, while dark molasses provides a distinctive flavor.

Corn syrup is made from the starch of corn and is available in light (white or colorless), golden (in Canada) and dark varieties. Popular in baking, it does not crystallize and it makes baked products brown more quickly than granulated sugar. It's used here in many of the glazes.

Nuts

Nuts provide good nutritional value. They also add flavor and texture to donuts and look great on top of the iced finished donut. I tend to purchase large bags of nuts and vacuum pack the remainder and store in the freezer.

To toast nuts: Preheat oven to 350°F (180°C). Spread nuts on a baking sheet and bake for 6 to 8 minutes, depending on the size of nuts, checking a few times to make sure they don't burn, until golden and fragrant. Allow to cool before chopping or using.

Flavorings and Spices
Vanilla Extracts

Pure vanilla extract is created by soaking vanilla beans in bourbon or vodka and then aging the liquid. The flavor and aroma are unmistakable. Do not scrimp on the quality or delete the vanilla from your recipes. Vanilla enhances all of the other ingredients. Vanilla is the only edible part of a certain species of orchid. (For a list of companies for vanilla extract, see Sources, page 217.) There are three main types of vanilla extracts as listed by region:

Madagascar: For baking, this is by far the best. Whenever vanilla is going to be heated in your baking, use this vanilla.

Mexico: Mexican vanilla beans are good quality (in fact this is where the other vanilla plants stem from originally), however, some vanilla extract sold in Mexico is not real and contains harmful ingredients, even though is it labeled "real." Be cautious when buying vanilla from Mexico and make sure it is genuine. It should state on the packaging that it contains "no coumarin." If the price seems too good to be true, it probably isn't real vanilla. Many companies purchase Mexican beans and produce vanilla outside of Mexico. These are generally good-quality extracts.

Tahiti: For unbaked sweets and desserts such as icings, ice cream and the like. Tahitian vanilla beans tend to have a "flowery" aroma and taste.

Imitation vanilla is created with man-made products and barely resembles what it attempts to imitate. Despite being one-tenth the cost of the real thing, it is not worth substituting for pure vanilla extract.

Extracts and Flavorings

Extracts and flavorings are made by infusing alcohol with the rind of the fruit. They can dissipate if left open and change flavor in heat. You can buy some extracts in supermarkets but for specialty flavors such as cherry and lime you may need to go to a baking supply store or online, see Sources, page 217.

Spices

I tend to purchase all of my spices from a spice store (see Sources, page 217). The spices are fresher, ground in small batches and I like to support the local business owner. Keep spices tightly sealed and store in a cool, dark, dry place. For the best flavor, purchase whole spices and grind them as you need them. Use ground spices within 2 years and whole spices within 3.

Chocolates

I feel chocolate is like wine. Many people enjoy store brands and some only use European varieties. I use a variety of chocolates in my donuts and icings. Only use chocolate chips when it is stated because they react differently in baking. Use block or bars and chop the chocolate up when called for in everything else.

Unsweetened chocolate: Made without sugar, it is pure chocolate liquor that has been cooled and formed into bars

Cocoa powder: Both natural and Dutch-process cocoa powder are available. I prefer to use Dutch-process cocoa powder but it can be harder to find. It is processed with alkali, which neutralizes the cocoa powder's natural acidity. The resulting cocoa powder is darker and richer in color and taste. Often a recipe will only work with natural or Dutch-process but for these donut recipes I found you can use them interchangeably with success.

Semisweet and bittersweet chocolate: These chocolates can be used interchangeably in most recipes without any change to the outcome other than taste. Bittersweet must contain at least 35% chocolate liquor. Semisweet must contain at least 15 to 35% chocolate liquor.

Milk chocolate: It must contain at least 10% chocolate liquor and 12% milk solids.

Making Donuts Step-by-Step

Orange Yeast Donuts...14

   Making Raised Donuts..................................16

Lemon Mist Donuts 18

   Making Cake-Based Donuts 19

Apple Spice Donuts..20

   Making Baked Donuts 21

Fresh Jelly Donuts 22

   Making Filled (injected) Donuts 23

Anjou Pear Fritters..24

   Making Fritters..25

Island Bites 26

   Making One-Bite Donuts............................27

Honey-Glazed Bow Ties 28

   Making Bow Ties 29

Twisted Praline Pecan New Orleans Donuts 30

   Making Twists...31

Orange Yeast Donuts

**Makes about
12 donuts**

When I was in pastry
school we learned how
to make these light,
airy donuts. I enjoy the
subtle orange taste that
is not overpowering.

Finishing suggestions

Icings: Honey Glaze
(page 200), Maple Glaze
(page 201), Milk Chocolate
Glaze (page 201), Orange
Glaze (page 202) or Sunset
Orange Glaze (page 204).

- Stand mixer with paddle attachment
- 3-inch (7.5 cm) round donut cutter
- Baking sheet, lined with parchment paper
- Digital candy/deep-fry thermometer

¾ cup + 1 tbsp	whole milk, warmed to 110°F (43°C)	190 mL
1	package (¼ oz/8 g) quick-rising (instant) yeast	1
2	egg whites	2
2 tbsp	canola oil	30 mL
1 tsp	orange extract	5 mL
2¾ cups	all-purpose flour, divided (approx.)	675 mL
1 tbsp	granulated sugar	15 mL
⅛ tsp	salt	0.5 mL
	Canola oil	

1. In mixer bowl, sprinkle yeast over milk and stir with a fork. Let stand until foamy, about 5 minutes.

2. Attach bowl to mixer fitted with paddle attachment and add egg whites, oil, orange extract, 1 cup (250 mL) of the flour, sugar and salt to yeast mixture. Let stand in bowl for 10 minutes. On low speed, mix just until blended, then gradually add just enough of the remaining flour until dough starts to pull away from sides of bowl. Increase speed to medium and beat for 1 minute.

3. Transfer dough to a large oiled bowl and cover with plastic wrap. Let rise in a warm, draft-free place until doubled in volume, about 30 minutes.

4. On a floured work surface, roll out dough to slightly thicker than ¼ inch (0.5 cm). If dough is tacky, dust with additional flour. Cut dough with cutter into 12 donuts, re-rolling scraps as necessary. Place at least 1 inch (2.5 cm) apart on prepared baking sheet. Cover with a clean kitchen towel and let rise for 20 minutes.

Tip

When you are making ring-shaped donuts you may like to fry up the center holes for a treat. Depending on the size of the hole, your frying time will have to be adjusted since they tend to fry faster. I sometimes like to test a donut hole just to see how the flavor of the donut is and what icing I will want to dress it with.

5. Meanwhile, in a large, deep pot or deep fryer, heat about 4 inches (10 cm) oil over medium heat until temperature registers 360°F (182°C). Deep-fry 4 donuts at a time in hot oil, turning once with wooden chopsticks, until golden brown, about 15 seconds per side. Using a slotted spoon, transfer to paper towels to absorb excess oil. Fry remaining donuts, adjusting heat as necessary between batches to maintain oil temperature.

6. Let donuts cool completely prior to icing.

*Step-by-step techniques
on next page...*

See the step-by-step photographs on photo pages A1 and A2. ▼

Making Raised Donuts

1. Once the yeast is foamy, add the egg(s), flavoring ingredients, a portion of the flour and oil (or butter) called for. Let it stand for 10 minutes to help the yeast continue to ferment before mixing the dough which helps dough rise. Mix the yeast and dough ingredients on low speed until they are just incorporated (the mixture will be quite sticky at this stage).

2. With the mixer running on low, gradually add more of the remaining flour to incorporate just enough flour to make a soft dough that isn't sticky. Be careful not to add too much, which would cause the dough to be dry. The amount of flour you need will vary depending on the room temperature and humidity in the air and the flour you are using.

3. Once enough flour is incorporated, the dough will be dry enough to leave the sides of the mixer bowl clean without any bits of dough sticking to it. It should hold together yet feel soft but not sticky when you gently squeeze it.

4. Place the dough in an oiled bowl (so it comes out easily), cover with plastic wrap and let it rise in a warm, draft-free place until it is doubled in volume. This should take about 30 minutes but may take longer in cool, dry weather.

5. Dump the fully risen dough out onto a large surface dusted with flour for rolling. Press dough with your hands to flatten the dough, removing any large air bubbles that have formed during rising, to make it easier to roll.

6. Use a French tapered or box rolling pin (see page 7) to roll out the dough. While rolling, dust the surface under the dough, the top of the dough and the pin with just enough flour to prevent it from sticking. Try not to add too much flour as this can make the donuts dry. Roll the dough so it's just slightly thicker than $\frac{1}{4}$ inch (0.5 cm), but not quite $\frac{1}{2}$ inch (1 cm) thick and even thickness all the way across.

7. Dip the cutting edge of the cutter in flour and start cutting out donuts around the edges of the dough. Press firmly, straight down, to cut the dough. Cut around the edge of the dough first, then cut donuts from the center, being careful not to overlap any previously cut donuts. Dip the cutter in flour as necessary to keep the dough from sticking.

8. Lift cut donuts from rolling surface with an offset palate knife or your fingers and place them on a baking sheet lined with parchment paper leaving at least 1 inch (2.5 cm) between the donuts. Leaving room between the donuts allows room for rising and makes it easier to lift the donuts off the sheet after they've risen.

9. After 20 minutes, the donuts should look slightly puffy but they won't have gotten much larger.

10. Heat the oil while the donuts are rising, checking the temperature with a digital candy/deep-fry thermometer (see page 8). To safely add the donuts to the oil, hold the donut in your hand close to the surface of the oil, then gently release the donut into the oil, letting it slip into the oil without splashing. Remember the oil is very hot so keep your fingers away from the surface and don't drop the donut too quickly — the oil can splash and burn.

11. When the bottom is golden and the donut is puffed, use two wooden chopsticks to flip donuts in oil to cook the second side. The chopsticks are easy to handle, won't crush the donuts and help prevent the oil from splashing as can happen when you use a large spoon or spatula.

12. Use a slotted spatula to lift cooked donuts from the oil, allowing as much oil to drain off as possible, while working quickly so remaining donuts don't get overcooked. The paper towel on the baking sheet will absorb excess oil, preventing donuts from being greasy. Be sure to leave space between the donuts to allow air circulation and prevent them from steaming. If using a sugar or dust, toss the donuts when warm. If icing and/or filling, let the donuts cool completely on the paper towel.

Lemon Mist Donuts

● ●

**Makes about
18 donuts**

This donut is a light
and flavorful cake donut
with zesty taste.

● ● ● ● ● ● ● ● ● ● ● ● ● ● ● ● ● ●

Finishing suggestions

Icing: Citrus Sugar
(page 205).

Filling (cut donuts in
half): Lemon Zest Filling
(page 213).

● Stand mixer with paddle attachment
● Digital candy/deep-fry thermometer
● 5- by 2-inch (12.5 by 5 cm) bar cutter, optional
● Baking sheet, lined with parchment paper

1½ cups	cake flour	375 mL
1 cup	all-purpose flour, divided	250 mL
2 tsp	baking powder	10 mL
1 tsp	salt	5 mL
½ tsp	baking soda	2 mL
1 cup	granulated sugar	250 mL
2	large eggs, beaten	2
1	large egg yolk, beaten	1
¼ cup	whole milk	60 mL
¼ cup	unsalted butter, melted and cooled	60 mL
2 tsp	grated lemon zest	10 mL
1 tbsp	freshly squeezed lemon juice	15 mL
	Canola oil	

1. In a bowl, whisk together cake flour, ½ cup (125 mL) of the all-purpose flour, baking powder, salt and baking soda. Set aside.

2. In mixer bowl fitted with paddle attachment, combine sugar, eggs, egg yolk, milk, butter, lemon zest and juice. On low speed, mix until well combined. Add dry ingredients and mix until incorporated. Gradually mix in more of the flour, as necessary, until dough starts to come together and is the consistency of biscuit dough. Cover and refrigerate for 10 minutes.

3. Meanwhile, in a large, deep pot or deep fryer, heat about 4 inches (10 cm) oil over medium heat until temperature registers 360°F (182°C).

4. On a floured work surface, roll out dough to slightly thicker than ¼ inch (0.5 cm). If dough is tacky, dust with additional flour. Cut dough with cutter into 18 donuts (or cut with a knife or pizza cutter into 5- by 2-inch/12.5 by 5 cm rectangles), re-rolling scraps as necessary. Place at least 1 inch (2.5 cm) apart on prepared baking sheet.

5. Deep-fry 4 donuts at a time in hot oil, turning once with wooden chopsticks, until golden brown,

about 25 seconds per side. Using a slotted spatula, transfer to paper towels to absorb excess oil. Fry remaining donuts, adjusting heat as necessary between batches to maintain oil temperature.

See the step-by-step photographs on photo page B. ▼

6. Toss warm donuts with Citrus Sugar, if using. Let cool completely and fill with Lemon Zest Filling, if desired.

Making Cake-Based Donuts

1. Use the mixer on low speed to combine the dry ingredients with the wet ingredients just until you can no longer see any dry ingredients.

2. Gradually mix in just enough flour to prevent the dough from being sticky without making it too dry. It should resemble a biscuit dough for nice, tender donuts. Adding too much flour can make the donuts crumbly. Cover and refrigerate for 10 minutes to chill the dough slightly making it easier to roll out.

3. Use a French or box rolling pin (see page 7) to roll out the dough into a rough rectangle to make it easier to cut bar shapes. While rolling, dust the surface under the dough, the top of the dough and the pin with just enough flour to prevent it from sticking. Try not to add too much flour as this can make the donuts dry. Roll the dough so it's just slightly thicker than $\frac{1}{4}$ inch (0.5 cm), but not quite $\frac{1}{2}$ inch (1 cm) thick and even thickness all the way across.

4. Dip the cutting edge of bar-shaped cutter in flour, start at one edge of the dough and press firmly, straight down, to cut the dough. Dip the cutter in flour as necessary to keep the dough from sticking. If you don't have a bar-shaped cutter you can use a pizza cutter or knife and a ruler to cut the rectangles.

5. To cut donuts for filling, hold a serrated knife in one hand and place the other hand on top of one bar lengthwise to hold it in place. Place the knife horizontally along the center of one long side of the donut and use a gentle sawing motion to slice donut, almost, but not all the way across, leaving a "hinge" at the opposite long edge (or cut all the way through if specified in the recipe).

6. Hold the "lid" of the donut in one hand and open the donut at the cut without separating it at the hinge. Hold the filled pastry bag in the other hand and pipe cream onto bottom of cut donut, covering evenly while leaving a small border around the edge without filling. Gently replace the lid of the donut, squeezing just enough to close without squishing out the cream.

Apple Spice Donuts

Just like a piece of apple pie, but in a donut.

Finishing suggestions

Icings: Honey Glaze (page 200) or Simple Sugar Glaze (page 205).

Fillings (cut donuts in half): Bavarian Cream Custard (page 209) or Banana Cream Filling (page 208).

- Preheat oven to 325°F (160°C)
- Two 6-well donut pans, sprayed with nonstick spray

2½ cups	cake flour	625 mL
1 cup	granulated sugar	250 mL
2½ tsp	baking powder	12 mL
2 tsp	ground cinnamon	10 mL
1 tsp	freshly ground nutmeg	5 mL
½ tsp	salt	2 mL
2	large eggs, beaten	2
¾ cup	whole milk	175 mL
2 tbsp	canola oil	30 mL
1 tsp	vanilla extract	5 mL
1½ cups	finely chopped apples	375 mL

1. In a large bowl, whisk together flour, sugar, baking powder, cinnamon, nutmeg and salt. Set aside.

2. In another bowl, whisk together eggs, milk, oil and vanilla. Add to flour mixture and mix with a rubber spatula just until incorporated. Fold in apples.

3. Spoon batter into resealable freezer bag or pastry bag (see page 8) and fill each prepared well two-thirds full.

4. Bake in preheated oven until donut springs back when lightly touched, 10 to 14 minutes.

5. Let donuts cool in pans on a rack for 5 minutes. Turn out of pans onto rack and let cool completely prior to icing and/or filling.

See the step-by-step photographs on photo page C. ▶

Making Baked Donuts

1. Use a whisk to easily and thoroughly incorporate the dry ingredients together.

2. Whisk the wet ingredients thoroughly until evenly blended. You don't need to whisk until foamy or thick.

3. Pour the wet ingredients into the dry ingredients and use a rubber spatula to combine the two mixtures just until you can't see any traces of dry. Avoid overmixing to keep the donuts tender. When adding fruit or other flavoring ingredients, use the spatula to gently fold into the batter just until they are evenly distributed.

4. To easily and neatly transfer the batter to the pan, set a resealable freezer bag or pastry bag in a tall glass (this holds the bag while you fill it), then pour the batter into the bag. Be careful not to get any batter on the resealable seam of the bag.

5. Squeeze the batter into one corner of the bag, removing all of the air pockets, then cut off the corner of the bag, if necessary, to make a hole about ¾ inch (2 cm) wide. If using a pastry bag you may not need a tip if the hole is the right size. If you do need a tip, use a large plain tip.

6. Pipe the batter into the sprayed donut pan. Fill each well about two-thirds full of batter, being sure to fill each with the same amount of batter so they bake evenly. You want to leave enough room for the donuts to rise. If you fill the wells too much, the batter will flow across the center and fill in where there should be a hole.

Fresh Jelly Donuts

I love to overfill this donut with fresh jelly. When you take the first bite the jelly squirts out!

Finishing suggestions

Icings: Honey Glaze (page 200).

Variations

Fillings (injected): Instead of the Raspberry Filling, try Fresh Cherry Filling (page 211), Lemon Zest Filling (page 213) or Strawberry Filling (page 214).

Topping: Dust with confectioner's (icing) sugar.

- Stand mixer with paddle attachment
- 4-inch (10 cm) round cutter
- Baking sheet, lined with parchment paper
- Digital candy/deep-fry thermometer

¾ cup + 1 tbsp	whole milk, warmed to 110°F (43°C)	190 mL
1	package (¼ oz/8 g) quick-rising (instant) yeast	1
1	large egg	1
1	egg white	1
2 tbsp	unsalted butter, melted	30 mL
1 tsp	vanilla extract	5 mL
2¾ cups	all-purpose flour, divided (approx.)	675 mL
1 tbsp	granulated sugar	15 mL
⅛ tsp	salt	0.5 mL
	Canola oil	
	Raspberry Filling (Variation, page 214)	

1. In mixer bowl, sprinkle yeast over milk and stir with a fork. Let stand until foamy, about 5 minutes.

2. Attach bowl to mixer fitted with paddle attachment and add egg, egg white, butter, vanilla, 1 cup (250 mL) of the flour, sugar and salt to yeast mixture. Let stand in bowl for 10 minutes. On low speed, mix just until blended, then gradually add just enough of the remaining flour until dough starts to pull away from sides of bowl. Increase speed to medium and beat for 1 minute.

3. Transfer dough to a large oiled bowl and cover with plastic wrap. Let rise in a warm, draft-free place until doubled in volume, about 30 minutes.

4. On a floured work surface, roll out dough to slightly thicker than ¼ inch (0.5 cm). If dough is tacky, dust with additional flour. Cut dough with cutter into 12 donuts, re-rolling scraps as necessary. Place at least 1 inch (2.5 cm) apart on prepared baking sheet. Cover with a clean kitchen towel and let rise for 20 minutes.

5. Meanwhile, in a large, deep pot or deep fryer, heat about 4 inches (10 cm) oil over medium heat until temperature registers 360°F (182°C). Deep-fry 4 donuts

at a time in hot oil, turning once with wooden chopsticks, until golden brown, about 15 seconds per side. Using a slotted spoon, transfer to paper towels to absorb excess oil. Fry remaining donuts, adjusting heat as necessary between batches to maintain oil temperature.

6. Let donuts cool completely and then fill with jelly using a pastry bag fitted with Bismarck or plain tip (see page 8). If desired, ice with the glaze or dust with sugar.

See the step-by-step photographs on photo page D. ▼

Making Filled (injected) Donuts

1. Use a French tapered or box rolling pin (see page 7) to roll out the dough. While rolling, dust the surface under the dough, the top of the dough and the pin with just enough flour to prevent it from sticking. Try not to add too much flour as this can make the donuts dry. Roll the dough so it's just slightly thicker than $\frac{1}{4}$ inch (0.5 cm), but not quite $\frac{1}{2}$-inch (1 cm) thick and even thickness all the way across.

2. Dip the cutting edge of the cutter in flour and start cutting out donuts around the edges of the dough. Press firmly, straight down, to cut the dough. Cut around the edge of the dough first, then cut donuts from the center, being careful not to overlap any previously cut donuts. Dip the cutter in flour as necessary to keep the dough from sticking.

3. Let the fried donuts cool completely on baking sheets lined with paper towel. The paper towel absorbs the excess oil and prevents the donuts from being greasy. Make sure they're completely cool to avoid gummy filled donuts.

4. Fit a pastry bag with a Bismarck tip (see page 8), which pokes a hole in the donut, allowing the filling to be injected. If you don't have a Bismarck tip, use a medium-size star tip.

5. To fill donuts, hold the donut in one hand and the filled pastry bag in the other. Insert the tip in center of the donut on the side and, using gentle pressure, squeeze the filling into the donut. You'll know the donut is getting full when it feels heavier. Avoid squeezing too forcefully or quickly to prevent the filling from breaking through the donut walls.

6. After filling donuts, place them on a plate. For a final garnish, place confectioner's sugar in a fine sieve and shake over donuts. Serve promptly.

Anjou Pear Fritters

Makes about 12 donuts

Pump your donuts up a notch by including fresh pears in the dough.

Finishing suggestions

Icings: Autumn Spiced Sugar (page 204), Honey Glaze (page 200) or Simple Sugar Glaze (page 205).

- Stand mixer with paddle attachment
- Baking sheet, lined with parchment paper
- Digital candy/deep-fry thermometer

¾ cup	whole milk, warmed to 110°F (43°C)	175 mL
1	package (¼ oz/8 g) quick-rising (instant) yeast	1
2	large egg whites	2
2 tbsp	canola oil	30 mL
1 tsp	vanilla extract	5 mL
2¾ cups	all-purpose flour, divided (approx.)	675 mL
2 tbsp	granulated sugar	30 mL
⅛ tsp	salt	0.5 mL
2	medium Anjou pears, peeled and diced	2
	Canola oil	

1. In mixer bowl, sprinkle yeast over milk and stir with a fork. Let stand until foamy, about 5 minutes.

2. Attach bowl to mixer fitted with paddle attachment and add egg whites, oil, vanilla, 1 cup (250 mL) of the flour, sugar and salt to yeast mixture. Let stand in bowl for 10 minutes. On low speed, mix just until blended, then gradually add just enough of the remaining flour until dough starts to pull away from sides of bowl. Increase speed to medium and beat for 1 minute.

3. Turn dough out onto a floured work surface. Knead in diced pears with your hands until evenly distributed. (Additional flour may be needed, depending on the juice of the fresh pears. Add just enough to keep dough from getting sticky.)

4. Transfer dough to a large oiled bowl and cover with plastic wrap. Let rise in a warm, draft-free place until doubled in volume, about 30 minutes.

5. On a floured work surface, press dough out to a rectangle, about 12 by 8 inches (30 by 20 cm) and to ¾-inch (2 cm) thickness. Cut dough into 12 equal rectangles and press edges to neaten. Place at least 1 inch (2.5 cm) apart on prepared baking sheet. Cover with a clean kitchen towel and let rise for 20 minutes.

6. Meanwhile, in a large, deep pot or deep fryer, heat about 4 inches (10 cm) oil over medium heat until temperature registers 360°F (182°C). Deep-fry 4 donuts at a time in hot oil, turning once with wooden chopsticks until golden brown, about 30 seconds per side (the donuts will sink to the bottom of the fryer and then float to the top). Using a slotted spoon, transfer to paper towels to absorb excess oil. Fry remaining donuts, adjusting heat as necessary between batches to maintain oil temperature.

See the step-by-step photographs on photo page E. ▼

7. Toss warm fritters in Autumn Spiced Sugar, if using, or let fritters cool completely prior to icing.

Making Fritters

1. Dump the risen dough onto a floured work surface. Pat dough out with your hands into a rectangle, about 12 by 8 inches (30 by 20 cm) and to ¾-inch (2 cm) thickness.

2. Fritters are a less uniform shape than donuts cut with a shaped cutter. Use a bench scraper or knife and cut the rectangle in half lengthwise. Next, cut rectangle in half crosswise, then cut each half crosswise twice to make 12 equal rectangles.

3. With the sides of your hands, press the top edges of dough downward so you get tight mounds that are the size of a small loaf and you do not see any cut edges. This keeps the fritters more uniform looking when fried.

4. Cover the fritters with a clean, lint-free towel. A towel won't stick to the donuts as plastic wrap tends to do. Let them rise in a warm, draft-free place for 20 minutes. This allows them to get slightly puffier, making the fritters airy and tender.

5. To transfer the fritters to the oil, place one fritter on a slotted spatula, then lower the spatula into the hot oil, allowing the fritter to float off the spatula. This prevents the oil from splashing and helps keep the fritter from losing its shape.

6. To coat fritters in Autumn Spiced Sugar, as soon as you're finished frying all of the fritters and while they are still warm but cool enough to handle them safely, toss one fritter at a time in a bowl of the sugar to evenly coat. Gently shake off excess sugar then place fritters on a wire rack set over a baking sheet and let them cool.

Island Bites

**Makes about
24 donuts**

These macadamia nut donut bites are packed with flavor that will make you dance the hula.

Finishing suggestions

Icing: Honey Glaze (page 200).

Fillings (injected): White Chocolate Macadamia Mousse Filling (page 216).

Topping: Dust with confectioner's (icing) sugar.

- Food processor
- Stand mixer with paddle attachment
- 2-inch (5 cm) round cutter
- Baking sheet, lined with parchment paper
- Digital candy/deep-fry thermometer

¾ cup + 1 tbsp	whole milk, warmed to 110°F (43°C)	190 mL
1	package (¼ oz/8 g) quick-rising (instant) yeast	1
1¾ cups	all-purpose flour (approx.)	425 mL
1½ cups	macadamia nuts	375 mL
1 tbsp	granulated sugar	15 mL
⅛ tsp	salt	0.5 mL
1	large egg	1
1	large egg white	1
2 tbsp	unsalted butter, softened	30 mL
1 tsp	vanilla extract	5 mL
	Canola oil	

1. In mixer bowl, sprinkle yeast over milk and stir with a fork. Let stand until foamy, about 5 minutes.

2. In food processor fitted with metal blade, combine flour, macadamia nuts, sugar and salt and process for 15 seconds or until nuts are finely ground. Set aside.

3. Attach bowl to mixer fitted with paddle attachment and add egg, egg white, butter, vanilla and 1 cup (250 mL) of the flour mixture to the yeast mixture. Let stand in bowl for 10 minutes. On low speed, mix just until blended, then gradually add just enough of the remaining flour until dough starts to pull away from sides of bowl. Increase speed to medium and beat for 1 minute.

4. Transfer dough to a large oiled bowl and cover with plastic wrap. Let rise in a warm, draft-free place until doubled in volume, about 30 minutes.

5. Turn dough out onto a floured work surface. Roll out dough to slightly thicker than ¼ inch (0.5 cm). If dough is tacky, dust with additional flour. Cut dough with cutter into 24 donuts, re-rolling scraps as necessary. Place at least 1 inch (2.5 cm) apart on prepared baking sheet. Cover with a clean kitchen towel and let rise for 20 minutes.

6. Meanwhile, in a large, deep pot or deep fryer, heat about 4 inches (10 cm) oil over medium heat until temperature registers 360°F (182°C). Deep-fry 6 donuts at a time in hot oil, turning once with wooden chopsticks, until golden brown, about 15 seconds per side. Using a slotted spoon, transfer to paper towels to absorb excess oil. Fry remaining donuts, adjusting heat as necessary between batches to maintain oil temperature.

7. Let donuts cool completely prior to icing, filling or topping.

See the step-by-step photographs on photo page F. ▼

Making One-Bite Donuts

1. Fry about 6 donuts at a time in the hot oil. Depending on the diameter of your pot, you may only be able to fry 4 or 5 at a time to avoid crowding. It's important that there is plenty of room for the donuts to float in the oil without sticking together. As well, adding too many at a time can cool down the oil, causing greasy donuts.

2. Once the donuts are cooked, remove them with a slotted spoon 2, or even 3, at a time to get them out of the oil quickly and prevent the donuts from overcooking. This is important any time you're cooking more donuts in a batch.

3. To fill donuts, hold the donut in one hand and the filled pastry bag fitted with a Bismarck tip in the other. Insert the tip in center of the donut on the side and using gentle pressure, squeeze the filling into the donut. You'll know the donut is getting full when it feels heavier. Avoid squeezing too forcefully or quickly to prevent the filling from breaking through the donut walls.

4. To glaze donuts, let them cool completely, making the glaze while they cool. Using two fingers to hold the donut, dip one at a time, into glaze submerging completely to fully coat. Lift out of the glaze and gently shake excess glaze off.

5. Immediately after dipping donuts into the glaze, place them on a wire rack set over a baking sheet. This allows any excess glaze to drip off onto the sheet, rather than pooling under the donut, and lets the donut dry evenly and efficiently.

6. Instead of glazing the donuts, you can roll donuts in confectioner's (icing) sugar. After filling donuts, place confectioner's sugar in a bowl and roll donuts in the sugar. Serve promptly.

Honey-Glazed Bow Ties

Makes about 18 donuts

This larger donut is in the shape of a bow tie.

Finishing suggestions

Icing: Honey Glaze (page 200).

- Stand mixer with paddle attachment
- 4-inch (10 cm) round donut cutter
- Baking sheet, lined with parchment paper
- Digital candy/deep-fry thermometer

1½ cups	whole milk, warmed to 110°F (43°C)	375 mL
2	packages (each ¼ oz/8 g) quick-rising (instant) yeast	2
1	large egg	1
2	egg whites	2
¼ cup	unsalted butter, softened	60 mL
2 tbsp	canola oil	30 mL
2 tsp	vanilla extract	10 mL
5¼ cups	all-purpose flour, divided (approx.)	1.3 L
2 tbsp	granulated sugar	30 mL
¼ tsp	salt	1 mL
	Canola oil	

1. In mixer bowl, sprinkle yeast over milk and stir with a fork. Let stand until foamy, about 5 minutes.

2. Attach bowl to mixer fitted with paddle attachment and add egg, egg whites, butter, oil, vanilla, 2 cups (500 mL) of the flour, sugar and salt to yeast mixture. Let stand in bowl for 10 minutes. On low speed, mix just until blended, then gradually add just enough of the remaining flour until dough starts to pull away from sides of bowl. Increase speed to medium and beat for 1 minute.

3. Divide dough into two equal pieces. Transfer dough to two large oiled bowls and cover with plastic wrap. Let rise in a warm, draft-free place until doubled in volume, about 30 minutes.

4. On a floured work surface, working with one piece at a time, roll out dough to slightly thicker than ¼ inch (0.5 cm). If dough is tacky, dust with additional flour. Cut dough with cutter into 18 donuts, re-rolling scraps as necessary. Working with one donut at a time, stretch the ring to an oval about 4 inches (10 cm) long. Twist into a figure eight and press the center so the two layers of dough stick together, creating a "bow tie." Place at least 1 inch (2.5 cm) apart on prepared baking sheet. Cover with a clean kitchen towel and let rise for 20 minutes.

5. Meanwhile, in a large, deep pot or deep fryer, heat about 4 inches (10 cm) oil over medium heat until temperature registers 360°F (182°C). Deep-fry 3 donuts at a time in hot oil, turning once with wooden chopsticks, until golden brown, about 15 seconds per side. Using a slotted spoon, transfer to paper towels to absorb excess oil. Fry remaining donuts, adjusting heat as necessary between batches to maintain oil temperature.

6. Let donuts cool completely prior to icing.

See the step-by-step photographs on photo page G. ▶

Making Bow Ties

1. Start a bow tie by cutting regular ring-shaped donuts. Use your fingers to gently stretch the ring of dough to an oval about 4 inches (10 cm) long.

2. Hold each end of the oval between your fingers, then rotate one hand away from you and the other hand toward you to twist the ring into a figure eight. Place on the parchment-lined baking sheet and gently press at the center to seal the two layers of dough together to help hold the bow tie shape. If the dough is not sticking together, brush any excess flour off and brush with a little water.

Twisted Praline Pecan New Orleans Donuts

**Makes about
12 donuts**

A donut shop opened in the Big Easy called Blue Dot Donuts. It's owned by city police officers and they have so many great flavors, such as this one.

Finishing suggestions
Icing: Honey Glaze (page 200).

- Stand mixer with paddle attachment
- Pizza cutter
- Baking sheet, lined with parchment paper
- Digital candy/deep-fry thermometer

¾ cup	whole milk, warmed to 110°F (43°C)	175 mL
1	package (¼ oz/8 g) quick-rising (instant) yeast	1
1	large egg	1
2 tbsp	unsalted butter, melted	30 mL
1 tsp	vanilla extract	5 mL
2¾ cups	all-purpose flour, divided (approx.)	675 mL
2 tbsp	granulated sugar	30 mL
½ tsp	salt	2 mL
¼ cup	packed brown sugar	60 mL
¼ cup	chopped pecans	60 mL
1½ tsp	ground cinnamon	7 mL
½ tsp	freshly ground nutmeg	2 mL
	Canola oil	

1. In mixer bowl, sprinkle yeast over milk and stir with a fork. Let stand until foamy, about 5 minutes.

2. Attach bowl to mixer fitted with paddle attachment and add egg, butter, vanilla, 1 cup (250 mL) of the flour, granulated sugar and salt to yeast mixture. Let stand in bowl for 10 minutes. On low speed, mix just until blended, then add just enough of the remaining flour until dough starts to pull away from sides of bowl. Increase speed to medium and beat for 1 minute.

3. Transfer dough to a large oiled bowl and cover with plastic wrap. Let rise in a warm, draft-free place until doubled in volume, about 30 minutes.

4. Meanwhile in a small bowl, combine brown sugar, pecans, cinnamon and nutmeg. Set aside.

5. Turn dough out onto a floured work surface. Roll out to a rectangle about 24 by 18 inches (60 by 45 cm) and about ¼ inch (0.5 cm) thick with one long side closest to you. If dough is tacky, dust with additional flour.

Sprinkle pecan mixture on top. Starting with one short side, fold dough in half from left to right. Cut dough lengthwise with a pizza cutter into 12 strips, about 1 inch (2.5 cm) thick. Fold each strip in half and twist. Place at least 1 inch (2.5 cm) apart on prepared baking sheet. Cover with a clean kitchen towel and let rise for 20 minutes.

6. Meanwhile, in a large, deep pot or deep fryer, heat about 4 inches (10 cm) oil over medium heat until temperature registers 360°F (182°C). Deep-fry 3 donuts at a time in hot oil, turning once with wooden chopsticks, until golden brown, about 15 seconds per side. Using a slotted spatula, transfer to paper towels to absorb excess oil. Fry remaining donuts, adjusting heat as necessary between batches to maintain oil temperature.

7. Let donuts cool completely prior to icing.

See the step-by-step photographs on photo page G. ▼

Making Twists

1. Sprinkle the pecan mixture as evenly as possible over the rolled dough right to the edges.

2. Hold the dough at two corners of one short edge of the rectangle and quickly fold in half toward opposite short edge (like folding a book) to enclose the pecan filling between two layers of dough. Gently press the two layers together.

3. Now use a pizza cutter to cut the rectangle lengthwise into strips. To get strips of even width, start by cutting the rectangle in half lengthwise, then cut each side in half so you have 4 wide strips. Next, cut each strip twice to make 3 strips from each, making a total of 12 equal strips. Between cuts, dip the edge in flour as necessary to prevent the blade from sticking to the dough.

4. Hold a strip at one short side and fold in half toward opposite short side and flatten (so you have 4 layers of dough and 2 of pecan filling). Next, hold one end of the folded strip with each hand and rotate one hand away from you and the other hand toward you, twisting the strip twice. Place on a baking sheet lined with parchment paper and gently press down on twist to help hold the shape.

Deep-Frying Tips for Donut Making

When making donuts or any fried foods, safety is the number one factor. When you decide which pot or vessel you will be using to make your donuts, test it out by adding water first to the desired depth. Then measure that water so you know how much oil you will need. Leave at least 2 to 3 inches (5 to 7.5 cm) above the surface of the oil to allow room for bubbling up and also so the oil won't splatter when you turn the donuts. Never leave the vessel with the oil heating unattended. In a matter of seconds the oil could create a fire. Make sure you have a kitchen fire extinguisher always close by no matter what you are making. Also, have a lid the size of the vessel handy to smother any flame ups.

The oil I used throughout the book was canola. It is consistent and gives a better crust on the fried donut. The oil also lasted longer than others I worked with. When you are making donuts and want to use the oil a second or third time, brush the excess flour from the donut prior to frying because the flour is what causes the oil to get cloudy and give off a burnt taste.

Make sure your temperature is accurate because if the oil is not hot enough your donut may be gummy or raw in the middle, or if the temperature is too hot the sides of the donuts will be burnt. Make sure you check the temperature after each batch of donuts, adjusting the heat higher or lower. When you place your raw donuts into the oil the temperature will drop so watch it.

After the oil has completely cooled down, strain out the bits of donuts left and place back into the container. (Make sure the oil is completely cold or it will melt the plastic container.) When you pour the oil back in you will be able to see the color and the aroma. I judge the oil by the taste too, so put a little on your finger and see if it has a pleasant taste. If so you can store it for about 3 to 4 weeks. Again, prior to use taste again. You do not want to use oil that has gone rancid. Finding this out after you have fried a new batch of donuts would be upsetting.

Making Raised Donuts

(see pages 16–17 for detailed step-by-step instructions)

Mix the yeast and dough ingredients until just incorporated.

Gradually add more of the remaining flour; just enough to make a soft dough.

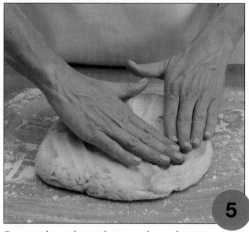

Dough will be dry enough to leave the sides of the mixer bowl clean.

Place dough in an oiled bowl, cover and let rise until doubled in volume.

Press dough with your hands to flatten it for rolling.

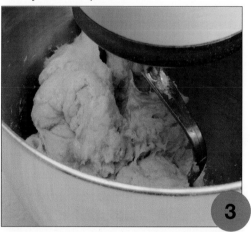

Roll the dough out to slightly more than ¼-inch (0.5 cm) thickness.

continued next page... **A1.**

Making Raised Donuts (continued)

(see pages 16–17 for detailed step-by-step instructions)

7

Dip cutter in flour and cut out donuts, beginning at edge of dough.

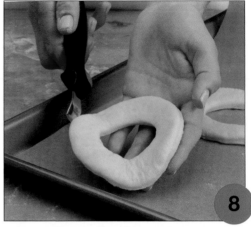

8

Lift cut donuts and place 1 inch (2.5 cm) apart on lined baking sheet.

9

After 20 minutes, donuts should look slightly puffy.

10

Hold donut close to the surface of oil; gently let it slip in without splashing.

11

When bottoms are golden and donuts are puffed, use chopsticks to flip them.

A2.

12

Use a slotted spatula to lift donuts from oil, draining well, and place on paper towel–lined baking sheet.

Making Cake-Based Donuts

(see page 19 for detailed step-by-step instructions)

Mix wet and dry ingredients until just combined, then add more flour.

Dough should resemble biscuit dough; not sticky, but not too dry.

Use a French or box rolling pin to roll out dough.

Dip bar cutter into flour and cut bars in a row starting at one end of dough.

Cut donut horizontally, going almost, but not all the way through, leaving a hinge on one side.

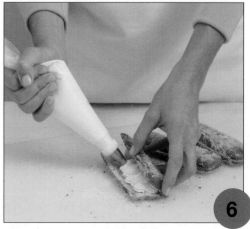

Carefully raise "lid" of donut and pipe cream onto bottom half, covering evenly without overfilling.

B.

Making Baked Donuts

(see page 21 for detailed step-by-step instructions)

Use a whisk to thoroughly incorporate the dry ingredients together.

Whisk wet ingredients together until evenly blended.

Pour wet ingredients into dry and combine with a rubber spatula.

Set a resealable freezer bag into a glass and carefully pour batter into it.

Squeeze batter into one corner of the bag, removing all of the air pockets.

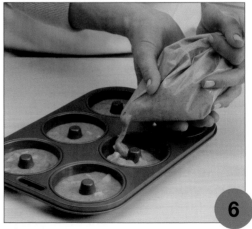

Pipe the batter into the sprayed donut pan, leaving room for donuts to rise.

C.

Making Filled (injected) Donuts

(see page 23 for detailed step-by-step instructions)

Roll the dough out to slightly more than ¼-inch (0.5 cm) thickness.

Dip cutter in flour and cut donuts starting at edge of dough.

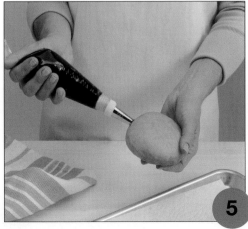

Let fried donuts cool completely on paper towel–lined baking sheets.

Fit a pastry bag with a Bismarck tip.

Insert tip in center of one side of donut and gently squeeze filling into it.

To garnish, place confectioner's sugar in a fine sieve and shake over donuts.

D.

Making Fritters

(see page 25 for detailed step-by-step instructions)

Pat dough out with your hands to a rectangle, 12 by 8 inches (30 by 20 cm).

Use bench scraper to cut dough into 12 rectangles.

With the sides of your hands press edges of dough downward to neaten.

Cover the fritters with a clean, lint-free towel and let them rise.

Using slotted spatula, lower fritter into oil and allow to float off spatula.

Coat fritters in Autumn Spiced Sugar while donuts are still warm.

E.

Making One-Bite Donuts

(see page 27 for detailed step-by-step instructions)

1

Fry about 6 donuts at a time in the hot oil. Avoid overcrowding.

2

When done, promptly remove donuts 2 or 3 at a time to prevent overcooking.

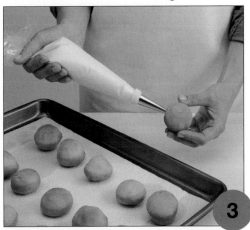

3

To fill, insert Bismarck tip into side of donut and gently squeeze pastry bag.

4

Let donuts cool completely before glazing.

5

Using two fingers, dip donuts in glaze, submerging completely. Shake off excess glaze and place on wire rack.

6

Or, instead of glazing, roll each donut in confectioner's sugar.

F.

Making Bow Ties (Ga.) (see page 29 for detailed step-by-step instructions)

Cut a regular ring-shaped donut and stretch it into a 4-inch (10 cm) oval.

Twist each ring into a figure eight, then lay on baking sheet and press center.

Making Twists (Gb.) (see page 31 for detailed step-by-step instructions)

Sprinkle the pecan mixture evenly right to the edges of the dough.

Hold dough at short edge and fold in half, like a book.

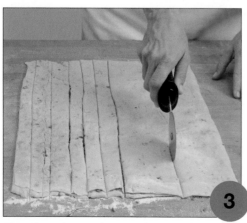

Cut dough, as directed, into 12 equal 1-inch (2.5 cm) strips.

Fold each strip in half and twist. Place on parchment–lined baking sheet.

G.

Raised Donuts

• •

You **cannot beat** a perfectly raised donut. It is very versatile. You can form the dough into rounds, bars, cinnamon-roll shapes and more. Most raised donuts need a sugar glaze, dusting of sugar or filling to add sweetness and round out the flavor. A full plate of raised donuts with a variety of icings and fillings is a sight to behold.

Black Forest Donut Bars 34

Blueberry Raised Donuts 36

Cinnamon Honey Donuts 38

Fresh Cherry Donuts 40

Fresh Vanilla Bean Donuts 42

Key Lime Donuts 44

Light-as-Air Glazed Donuts 46

Mandarin Orange Donuts 48

Mocha Raised Donuts 50

Perfect Chocolate–Glazed Donuts 52

Persian Walnut Donuts 54

Potato Flour Donuts 56

Pretzel Twist Donuts 58

Maple Bars 60

Black Forest Donut Bars

**Makes about
18 donuts**

A dark chocolate bar topped with cherry filling will remind you of a rich piece of black forest cake all in one donut.

- Stand mixer with paddle attachment
- 5- by 2-inch (12.5 by 5 cm) bar cutter, optional
- Baking sheet, lined with parchment paper
- Digital candy/deep-fry thermometer

¾ cup + 1 tbsp	whole milk, warmed to 110°F (43°C)	190 mL
1	package (¼ oz/8 g) quick-rising (instant) yeast	1
1	large egg	1
2 tbsp	canola oil	30 mL
½ tsp	cherry extract	2 mL
2 cups	all-purpose flour, divided (approx.)	500 mL
½ cup	unsweetened cocoa powder	125 mL
⅓ cup	granulated sugar	75 mL
⅛ tsp	salt	0.5 mL
	Canola oil	
	Fresh Cherry Filling (page 211)	

1. In mixer bowl, sprinkle yeast over milk and stir with a fork. Let stand until foamy, about 5 minutes.

2. Attach bowl to mixer fitted with paddle attachment and add egg, oil, cherry extract, ½ cup (125 mL) of the flour, cocoa powder, sugar and salt to yeast mixture. Let stand in bowl for 10 minutes. On low speed, mix just until blended, then gradually add just enough of the remaining flour until dough starts to pull away from sides of bowl. Increase speed to medium and beat for 1 minute.

3. Transfer dough to a large oiled bowl and cover with plastic wrap. Let rise in a warm, draft-free place until doubled in volume, about 30 minutes.

Finishing suggestions

Icing: Honey Glaze
(page 200).

4. Turn dough out onto a floured work surface. Roll out dough to slightly thicker than ¼ inch (0.5 cm). If dough is tacky, dust with additional flour. Cut dough with cutter into 18 donuts (or cut with a knife or pizza cutter into 5- by 2-inch/12.5 by 5 cm rectangles), re-rolling scraps as necessary. Place at least 1 inch (2.5 cm) apart on prepared baking sheet. Cover with a clean kitchen towel and let rise for 20 minutes.

5. Meanwhile, in a large, deep pot or deep fryer, heat about 4 inches (10 cm) oil over medium heat until temperature registers 360°F (182°C). Deep-fry 3 to 4 donuts at a time in hot oil, turning once with wooden chopsticks, until puffy, about 20 seconds per side. Using a slotted spatula, transfer to paper towels to absorb excess oil. Fry remaining donuts, adjusting heat as necessary between batches to maintain oil temperature.

6. After donuts have cooled completely, slice in half horizontally, leaving the back attached like a "hinge" and spoon about 2 tbsp (30 mL) cherry filling onto bottom of each. If desired, donuts may now be glazed on the top only.

Blueberry Raised Donuts

**Makes about
24 donuts**

Using dried blueberries make a powerful flavored donut. I like them a little smaller then the normal donut.

Tip

Dried blueberries work much better in these donuts since fresh or frozen blueberries will color the dough blue and the flavor will not be as rich.

- Stand mixer with paddle attachment
- 2-inch (5 cm) round cutter
- Baking sheet, lined with parchment paper
- Digital candy/deep-fry thermometer

¾ cup	whole milk, warmed to 110°F (43°C)	175 mL
1	package (¼ oz/8 g) quick-rising (instant) yeast	1
1	large egg	1
2 tbsp	canola oil	30 mL
1 tsp	vanilla extract	5 mL
2¾ cups	all-purpose flour, divided (approx.)	675 mL
½ cup	dried blueberries (see Tip, left)	125 mL
1 tbsp	granulated sugar	15 mL
⅛ tsp	salt	0.5 mL
	Canola oil	

1. In mixer bowl, sprinkle yeast over milk and stir with a fork. Let stand until foamy, about 5 minutes.

2. Attach bowl to mixer fitted with paddle attachment and add egg, oil, vanilla, 1 cup (250 mL) of the flour, blueberries, sugar and salt to yeast mixture. Let stand in bowl for 10 minutes. On low speed, mix just until blended, then gradually add just enough of the remaining flour until dough starts to pull away from sides of bowl. Increase speed to medium and beat for 1 minute.

3. Transfer dough to a large oiled bowl and cover with plastic wrap. Let rise in a warm, draft-free place until doubled in volume, about 30 minutes.

Finishing suggestions

Icings: Honey Glaze (page 200) or Lavender Sugar Dust (page 206).

Filling (injected): Blueberry Filling (page 212).

4. On a floured work surface, roll out dough to slightly thicker than $1/4$ inch (0.5 cm). If dough is tacky, dust with additional flour. Cut dough with cutter into 24 donuts, re-rolling scraps as necessary. Place at least 1 inch (2.5 cm) apart on prepared baking sheet. Cover with a clean kitchen towel and let rise for 20 minutes.

5. Meanwhile, in a large, deep pot or deep fryer, heat about 4 inches (10 cm) oil over medium heat until temperature registers 360°F (182°C). Deep-fry 6 donuts at a time in hot oil, turning once with wooden chopsticks, until golden brown, about 15 seconds per side. Using a slotted spatula, transfer to paper towels to absorb excess oil. Fry remaining donuts, adjusting heat as necessary between batches to maintain oil temperature.

6. Let donuts cool in pans on a rack for 5 minutes. Turn out of pans onto rack and toss with Lavender Sugar Dust, if using, or let cool completely prior to icing and/or filling.

Cinnamon Honey Donuts

● ●

Makes about 18 donuts

This is a cross between a cinnamon roll and a donut.

● ● ● ● ● ● ● ● ● ● ● ● ● ● ● ● ●

Variations

Instead of Honey Glaze you could use Autumn Spiced Sugar (page 204). Let donuts cool in pans on a rack for 5 minutes. Turn out of pans onto rack and toss with sugar.

Add ½ cup (125 mL) chopped pecans to the filling.

● Stand mixer with paddle attachment
● Baking sheet, lined with parchment paper
● Digital candy/deep-fry thermometer

¾ cup	whole milk, warmed to 110°F (43°C)	175 mL
1	package (¼ oz/8 g) quick-rising (instant) yeast	1
2	large eggs	2
2 tbsp	unsalted butter, melted	30 mL
1 tsp	vanilla extract	5 mL
2¾ cups	all-purpose flour, divided (approx.)	675 mL
⅓ cup	packed brown sugar, divided	75 mL
⅛ tsp	salt	0.5 mL
2 tsp	ground cinnamon	10 mL
1 tsp	freshly ground nutmeg	5 mL
	Canola oil	
	Honey Glaze (page 200)	

1. In mixer bowl, sprinkle yeast over milk and stir with a fork. Let stand until foamy, about 5 minutes.

2. Attach bowl to mixer fitted with paddle attachment and add eggs, butter, vanilla, 1 cup (250 mL) of the flour, 1 tbsp (15 mL) of the brown sugar and salt to yeast mixture. Let stand in bowl for 10 minutes. On low speed, mix just until blended, then gradually add just enough of the remaining flour until dough starts to pull away from sides of bowl. Increase speed to medium and beat for 1 minute.

3. Transfer dough to a large oiled bowl and cover with plastic wrap. Let rise in a warm, draft-free place until doubled in volume, about 30 minutes.

4. Meanwhile, in a small bowl, combine remaining ¼ cup (60 mL) of brown sugar, cinnamon and nutmeg. Set aside.

5. On a floured work surface, roll out dough to about 18 by 12 inches (45 by 30 cm) and about $\frac{1}{4}$ inch (0.5 cm) thick. If dough is tacky, dust with additional flour.

6. Sprinkle cinnamon-sugar mixture on top. Starting at one long side, roll up dough jelly-roll style to create a long rolled log. Pinch edge to seal as you would for cinnamon rolls. Cut dough crosswise into 18 equal pieces. Place, cut side up, at least 1 inch (2.5 cm) apart on prepared baking sheet. Cover with a clean kitchen towel and let rise for 20 minutes.

7. Meanwhile, in a large, deep pot or deep fryer, heat about 4 inches (10 cm) oil over medium heat until temperature registers 360°F (182°C). Deep-fry 3 donuts at a time in hot oil, turning once with wooden chopsticks, until golden brown, about 30 seconds per side. Using a slotted spatula, transfer to paper towels to absorb excess oil. Fry remaining donuts, adjusting heat as necessary between batches to maintain oil temperature.

8. Let donuts cool completely prior to glazing with Honey Glaze.

Fresh Cherry Donuts

**Makes about
18 donuts**

When you see fresh
cherries in the farmer's
market, make sure
you try these flavorful
donuts.

Tip

When you are making
ring-shaped donuts you
may like to fry up the
center holes for a treat.
Depending on the size of
the hole, your frying time
will have to be adjusted
since they tend to fry
faster. I sometimes like to
test a donut hole just to
see how the flavor of the
donut is and what icing I
will want to dress it with.

- Stand mixer with paddle attachment
- 3-inch (7.5 cm) round cutter
- Baking sheet, lined with parchment paper
- Digital candy/deep-fry thermometer

¾ cup	whole milk, warmed to 110°F (43°C)	175 mL
1	package (¼ oz/8 g) quick-rising (instant) yeast	1
1	large egg	1
2 tbsp	unsalted butter, melted	30 mL
1 tsp	vanilla extract	5 mL
1 tsp	cherry extract	5 mL
3 cups	all-purpose flour, divided (approx.)	750 mL
1 tbsp	granulated sugar	15 mL
⅛ tsp	salt	0.5 mL
½ cup	cherries, finely chopped	125 mL
	Canola oil	

1. In mixer bowl, sprinkle yeast over milk and stir with a fork. Let stand until foamy, about 5 minutes.

2. Attach bowl to mixer fitted with paddle attachment and add egg, butter, vanilla and cherry extracts, 1 cup (250 mL) of the flour, sugar and salt to yeast mixture. Let stand in bowl for 10 minutes. On low speed, mix just until blended, then gradually add just enough of the remaining flour until dough starts to pull away from sides of bowl. Increase speed to medium and beat for 1 minute. On low speed, mix in cherries, adding more flour if dough starts to stick to sides of bowl.

3. Transfer dough to a large oiled bowl and cover with plastic wrap. Let rise in a warm, draft-free place until doubled in volume, about 30 minutes.

Finishing suggestions

Icings: Honey Glaze
(page 200) or Simple
Sugar Glaze (page 205).

4. Turn dough out onto a floured work surface. Roll out dough to slightly thicker than $\frac{1}{4}$ inch (0.5 cm). If dough is tacky, dust with additional flour. Cut dough with cutter into 18 donuts, re-rolling scraps as necessary. Place at least 1 inch (2.5 cm) apart on prepared baking sheet. Cover with a clean kitchen towel and let rise for 20 minutes.

5. Meanwhile, in a large, deep pot or deep fryer, heat about 4 inches (10 cm) oil over medium heat until temperature registers 360°F (182°C). Deep-fry 3 to 4 donuts at a time in hot oil, turning once with wooden chopsticks, until golden brown, about 15 seconds per side. Using a slotted spatula, transfer to paper towels to absorb excess oil. Fry remaining donuts, adjusting heat as necessary between batches to maintain oil temperature.

6. Let donuts cool completely prior to icing.

Fresh Vanilla Bean Donuts

**Makes about
12 donuts**

Fresh vanilla beans
create little dark specks
in the dough. They are
a burst of flavor.

Tip

If vanilla beans are
unavailable, use 1 tbsp
(15 mL) vanilla extract or
paste.

- Stand mixer with paddle attachment
- 3-inch (7.5 cm) round donut cutter
- Baking sheet, lined with parchment paper
- Digital candy/deep-fry thermometer

¾ cup + 1 tbsp	whole milk	190 mL
1	vanilla bean, split lengthwise (see Tip, left)	1
1	package (¼ oz/8 g) quick-rising (instant) yeast	1
1	large egg	1
2 tbsp	canola oil	30 mL
2¾ cups	all-purpose flour, divided (approx.)	675 mL
1 tbsp	granulated sugar	15 mL
⅛ tsp	salt	0.5 mL
	Canola oil	

1. In a small saucepan, combine milk and vanilla bean. Heat over medium heat to 110°F (43°C). With fingers, press seeds out of the pod into the milk and stir to distribute. Strain through a fine-mesh sieve into mixer bowl. Discard vanilla pod or reserve for another use. Sprinkle yeast over milk mixture and stir with a fork. Let stand until foamy, about 5 minutes.

2. Attach bowl to mixer fitted with paddle attachment and add egg, oil, 1 cup (250 mL) of the flour, sugar and salt to yeast mixture. Let stand in bowl for 10 minutes. On low speed, mix just until blended, then gradually add just enough of the remaining flour until dough starts to pull away from sides of bowl. Increase speed to medium and beat for 1 minute.

3. Transfer dough to a large oiled bowl and cover with plastic wrap. Let rise in a warm, draft-free place until doubled in volume, about 30 minutes.

Finishing suggestions

Icings: Belgian Chocolate Ganache Glaze (page 197), Milk Chocolate Glaze (page 201) or Truffle Fudge Icing (page 196).

4. On a floured work surface, roll out dough to slightly thicker than $\frac{1}{4}$ inch (0.5 cm). If dough is tacky, dust with additional flour. Cut dough with cutter into 12 donuts, re-rolling scraps as necessary. Place at least 1 inch (2.5 cm) apart on prepared baking sheet. Cover with a clean kitchen towel and let rise for 20 minutes.

5. Meanwhile, in a large, deep pot or deep fryer, heat about 4 inches (10 cm) oil over medium heat until temperature registers 360°F (182°C). Deep-fry 4 donuts at a time in hot oil, turning once with wooden chopsticks, until golden brown, about 15 seconds per side. Using a slotted spatula, transfer to paper towels to absorb excess oil. Fry remaining donuts, adjusting heat as necessary between batches to maintain oil temperature.

6. Let donuts cool completely prior to icing.

Key Lime Donuts

**Makes about
12 donuts**

You will think you are
in the Florida Keys
while enjoying these
donuts packed with
lime flavor.

Tip

If you have a hard time
finding Key limes you can
use the same amount of
regular limes.

- Stand mixer with paddle attachment
- 3-inch (7.5 cm) round donut cutter
- Baking sheet, lined with parchment paper
- Digital candy/deep-fry thermometer

½ cup	whole milk, warmed to 110°F (43°C)	125 mL
1	package (¼ oz/8 g) quick-rising (instant) yeast	1
1 tsp	grated Key lime zest (see Tip, left)	5 mL
¼ cup	freshly squeezed Key lime juice	60 mL
1	large egg	1
2 tbsp	canola oil	30 mL
1 tsp	lime extract	5 mL
2¾ cups	all-purpose flour, divided (approx.)	675 mL
1 tbsp	granulated sugar	15 mL
⅛ tsp	salt	0.5 mL
	Canola oil	

1. In mixer bowl, sprinkle yeast over milk and stir with a fork. Let stand until foamy, about 5 minutes.

2. Attach bowl to mixer fitted with paddle attachment and add lime zest, lime juice, egg, oil, lime extract, 1 cup (250 mL) of the flour, sugar and salt to yeast mixture. Let stand in bowl for 10 minutes. On low speed, mix just until blended, then gradually add just enough of the remaining flour until dough starts to pull away from sides of bowl. Increase speed to medium and beat for 1 minute.

3. Transfer dough to a large oiled bowl and cover with plastic wrap. Let rise in a warm, draft-free place until doubled in volume, about 30 minutes.

Finishing suggestions

Icings: Honey Glaze (page 200) or Sunset Orange Glaze (page 204).

Topping: Sprinkle freshly glazed donuts with colorful sprinkles.

4. On a floured work surface, roll out dough to slightly thicker than $1/4$ inch (0.5 cm). If dough is tacky, dust with additional flour. Cut dough with cutter into 12 donuts, re-rolling scraps as necessary. Place at least 1 inch (2.5 cm) apart on prepared baking sheet. Cover with a clean kitchen towel and let rise for 20 minutes.

5. Meanwhile, in a large, deep pot or deep fryer, heat about 4 inches (10 cm) oil over medium heat until temperature registers 360°F (182°C). Deep-fry 4 donuts at a time in hot oil, turning once with wooden chopsticks, until golden brown, about 15 seconds per side. Using a slotted spatula, transfer to paper towels to absorb excess oil. Fry remaining donuts, adjusting heat as necessary between batches to maintain oil temperature.

6. Let donuts cool completely prior to icing and/or topping.

Light-as-Air Glazed Donuts

This is a light airy donut that is made with rice flour.

Tip

For step-by-step photos of glazing, see photo page F.

Variation

Replace Honey Glaze with Sunset Orange Glaze (page 204).

- Stand mixer with paddle attachment
- 3-inch (7.5 cm) round donut cutter
- Baking sheet, lined with parchment paper
- Digital candy/deep-fry thermometer

1 cup + 1 tbsp	whole milk, warmed to 110°F (43°C)	190 mL
2	packages (¼ oz/8 g) quick-rising (instant) yeast	2
3	egg whites	3
3 tbsp	canola oil	45 mL
2 tsp	vanilla extract	10 mL
3 cups	all-purpose flour, divided (approx.)	750 mL
¾ cup	rice flour	175 mL
1½ tbsp	granulated sugar	22 mL
1 tsp	salt	5 mL
	Canola oil	
	Honey Glaze (page 200)	

1. In mixer bowl, sprinkle yeast over milk and stir with a fork. Let stand until foamy, about 5 minutes.

2. Attach bowl to mixer fitted with paddle attachment and add egg whites, oil, vanilla, 1 cup (250 mL) of the all-purpose flour, rice flour, sugar and salt to yeast mixture. Let stand in bowl for 10 minutes. On low speed, mix just until blended, then gradually add just enough of the remaining flour until dough starts to pull away from sides of bowl. Increase speed to medium and beat for 1 minute.

3. Transfer dough to a large oiled bowl and cover with plastic wrap. Let rise in a warm, draft-free place until doubled in volume, about 30 minutes.

4. On a floured work surface, roll out dough to slightly thicker than $\frac{1}{4}$ inch (0.5 cm). If dough is tacky, dust with additional flour. Cut dough with cutter into 18 donuts, re-rolling scraps as necessary. Place at least 1 inch (2.5 cm) apart on prepared baking sheet. Cover with a clean kitchen towel and let rise for 20 minutes.

5. Meanwhile, in a large, deep pot or deep fryer, heat about 4 inches (10 cm) oil over medium heat until temperature registers 360°F (182°C). Deep-fry 3 to 4 donuts at a time in hot oil, turning once with wooden chopsticks, until golden brown, about 15 seconds per side. Using a slotted spatula, transfer to paper towels to absorb excess oil. Fry remaining donuts, adjusting heat as necessary between batches to maintain oil temperature.

6. While donuts are warm, glaze in Honey Glaze and place on a rack to cool.

Mandarin Orange Donuts

**Makes about
12 donuts**

Small chunks of
mandarin oranges burst
with flavor in these
fritter-type donuts.

- Stand mixer with paddle attachment
- Baking sheet, lined with parchment paper
- Digital candy/deep-fry thermometer

¾ cup	whole milk, warmed to 110°F (43°C)	175 mL
1	package (¼ oz/8 g) quick-rising (instant) yeast	1
2	egg whites	2
2 tbsp	unsalted butter, melted	30 mL
1 tsp	vanilla extract	5 mL
1 tsp	grated orange zest	5 mL
2¾ cups	all-purpose flour, divided (approx.)	675 mL
2 tbsp	granulated sugar	30 mL
⅛ tsp	salt	0.5 mL
½ cup	drained canned mandarin oranges, chopped	125 mL
	Canola oil	

1. In mixer bowl, sprinkle yeast over milk and stir with a fork. Let stand until foamy, about 5 minutes.

2. Attach bowl to mixer fitted with paddle attachment and add egg whites, butter, vanilla, orange zest, 1 cup (250 mL) of the flour, sugar and salt to yeast mixture. Let stand in bowl for 10 minutes. On low speed, mix just until blended, then gradually add just enough of the remaining flour until dough starts to pull away from sides of bowl. Increase speed to medium and beat for 1 minute.

3. Turn dough out onto a floured work surface. Knead chopped mandarin oranges into dough with your hands. (Additional flour may be needed depending on the moisture of the mandarin oranges. Add just enough to keep dough from getting sticky.)

Finishing suggestions

Icings: Honey Glaze (page 200) or Sunset Orange Glaze (page 204).

4. Transfer dough to a large oiled bowl and cover with plastic wrap. Let rise in a warm, draft-free place until doubled in volume, about 30 minutes.

5. On a floured work surface, press dough out to a rectangle, about 12 by 8 inches (30 by 20 cm) and to ³⁄₄-inch (2 cm) thickness. Cut dough into 12 equal rectangles and press edges to neaten. Place at least 1 inch (2.5 cm) apart on prepared baking sheet. Cover with a clean kitchen towel and let rise for 20 minutes.

6. Meanwhile, in a large, deep pot or deep fryer, heat about 4 inches (10 cm) oil over medium heat until temperature registers 360°F (182°C). Deep-fry 4 fritters at a time in hot oil, turning once with wooden chopsticks, until golden brown, about 30 seconds per side (the donuts will sink to the bottom of the fryer and then float to the top). Using a slotted spatula, transfer to paper towels to absorb excess oil. Fry remaining donuts, adjusting heat as necessary between batches to maintain oil temperature.

7. Let donuts cool completely prior to icing.

Mocha Raised Donuts

**Makes about
12 donuts**

A light hint of coffee
pairs perfectly with an
espresso.

Tip

For step-by-step photos of
glazing, see photo page F.

- Stand mixer with paddle attachment
- 3-inch (7.5 cm) round donut cutter
- Baking sheet, lined with parchment paper
- Digital candy/deep-fry thermometer

¾ cup	whole milk, warmed to 110°F (43°C)	175 mL
1	package (¼ oz/8 g) quick-rising (instant) yeast	1
1	large egg	1
2 tbsp	unsalted butter, melted	30 mL
1 tbsp	instant espresso powder	15 mL
1 tsp	vanilla extract	5 mL
2¾ cups	all-purpose flour, divided	675 mL
1 tbsp	granulated sugar	15 mL
⅛ tsp	salt	0.5 mL
	Canola oil	

1. In mixer bowl, sprinkle yeast over milk and stir with a fork. Let stand until foamy, about 5 minutes.

2. Attach bowl to mixer fitted with paddle attachment and add egg, butter, espresso powder, vanilla, 1 cup (250 mL) of the flour, sugar and salt to yeast mixture. Let stand in bowl for 10 minutes. On low speed, mix just until blended, then gradually add just enough of the remaining flour until dough starts to pull away from sides of bowl. Increase speed to medium and beat for 1 minute.

3. Transfer dough to a large oiled bowl and cover with plastic wrap. Let rise in a warm, draft-free place until doubled in volume, about 30 minutes.

Finishing suggestions

Icings: Mocha Glaze
(page 202) or Bittersweet
Chocolate Glaze
(page 197)

4. On a floured work surface, roll out dough to slightly thicker than $\frac{1}{4}$ inch (0.5 cm). If dough is tacky, dust with additional flour. Cut dough with cutter into 12 donuts, re-rolling scraps as necessary. Place at least 1 inch (2.5 cm) apart on prepared baking sheet. Cover with a clean kitchen towel and let rise for 20 minutes.

5. Meanwhile, in a large, deep pot or deep fryer, heat about 4 inches (10 cm) oil over medium heat until temperature registers 360°F (182°C). Deep-fry 4 donuts at a time in hot oil, turning once with wooden chopsticks, until puffy, about 15 to 20 seconds per side. Using a slotted spatula, transfer to paper towels to absorb excess oil. Fry remaining donuts, adjusting heat as necessary between batches to maintain oil temperature.

6. Let donuts cool completely and then dip in prepared glaze.

Perfect Chocolate–Glazed Donuts

Makes about 12 donuts

Here we have light yet rich chocolate donuts with a simple chocolate glaze.

Tip

For step-by-step photos of glazing, see photo page F.

- Stand mixer with paddle attachment
- 3-inch (7.5 cm) round donut cutter
- Baking sheet, lined with parchment paper
- Digital candy/deep-fry thermometer

¾ cup + 1 tbsp	whole milk, warmed to 110°F (43°C)	190 mL
1	package (¼ oz/8 g) quick-rising (instant) yeast	1
1	large egg	1
2 tbsp	unsalted butter, melted	30 mL
1 tsp	vanilla extract	5 mL
2 cups	all-purpose flour, divided (approx.)	500 mL
½ cup	unsweetened cocoa powder	125 mL
⅓ cup	granulated sugar	75 mL
⅛ tsp	salt	0.5 mL
	Canola oil	
	Milk Chocolate Glaze (page 201)	

1. In mixer bowl, sprinkle yeast over milk and stir with a fork. Let stand until foamy, about 5 minutes.

2. Attach bowl to mixer fitted with paddle attachment and add egg, butter, vanilla, ½ cup (125 mL) of the flour, cocoa powder, sugar and salt to yeast mixture. Let stand in bowl for 10 minutes. On low speed, mix just until blended, then gradually add just enough of the remaining flour until dough starts to pull away from sides of bowl. Increase speed to medium and beat for 1 minute.

3. Transfer dough to a large oiled bowl and cover with plastic wrap. Let rise in a warm, draft-free place until doubled in volume, about 30 minutes.

4. On a floured work surface, roll out dough to slightly thicker than ¼ inch (0.5 cm). If dough is tacky, dust with additional flour. Cut dough with cutter into 12 donuts, re-rolling scraps as necessary. Place at least 1 inch (2.5 cm) apart on prepared baking sheet. Cover with a clean kitchen towel and let rise for 20 minutes.

Variations

Instead of Milk Chocolate Glaze, use Dulce de Leche Glaze (page 199), Honey Glaze (page 200), Mocha Glaze (page 202), Truffle Fudge Icing (page 196) or Bittersweet Chocolate Glaze (page 197).

5. Meanwhile, in a large, deep pot or deep fryer, heat about 4 inches (10 cm) oil over medium heat until temperature registers 360°F (182°C). Deep-fry 4 donuts at a time in hot oil, turning once with wooden chopsticks, until puffy, about 20 seconds per side. Using a slotted spatula, transfer to paper towels to absorb excess oil. Fry remaining donuts, adjusting heat as necessary between batches to maintain oil temperature.

6. Let donuts cool completely prior to icing with Milk Chocolate Glaze.

Persian Walnut Donuts

Makes about 36 donuts

While walking the streets of Paris you'll find these much smaller versions of donuts, called Persian — sometimes with nuts or a thick icing.

Tip

This is a large batch of donuts so if you can fit more donuts at a time in your pot it will speed up frying time. However, you need to avoid crowding the pan and cooling the oil down too much.

- Stand mixer with paddle attachment
- Baking sheet, lined with parchment paper
- Digital candy/deep-fry thermometer

1½ cups	whole milk, warmed to 110°F (43°C)	375 mL
2	packages (each ¼ oz/8 g) quick-rising (instant) yeast	2
2	large eggs	2
2	egg whites	2
¼ cup	unsalted butter, melted	60 mL
2 tsp	vanilla extract	10 mL
5¼ cups	all-purpose flour, divided (approx.)	1.3 L
½ cup	chopped walnuts	125 mL
1 tbsp	granulated sugar	15 mL
1 tsp	salt	5 mL
½ cup	packed brown sugar	125 mL
1 tbsp	ground cinnamon	15 mL
2 tsp	freshly ground nutmeg	10 mL
	Canola oil	

1. In mixer bowl, sprinkle yeast over milk and stir with a fork. Let stand until foamy, about 5 minutes.

2. Attach bowl to mixer fitted with paddle attachment and add eggs, egg whites, butter, vanilla, 2 cups (500 mL) of the flour, walnuts, granulated sugar and salt to yeast mixture. Let stand in bowl for 10 minutes. On low speed, mix just until blended, then gradually add just enough of the remaining flour until dough starts to pull away from sides of bowl. Increase speed to medium and beat for 1 minute.

3. Divide dough into two equal pieces. Transfer dough to two large oiled bowls and cover with plastic wrap. Let rise in a warm, draft-free place until doubled in volume, about 30 minutes.

Finishing suggestions

Icings: Honey Glaze (page 200) or Simple Sugar Glaze (page 205).

4. Meanwhile in a small bowl, combine brown sugar, cinnamon and nutmeg. Set aside.

5. On a floured work surface, roll out one half of the dough to a rectangle about 18 by 12 inches (45 by 30 cm) and about $\frac{1}{4}$ inch (0.5 cm) thick. If dough is tacky, dust with additional flour.

6. Sprinkle half of the cinnamon-sugar mixture on top. Starting at one long edge, roll up dough jelly-roll style to create a long rolled log. Cut dough crosswise into 18 pieces. Place at least 1 inch (2.5 cm) apart on prepared baking sheet. Cover with a clean kitchen towel and let rise for 20 minutes. Repeat with remaining piece of dough and cinnamon-sugar mixture.

7. Meanwhile, in a large, deep pot or deep fryer, heat about 4 inches (10 cm) oil over medium heat until temperature registers 360°F (182°C). Deep-fry 3 to 6 donuts at a time in hot oil, turning once with wooden chopsticks, until golden brown, about 15 seconds per side. Using a slotted spatula, transfer to paper towels to absorb excess oil. Fry remaining donuts, adjusting heat as necessary between batches to maintain oil temperature.

8. Let donuts cool completely prior to icing.

Potato Flour Donuts

Makes about
18 donuts

Potato flour softens
the dough a bit and
produces a light donut.

Tip

Potato flour is a
buff-colored, heavier
flour with a definite
potato flavor made
from the actual potato,
including the potato skin.
It's not to be confused
with potato starch, a very
fine, pure white powder
with a bland taste, that
is made by removing the
potato peel, making the
potato into a slurry and
watery mix to extract the
starch, then dehydrated
to form a dry, powdered
starch.

- Stand mixer with paddle attachment
- 5- by 2-inch (12.5 by 5 cm) bar cutter, optional
- Baking sheet, lined with parchment paper
- Digital candy/deep-fry thermometer

¾ cup + 1 tbsp	whole milk, warmed to 110°F (43°C)	190 mL
1	package (¼ oz/8 g) quick-rising (instant) yeast	1
1	large egg	1
1	egg white	1
2 tbsp	unsalted butter, melted	30 mL
1 tsp	vanilla extract	5 mL
2 cups	all-purpose flour, divided (approx.)	500 mL
¾ cup	potato flour (see Tip, left)	175 mL
2 tbsp	granulated sugar	30 mL
⅛ tsp	salt	0.5 mL
	Canola oil	

1. In mixer bowl, sprinkle yeast over milk and stir with a fork. Let stand until foamy, about 5 minutes.

2. Attach bowl to mixer fitted with paddle attachment and add egg, egg white, butter, vanilla, 1 cup (250 mL) of the all-purpose flour, potato flour, sugar and salt to yeast mixture. Let stand in bowl for 10 minutes. On low speed, mix just until blended, then gradually add just enough of the remaining flour until dough starts to pull away from sides of bowl. Increase speed to medium and beat for 1 minute.

3. Transfer dough to a large oiled bowl and cover with plastic wrap. Let rise in a warm, draft-free place until doubled in volume, about 30 minutes.

Finishing suggestions

Icing: Honey Glaze (page 200).

Fillings (injected): Lemon Zest Filling (page 213), Raspberry Filling (Variation, page 214) or Strawberry Filling (page 214).

Filling (cut donuts in half): Fresh Cherry Filling (page 211).

4. On a floured work surface, roll out dough to slightly thicker than $\frac{1}{4}$ inch (0.5 cm). If dough is tacky, dust with additional flour. Cut dough with cutter into 18 donuts (or cut with a knife or pizza cutter into 5- by 2-inch/12.5 by 5 cm rectangles), re-rolling scraps as necessary. Place at least 1 inch (2.5 cm) apart on prepared baking sheet. Cover with a clean kitchen towel and let rise for 20 minutes.

5. Meanwhile, in a large, deep pot or deep fryer, heat about 4 inches (10 cm) oil over medium heat until temperature registers 360°F (182°C). Deep-fry 3 to 4 donuts at a time in hot oil, turning once with wooden chopsticks, until golden brown, about 15 seconds per side. Using a slotted spatula, transfer to paper towels to absorb excess oil. Fry remaining donuts, adjusting heat as necessary between batches to maintain oil temperature.

6. Let donuts cool completely prior to icing and/or filling.

Pretzel Twist Donuts

**Makes about
12 donuts**

Here's a donut twisted with a little spice inside.

Variation

Add ½ cup (125 mL) chopped pecans or walnuts to the dough after all the necessary flour has been added.

- Stand mixer with paddle attachment
- Pizza cutter
- Baking sheet, lined with parchment paper
- Digital candy/deep-fry thermometer

¾ cup + 1 tbsp	whole milk, warmed to 110°F (43°C)	190 mL
1	package (¼ oz/8 g) quick-rising (instant) yeast	1
2	egg whites	2
2 tbsp	canola oil	30 mL
1 tsp	vanilla extract	5 mL
2¾ cups	all-purpose flour, divided (approx.)	675 mL
2 tbsp	granulated sugar, divided	30 mL
⅛ tsp	salt	0.5 mL
2 tsp	ground cinnamon	10 mL
1 tsp	freshly ground nutmeg	5 mL
	Canola oil	

1. In mixer bowl, sprinkle yeast over milk and stir with a fork. Let stand until foamy, about 5 minutes.

2. Attach bowl to mixer fitted with paddle attachment and add egg whites, oil, vanilla, 1 cup (250 mL) of the flour, 1 tbsp (15 mL) of the sugar and salt to yeast mixture. Let stand in bowl for 10 minutes. On low speed, mix just until blended, then gradually add just enough of the remaining flour until dough starts to pull away from sides of bowl. Increase speed to medium and beat for 1 minute.

3. Transfer dough to a large oiled bowl and cover with plastic wrap. Let rise in a warm, draft-free place until doubled in volume, about 30 minutes.

4. Meanwhile in a small bowl, combine remaining 1 tbsp (15 mL) of sugar, cinnamon and nutmeg. Set aside.

Finishing suggestions

Icing: Honey Glaze
(page 200).

5. On a floured work surface, roll out dough to a rectangle about 24 by 18 inches (60 by 45 cm) and about ¼ inch (0.5 cm) thick with one long side closest to you. If dough is tacky, dust with additional flour. Sprinkle the cinnamon-sugar mixture on top. Starting with one short side, fold dough in half from left to right. Cut dough lengthwise with a pizza cutter into 12 strips, about 1 inch (2.5 cm) thick. Fold each strip in half and twist (see page 31). Place at least 1 inch (2.5 cm) apart on prepared baking sheet. Pinch both sides down. Cover with a clean kitchen towel and let rise for 20 minutes.

6. Meanwhile, in a large, deep pot or deep fryer, heat about 4 inches (10 cm) oil over medium heat until temperature registers 360°F (182°C). Deep-fry 3 donuts at a time in hot oil, turning once with wooden chopsticks, until golden brown, about 15 seconds per side. Using a slotted spatula, transfer to paper towels to absorb excess oil. Fry remaining donuts, adjusting heat as necessary between batches to maintain oil temperature.

7. Let donuts cool completely prior to icing.

Maple Bars

Most maple bars are just a plain bar with maple icing. I like my maple flavor throughout the entire donut.

Finishing suggestions
Icing: Maple Glaze (page 201).

- Stand mixer with paddle attachment
- 5- by 2-inch (12.5 by 5 cm) bar cutter, optional
- Baking sheet, lined with parchment paper
- Digital candy/deep-fry thermometer

$2/3$ cup	whole milk, warmed to 110°F (43°C)	150 mL
1	package ($1/4$ oz/8 g) quick-rising (instant) yeast	1
3 tbsp	pure maple syrup	45 mL
1	large egg	1
2 tbsp	canola oil	30 mL
$1/2$ tsp	maple extract	2 mL
$2\frac{3}{4}$ cups	all-purpose flour, divided (approx.)	675 mL
1 tbsp	granulated sugar	15 mL
$1/8$ tsp	salt	0.5 mL
	Canola oil	

1. In mixer bowl, sprinkle yeast over milk and stir with a fork. Let stand until foamy, about 5 minutes.

2. Attach bowl to mixer fitted with paddle attachment and add maple syrup, egg, oil, maple extract, 1 cup (250 mL) of the flour, sugar and salt to yeast mixture. Let stand in bowl for 10 minutes. On low speed, mix just until blended, then gradually add just enough of the remaining flour until dough starts to pull away from sides of bowl. Increase speed to medium and beat for 1 minute.

3. Transfer dough to a large oiled bowl and cover with plastic wrap. Let rise in a warm, draft-free place until doubled in volume, about 30 minutes.

4. On a floured work surface, roll out dough to slightly thicker than $1/4$ inch (0.5 cm). If dough is tacky, dust with additional flour. Cut dough with cutter or knife into 18 donuts, re-rolling scraps as necessary. Place at least 1 inch (2.5 cm) apart on prepared baking sheet. Cover with a clean kitchen towel and let rise for 20 minutes.

5. Meanwhile, in a large, deep pot or deep fryer, heat about 4 inches (10 cm) oil over medium heat until temperature registers 360°F (182°C). Deep-fry 3 to 4 donuts at a time in hot oil, turning once with wooden chopsticks, until golden brown, about 20 seconds per side. Using a slotted spatula, transfer to paper towels to absorb excess oil. Fry remaining donuts, adjusting heat between batches to maintain oil temperature. Let donuts cool prior to icing.

Cake-Based Donuts

● ●

My **favorite donut** would be a rich chocolate cake donut. You can create so many types of cake donuts with fillings, icings and glazes. Cake donuts stay fresher longer then any other type of donut. Most of the cake donuts can be mixed up by hand in no time. While donut shops have industrial equipment that press out cake donut batter directly into the hot oil, to make cake donuts at home, you'll have to roll out the dough and cut shapes as you do with raised donuts. It does take a bit more work than with a machine but it's definitely worth the effort.

Applesauce Donuts 62

Blackout Donuts. 64

Buttermilk Donuts 65

Cake Sticks 66

Candied Ginger Donut Stars. 67

Caramel Apple–Filled Bars 68

Chocolate Cake Donuts. 70

Coconut Donuts. 72

Whole Wheat Pecan Donuts 74

Fresh Peach Pecan Donuts 75

Fresh Strawberry and Cream Donuts 76

Lemon Crème Bars. 78

Peanut Chocolate Cake Donuts 80

Espresso Buttermilk Bars. 82

Pumpkin Nutmeg Spice Donuts 83

Pumpkin Bars 84

Red Velvet Chip Donut Bars 86

Rum Raisin Donuts. 88

Dark Devil's Food Donuts 90

Applesauce Donuts

These donuts remind
me of the apple country
I used to go to yearly
with my parents in the
fall.

Tip

When heating the oil
for deep-frying, keep a
close eye on it to be sure
it doesn't overheat, and
never leave the room
while the oil is on the
heat. Reduce the heat or
carefully remove the pot
from the burner when the
oil reaches the desired
temperature. Always keep
a metal lid that tightly fits
the pot handy to quickly
place on the pot should
the oil start to smoke or
burn.

- Stand mixer with paddle attachment
- Digital candy/deep-fry thermometer
- 5- by 2-inch (12.5 by 5 cm) bar cutter, optional
- Baking sheet, lined with parchment paper

4 cups	all-purpose flour, divided (approx.)	1 L
2 tsp	baking powder	10 mL
1 tsp	ground cinnamon	5 mL
1 tsp	salt	5 mL
1/2 tsp	freshly ground nutmeg	2 mL
1/2 tsp	baking soda	2 mL
1/4 tsp	ground allspice	1 mL
1 cup	packed brown sugar	250 mL
2	large eggs, beaten	2
1/2 cup	unsweetened applesauce	125 mL
1/4 cup	whole milk	60 mL
2 tbsp	unsalted butter, melted and cooled	30 mL
	Canola oil	

1. In a bowl, whisk together 3 cups (750 mL) of the flour, baking powder, cinnamon, salt, nutmeg, baking soda and allspice. Set aside.

2. In mixer bowl fitted with paddle attachment, combine brown sugar, eggs, applesauce, milk and butter. On low speed, mix until well combined. Add dry ingredients and mix until incorporated. Gradually mix in more of the remaining flour, as necessary, until dough starts to come together and is the consistency of biscuit dough. Cover and refrigerate for 10 minutes.

3. Meanwhile, in a large, deep pot or deep fryer, heat about 4 inches (10 cm) oil over medium heat until temperature registers 360°F (182°C) (see Tip, left).

Finishing suggestions

Icings: Autumn Spiced Sugar (page 204) or Maple Glaze (page 201).

4. On a floured work surface, roll out dough to slightly thicker than $\frac{1}{4}$ inch (0.5 cm). If dough is tacky, dust with additional flour. Cut dough with cutter into 22 donuts (or cut with a knife or pizza cutter into 5- by 2-inch/12.5 by 5 cm rectangles), re-rolling scraps as necessary. Place at least 1 inch (2.5 cm) apart on prepared baking sheet.

5. Deep-fry 3 to 4 donuts at a time in hot oil, turning once with wooden chopsticks, until golden brown, about 25 seconds per side. Using a slotted spatula, transfer to paper towels to absorb excess oil. Fry remaining donuts, adjusting heat as necessary between batches to maintain oil temperature.

6. Toss warm donuts with Autumn Spiced Sugar, if using, or let cool completely prior to icing.

Blackout Donuts

Makes about 18 donuts

The darkest and richest chocolate donuts on Earth.

Tip

Be careful not to over fry chocolate cake donuts. Test a few first and then taste to see if the texture and flavor is good and not overdone or undercooked.

Finishing suggestions

Icings: Belgian Chocolate Ganache Glaze (page 197), Milk Chocolate Glaze (page 201), Mocha Glaze (page 202), Bittersweet Chocolate Glaze (page 197) or Truffle Fudge Icing (page 196).

- Stand mixer with paddle attachment
- Digital candy/deep-fry thermometer
- 3-inch (7.5 cm) round donut cutter
- Baking sheet, lined with parchment paper

2¾ cups	all-purpose flour, divided (approx.)	675 mL
½ cup	unsweetened black cocoa powder	125 mL
1¼ tsp	baking powder	6 mL
1 tsp	salt	5 mL
½ tsp	baking soda	2 mL
1 cup	packed brown sugar	250 mL
3	large eggs, beaten	3
¼ cup	whole milk	60 mL
¼ cup	unsalted butter, melted and cooled	60 mL
2 tsp	vanilla extract	10 mL
	Canola oil	

1. In a bowl, whisk together 2 cups (500 mL) of the flour, cocoa powder, baking powder, salt and baking soda. Set aside.

2. In mixer bowl fitted with paddle attachment, combine brown sugar, eggs, milk, butter and vanilla. On low speed, mix until well combined. Add dry ingredients and mix until incorporated. Gradually mix in more of the remaining flour, as necessary, until dough starts to come together and is the consistency of biscuit dough. Cover and refrigerate for 10 minutes.

3. Meanwhile, in a large, deep pot or deep fryer, heat about 4 inches (10 cm) oil over medium heat until temperature registers 360°F (182°C).

4. On a floured work surface, roll out dough to slightly thicker than ¼ inch (0.5 cm). If dough is tacky, dust with additional flour. Cut dough with cutter into 18 donuts, re-rolling scraps as necessary. Place at least 1 inch (2.5 cm) apart on prepared baking sheet.

5. Deep-fry 4 donuts at a time in hot oil, turning once with wooden chopsticks, until puffy and firm, about 25 seconds per side. Using a slotted spatula, transfer to paper towels to absorb excess oil. Fry remaining donuts, adjusting heat as necessary between batches to maintain oil temperature.

6. Let donuts cool completely before icing.

Buttermilk Donuts

● ●

Makes about 12 donuts

Here's a rich and simple donut that you can mix up in one bowl.

● ● ● ● ● ● ● ● ● ● ● ● ● ●

Finishing suggestions

Icings: Autumn Spiced Sugar (page 204) or Citrus Sugar (page 205).

- Stand mixer with paddle attachment
- Digital candy/deep-fry thermometer
- 3-inch (7.5 cm) round donut cutter
- Baking sheet, lined with parchment paper

3 cups	all-purpose flour, divided (approx.)	750 mL
1½ tsp	baking powder	7 mL
1½ tsp	freshly ground nutmeg	7 mL
1 tsp	salt	5 mL
½ tsp	baking soda	2 mL
¾ cup	granulated sugar	175 mL
2	large eggs, beaten	2
¼ cup	buttermilk	60 mL
¼ cup	unsalted butter, melted and cooled	60 mL
	Canola oil	

1. In a bowl, whisk together 2½ cups (625 mL) of the flour, baking powder, nutmeg, salt and baking soda. Set aside.

2. In mixer bowl fitted with paddle attachment, combine sugar, eggs, buttermilk and butter. On low speed, mix until well combined. Add dry ingredients and mix until incorporated. Gradually mix in more of the remaining flour, as necessary, until dough starts to come together and is the consistency of biscuit dough. Cover and refrigerate for 10 minutes.

3. Meanwhile, in a large, deep pot or deep fryer, heat about 4 inches (10 cm) oil over medium heat until temperature registers 360°F (182°C).

4. On a floured work surface, roll out dough to slightly thicker than ¼ inch (0.5 cm). If dough is tacky, dust with additional flour. Cut dough with cutter into 12 donuts, re-rolling scraps as necessary. Place at least 1 inch (2.5 cm) apart on prepared baking sheet.

5. Deep-fry 4 donuts at a time in hot oil, turning once with wooden chopsticks, until golden brown, about 25 seconds per side. Using a slotted spoon, transfer to paper towels to absorb excess oil. Fry remaining donuts, adjusting heat as necessary between batches to maintain oil temperature.

6. Toss warm donuts with either Autumn Spiced Sugar or Citrus Sugar.

Cake Sticks

Makes about 24 donuts

Kids love these donuts as they are easy to eat and you can dip them into toppings for a party if you wish.

Tip

You can use a pizza cutter or knife, cutting dough into 2½- by 1½-inch (6 by 4 cm) rectangles.

Finishing suggestions

Icings: Autumn Spiced Sugar (page 204), Citrus Sugar (page 205) or Rose Petal Dust (page 206).

- Stand mixer with paddle attachment
- Digital candy/deep-fry thermometer
- 2½- by 1½-inch (6 by 4 cm) bar cutter (see Tip, left)
- Baking sheet, lined with parchment paper

2¾ cups	all-purpose flour, divided (approx.)	675 mL
1½ tsp	freshly ground nutmeg	7 mL
1¼ tsp	baking powder	6 mL
1 tsp	salt	5 mL
½ tsp	baking soda	2 mL
1 cup	granulated sugar	250 mL
3	large eggs, beaten	3
¼ cup	buttermilk	60 mL
¼ cup	unsalted butter, melted and cooled	60 mL
	Canola oil	

1. In a bowl, whisk together 2 cups (500 mL) of the flour, nutmeg, baking powder, salt and baking soda. Set aside.

2. In mixer bowl fitted with paddle attachment, combine sugar, eggs, buttermilk and butter. On low speed, mix until well combined. Add dry ingredients and mix until incorporated. Gradually mix in more of the remaining flour, as necessary, until dough starts to come together and is the consistency of biscuit dough. Cover and refrigerate for 10 minutes.

3. Meanwhile, in a large, deep pot or deep fryer, heat about 4 inches (10 cm) oil over medium heat until temperature registers 360°F (182°C).

4. On a floured work surface, roll out dough to slightly thicker than ¼ inch (0.5 cm). If dough is tacky, dust with additional flour. Cut dough with cutter into 24 donuts, re-rolling scraps as necessary. Place at least 1 inch (2.5 cm) apart on prepared baking sheet.

5. Deep-fry 4 to 6 donuts at a time in hot oil, turning once with wooden chopsticks, until golden brown, about 25 seconds per side. Using a slotted spoon, transfer to paper towels to absorb excess oil. Fry remaining donuts, adjusting heat as necessary between batches to maintain oil temperature.

6. Toss warm donuts with either Autumn Spiced Sugar, Citrus Sugar or Rose Petal Dust.

Candied Ginger Donut Stars

A perfect donut for the star in your life.

Tip

I use the food processor to combine the dry ingredients in this recipe since the candied ginger is very sticky and I want it to be well blended with the flour mixture so the flavor is evenly distributed through the donuts.

Finishing suggestions

Icings: Simple Sugar Glaze (page 205) or Raspberry Glaze (page 203).

- Food processor
- Stand mixer with paddle attachment
- Digital candy/deep-fry thermometer
- 3-inch (7.5 cm) star cutter

2¾ cups	all-purpose flour, divided (approx.)	675 mL
1 tbsp	finely chopped candied ginger	15 mL
1¼ tsp	baking powder	6 mL
1 tsp	salt	5 mL
½ tsp	baking soda	2 mL
1 cup	granulated sugar	250 mL
2	large eggs, beaten	2
1	large egg yolk, beaten	1
¼ cup	whole milk	60 mL
	Canola oil	

1. In food processor fitted with metal blade, combine 2 cups (500 mL) of the flour, candied ginger, baking powder, salt and baking soda and process for 20 seconds. Set aside.

2. In mixer bowl fitted with paddle attachment, combine sugar, eggs, egg yolk, milk and ¼ cup (60 mL) canola oil. On low speed, mix until well combined. Add dry ingredients and mix until incorporated. Gradually mix in more of the remaining flour, as necessary, until dough starts to come together and is the consistency of biscuit dough. Cover and refrigerate for 10 minutes.

3. Meanwhile, in a large, deep pot or deep fryer, heat about 4 inches (10 cm) oil over medium heat until temperature registers 360°F (182°C).

4. On a floured work surface, roll out dough to slightly thicker than ¼ inch (0.5 cm). If dough is tacky, dust with additional flour. Cut dough with cutter into 12 donuts, re-rolling scraps as necessary. Place at least 1 inch (2.5 cm) apart on prepared baking sheet.

5. Deep-fry 4 donuts at a time in hot oil, turning once with wooden chopsticks, until golden brown, about 25 seconds per side. Using a slotted spoon, transfer to paper towels to absorb excess oil. Fry remaining donuts, adjusting heat as necessary between batches to maintain oil temperature.

6. Let donuts cool completely prior to icing.

Caramel Apple–Filled Bars

Just like a caramel
apple but in a flavorful
donut.

- Stand mixer with paddle attachment
- Digital candy/deep-fry thermometer
- 5- by 2-inch (12.5 cm by 5 cm) bar cutter, optional
- Baking sheet, lined with parchment paper

3 cups	all-purpose flour, divided (approx.)	750 mL
1½ tsp	baking powder	7 mL
1 tsp	salt	5 mL
½ tsp	baking soda	2 mL
1 cup	granulated sugar	250 mL
2	large eggs, beaten	2
1	large egg yolk, beaten	1
¼ cup	whole milk	60 mL
¼ cup	unsalted butter, melted and cooled	60 mL
1 tsp	grated lemon zest	5 mL
1 tbsp	freshly squeezed lemon juice	15 mL
	Canola oil	
1	recipe Crisp Apple Filling (page 212)	1
1 cup	soft caramels, cut into quarters (about 6 oz/175 g)	250 mL

1. In a bowl, whisk together 2½ cups (625 mL) of the flour, baking powder, salt and baking soda. Set aside.

2. In mixer bowl fitted with paddle attachment, combine sugar, eggs, egg yolk, milk, butter, lemon zest and juice. On low speed, mix until well combined. Add dry ingredients and mix until incorporated. Gradually mix in more of the remaining flour, as necessary, until dough starts to come together and is the consistency of biscuit dough. Cover and refrigerate for 10 minutes.

3. Meanwhile, in a large, deep pot or deep fryer, heat about 4 inches (10 cm) oil over medium heat until temperature registers 360°F (182°C).

4. On a floured work surface, roll out dough to slightly thicker than ¼ inch (0.5 cm). If dough is tacky, dust with additional flour. Cut dough with cutter into 18 donuts (or cut with a knife or pizza cutter into 5- by 2-inch/12.5 by 5 cm rectangles), re-rolling scraps as necessary. Place at least 1 inch (2.5 cm) apart on prepared baking sheet.

5. Deep-fry 4 donuts at a time in hot oil, turning once with wooden chopsticks, until golden brown, about 25 seconds per side. Using a slotted spoon, transfer to paper towels to absorb excess oil. Fry remaining donuts, adjusting heat as necessary between batches to maintain oil temperature.

6. Let donuts cool completely. In a small bowl, combine filling and caramels. Slice donuts in half crosswise. Spoon filling onto bottoms, then sandwich with donut tops (see page 19). If desired, donuts may now be glazed or dusted on the top only.

Chocolate Cake Donuts

Makes about 18 donuts

When I go to a donut shop my first choice is a simple chocolate cake donut with a rich chocolate glaze.

Tip

When heating the oil for deep-frying, keep a close eye on it to be sure it doesn't overheat, and never leave the room while the oil is on the heat. Reduce the heat or carefully remove the pot from the burner when the oil reaches the desired temperature. Always keep a metal lid that tightly fits the pot handy to quickly place on the pot should the oil start to smoke or burn.

- Stand mixer with paddle attachment
- Digital candy/deep-fry thermometer
- 3-inch (7.5 cm) round donut cutter
- Baking sheet, lined with parchment paper

3 cups	all-purpose flour, divided (approx.)	750 mL
½ cup	unsweetened cocoa powder	125 mL
2 tsp	baking powder	10 mL
1 tsp	salt	5 mL
½ tsp	baking soda	2 mL
1 cup	packed brown sugar	250 mL
3	large eggs, beaten	3
¼ cup	unsalted butter, melted and cooled	60 mL
¼ cup	whole milk	60 mL
2 tsp	vanilla extract	10 mL
	Canola oil	

1. In a bowl, whisk together 2½ cups (625 mL) of the flour, cocoa powder, baking powder, salt and baking soda. Set aside.

2. In mixer bowl fitted with paddle attachment, combine brown sugar, eggs, butter, milk and vanilla. On low speed, mix until well combined. Add dry ingredients and mix until incorporated. Gradually mix in more of the remaining flour, as necessary, until dough starts to come together and is the consistency of biscuit dough. Cover and refrigerate for 10 minutes.

3. Meanwhile, in a large, deep pot or deep fryer, heat about 4 inches (10 cm) oil over medium heat until temperature registers 360°F (182°C).

4. On a floured work surface, roll out dough to slightly thicker than ¼ inch (0.5 cm). If dough is tacky, dust with additional flour. Cut dough with cutter into 18 donuts, re-rolling scraps as necessary. Place at least 1 inch (2.5 cm) apart on prepared baking sheet.

Finishing suggestions

Icings: Belgian Chocolate Ganache Glaze (page 197), Milk Chocolate Glaze (page 201), Mocha Glaze (page 202), Bittersweet Chocolate Glaze (page 197) or Truffle Fudge Icing (page 196).

Fillings (injected): Chocolate Fudge Filling (page 215).

5. Deep-fry 4 donuts at a time in hot oil, turning once with wooden chopsticks, until puffy and firm, about 25 seconds per side. Using a slotted spatula, transfer to paper towels to absorb excess oil. Fry remaining donuts, adjusting heat as necessary between batches to maintain oil temperature.

6. Let donuts cool completely before icing and/or filling.

Coconut Donuts

Makes about 12 donuts

These donuts are a taste of the islands with a hint of rum.

Tip

When you are making ring-shaped donuts you may like to fry up the center holes for a treat. Depending on the size of the hole, your frying time will have to be adjusted since they tend to fry faster. I sometimes like to test a donut hole just to see how the flavor of the donut is and what icing I will want to dress it with.

- Food processor
- Stand mixer with paddle attachment
- Digital candy/deep-fry thermometer
- 3-inch (7.5 cm) round donut cutter
- Baking sheet, lined with parchment paper

2½ cups	all-purpose flour, divided (approx.)	625 mL
1 cup	sweetened flaked coconut	250 mL
2 tsp	baking powder	10 mL
1 tsp	freshly ground nutmeg	5 mL
1 tsp	salt	5 mL
½ tsp	baking soda	2 mL
¾ cup	granulated sugar	175 mL
2	large eggs, beaten	2
¼ cup	whole milk	60 mL
2 tbsp	unsalted butter, melted and cooled	30 mL
¼ tsp	rum extract	1 mL
	Canola oil	

1. In food processor fitted with metal blade, combine 1¾ cups (425 mL) of the flour, coconut, baking powder, nutmeg, salt and baking soda and process for 20 seconds or until coconut is no longer visible. Set aside.

2. In mixer bowl fitted with paddle attachment, combine sugar, eggs, milk, butter and rum extract. On low speed, mix until well combined. Add dry ingredients and mix until incorporated. Gradually mix in more of the remaining flour, as necessary, until dough starts to come together and is the consistency of biscuit dough. Cover and refrigerate for 10 minutes.

3. Meanwhile, in a large, deep pot or deep fryer, heat about 4 inches (10 cm) oil over medium heat until temperature registers 360°F (182°C).

Finishing suggestions

Icings: Honey Glaze (page 200) or Lemon Zest Glaze (page 200).

Topping: Sprinkle freshly glazed donuts with toasted coconut.

4. On a floured work surface, roll out dough to slightly thicker than ¼ inch (0.5 cm). If dough is tacky, dust with additional flour. Cut dough with cutter into 12 donuts, re-rolling scraps as necessary. Place at least 1 inch (2.5 cm) apart on prepared baking sheet.

5. Deep-fry 4 donuts at a time in hot oil, turning once with wooden chopsticks, until golden brown, about 25 seconds per side. Using a slotted spatula, transfer to paper towels to absorb excess oil. Fry remaining donuts, adjusting heat as necessary between batches to maintain oil temperature.

6. Let donuts cool completely prior to icing or topping.

Whole Wheat Pecan Donuts

Makes about 12 donuts

Here's a deep nutty rich donut that is full of flavor and texture.

● ● ● ● ● ● ● ● ● ● ● ● ● ● ● ●

Finishing suggestions

Icing: Maple Glaze (page 201).

Topping: Sprinkle freshly glazed donuts with crushed pecans.

- Stand mixer with paddle attachment
- Digital candy/deep-fry thermometer
- 3-inch (7.5 cm) round donut cutter
- Baking sheet, lined with parchment paper

1 cup	all-purpose flour, divided (approx.)	250 mL
1 cup	whole wheat flour	250 mL
$\frac{1}{2}$ cup	pecan flour	125 mL
$1\frac{1}{2}$ tsp	baking powder	7 mL
1 tsp	ground cinnamon	5 mL
1 tsp	salt	5 mL
$\frac{1}{2}$ tsp	freshly ground nutmeg	2 mL
$\frac{1}{2}$ tsp	baking soda	2 mL
1 cup	granulated sugar	250 mL
2	large eggs, beaten	2
$\frac{1}{4}$ cup	whole milk	60 mL
	Canola oil	

1. In a bowl, whisk together $\frac{1}{2}$ cup (125 mL) of the all-purpose flour, whole wheat flour, pecan flour, baking powder, cinnamon, salt, nutmeg and baking soda. Set aside.

2. In mixer bowl fitted with paddle attachment, combine sugar, eggs, milk and $\frac{1}{4}$ cup (60 mL) canola oil. On low speed, mix until well combined. Add dry ingredients and mix until incorporated. Gradually mix in more of the remaining flour, as necessary, until dough starts to come together and is the consistency of biscuit dough. Cover and refrigerate for 10 minutes.

3. Meanwhile, in a large, deep pot or deep fryer, heat about 4 inches (10 cm) oil over medium heat until temperature registers 360°F (182°C).

4. On a floured work surface, roll out dough to slightly thicker than $\frac{1}{4}$ inch (0.5 cm). If dough is tacky, dust with additional flour. Cut dough with cutter into 12 donuts, re-rolling scraps as necessary. Place at least 1 inch (2.5 cm) apart on prepared baking sheet.

5. Deep-fry 4 donuts at a time in hot oil, turning once with wooden chopsticks, until golden brown, about 25 seconds per side. Using a slotted spoon, transfer to paper towels to absorb excess oil. Fry remaining donuts, adjusting heat as necessary between batches to maintain oil temperature.

6. Let donuts cool completely prior to icing or topping.

Fresh Peach Pecan Donuts

**Makes about
18 donuts**

Peaches and pecans
remind me of a
Southern donut stand
I found alongside
the road in Alabama
that sold peach pecan
donuts.

Finishing suggestions

Icings: Honey Glaze
(page 200) or Simple
Sugar Glaze (page 205).

- Stand mixer with paddle attachment
- Digital candy/deep-fry thermometer
- 3-inch (7.5 cm) round donut cutter
- Baking sheet, lined with parchment paper

2¾ cups	all-purpose flour, divided (approx.)	675 mL
1 cup	pecan flour	250 mL
1½ tsp	ground cinnamon	7 mL
1¼ tsp	baking powder	6 mL
1 tsp	salt	5 mL
½ tsp	baking soda	2 mL
1 cup	packed brown sugar	250 mL
2	large eggs, beaten	2
¼ cup	whole milk	60 mL
2 tbsp	unsalted butter, melted and cooled	30 mL
1	medium peach, peeled and diced	1
	Canola oil	

1. In a bowl, whisk together 2 cups (500 mL) of the all-purpose flour, pecan flour, cinnamon, baking powder, salt and baking soda. Set aside.

2. In mixer bowl fitted with paddle attachment, combine sugar, eggs, milk and butter. On low speed, mix until well combined. Add dry ingredients and mix until incorporated. Gradually mix in more of the flour, as necessary, until dough starts to come together and is the consistency of biscuit dough. Using a rubber spatula, stir in peaches. Cover and refrigerate for 10 minutes.

3. Meanwhile, in a large, deep pot or deep fryer, heat about 4 inches (10 cm) oil over medium heat until temperature registers 360°F (182°C).

4. On a floured work surface, roll out dough to slightly thicker than ¼ inch (0.5 cm). If dough is tacky, dust with additional flour. Cut dough with cutter into 18 donuts, re-rolling scraps as necessary. Place at least 1 inch (2.5 cm) apart on prepared baking sheet.

5. Deep-fry 4 donuts at a time in hot oil, turning once with wooden chopsticks, until golden brown, about 25 seconds per side. Using a slotted spatula, transfer to paper towels to absorb excess oil. Fry remaining donuts, adjusting heat as necessary between batches to maintain oil temperature.

6. Let donuts cool completely prior to icing.

Fresh Strawberry and Cream Donuts

Sweet strawberries make a donut that's great for a spring brunch or a tea party for kids.

- Stand mixer with paddle attachment
- Digital candy/deep-fry thermometer
- 3-inch (7.5 cm) round donut cutter
- Baking sheet, lined with parchment paper

3¼ cups	all-purpose flour, divided (approx.)	800 mL
1¾ tsp	baking powder	8 mL
1½ tsp	ground cinnamon	7 mL
1 tsp	salt	5 mL
½ tsp	baking soda	2 mL
1 cup	granulated sugar	250 mL
2	large eggs, beaten	2
¼ cup	heavy or whipping (35%) cream	60 mL
	Canola oil	
½ cup	chopped fresh strawberries	125 mL

1. In a bowl, whisk together 2½ cups (625 mL) of the flour, baking powder, cinnamon, salt and baking soda. Set aside.

2. In mixer bowl fitted with paddle attachment, combine sugar, eggs, cream and 2 tbsp (30 mL) canola oil. On low speed, mix until well combined. Add dry ingredients and mix until incorporated. Gradually mix in more of the remaining flour, as necessary, until dough starts to come together and is the consistency of biscuit dough. Using a rubber spatula, stir in strawberries. Cover and refrigerate for 10 minutes.

3. Meanwhile, in a large, deep pot or deep fryer, heat about 4 inches (10 cm) oil over medium heat until temperature registers 360°F (182°C).

Finishing suggestions

Icings: Rose Petal Dust
(page 206), Honey Glaze
(page 200) or Strawberry
Glaze (Variation, page 203).

**Fillings (cut donuts in
half):** Strawberry Filling
(page 214).

4. On a floured work surface, roll out dough to slightly
thicker than $\frac{1}{4}$ inch (0.5 cm). If dough is tacky, dust
with additional flour. Cut dough with cutter into
18 donuts, re-rolling scraps as necessary. Place at least
1 inch (2.5 cm) apart on prepared baking sheet.

5. Deep-fry 4 donuts at a time in hot oil, turning once
with wooden chopsticks, until golden brown, about
25 seconds per side. Using a slotted spatula, transfer to
paper towels to absorb excess oil. Fry remaining donuts,
adjusting heat as necessary between batches to maintain
oil temperature.

6. Toss warm donuts with Rose Petal Dust, if using, or let
cool completely prior to icing and/or filling.

Lemon Crème Bars

**Makes about
18 donuts**

Tart creamy filling will
make you pucker up
just after one bite.

- Stand mixer with paddle attachment
- Digital candy/deep-fry thermometer
- 5- by 2-inch (12.5 by 5 cm) bar cutter, optional
- Baking sheet, lined with parchment paper

3 cups	all-purpose flour, divided (approx.)	750 mL
1½ tsp	baking powder	7 mL
1 tsp	salt	5 mL
½ tsp	baking soda	2 mL
1 cup	granulated sugar	250 mL
2	large eggs, beaten	2
1	large egg yolk, beaten	1
¼ cup	whole milk	60 mL
¼ cup	unsalted butter, melted and cooled	60 mL
2 tsp	grated lemon zest	10 mL
1 tbsp	freshly squeezed lemon juice	15 mL
	Canola oil	
	Lemon Zest Filling (page 213)	

1. In a bowl, whisk together 2½ cups (625 mL) of the flour, baking powder, salt and baking soda. Set aside.

2. In mixer bowl fitted with paddle attachment, combine sugar, eggs, egg yolk, milk, butter, lemon zest and juice. On low speed, mix until well combined. Add dry ingredients and mix until incorporated. Gradually mix in more of the remaining flour, as necessary, until dough starts to come together and is the consistency of biscuit dough. Cover and refrigerate for 10 minutes.

3. Meanwhile, in a large, deep pot or deep fryer, heat about 4 inches (10 cm) oil over medium heat until temperature registers 360°F (182°C).

Finishing suggestions

Icings: Lemon Zest Glaze
(page 200) or dusted with
Citrus Sugar (page 205).

4. On a floured work surface, roll out dough to slightly thicker than $\frac{1}{4}$ inch (0.5 cm). If dough is tacky, dust with additional flour. Cut dough with cutter into 18 donuts (or cut with a knife or pizza cutter into 5- by 2-inch/12.5 by 5 cm rectangles), re-rolling scraps as necessary. Place at least 1 inch (2.5 cm) apart on prepared baking sheet.

5. Deep-fry 4 donuts at a time in hot oil, turning once with wooden chopsticks, until golden brown, about 25 seconds per side. Using a slotted spatula, transfer to paper towels to absorb excess oil. Fry remaining donuts, adjusting heat as necessary between batches to maintain oil temperature.

6. After donuts have cooled completely, slice in half horizontally leaving the back attached like a "hinge" (see page 19) and spoon about 2 tbsp (30 mL) Lemon Zest Filling onto bottom of each. If desired, donuts may now be glazed or dusted on the top only.

Peanut Chocolate Cake Donuts

Makes about 18 donuts

Grinding peanuts into the dough creates a crunchy nutty taste.

Tip

When heating the oil for deep-frying, keep a close eye on it to be sure it doesn't overheat, and never leave the room while the oil is on the heat. Reduce the heat or carefully remove the pot from the burner when the oil reaches the desired temperature. Always keep a metal lid that tightly fits the pot handy to quickly place on the pot should the oil start to smoke or burn.

- Food processor
- Stand mixer with paddle attachment
- Digital candy/deep-fry thermometer
- 3-inch (7.5 cm) round donut cutter
- Baking sheet, lined with parchment paper

2½ cups	all-purpose flour, divided (approx.)	625 mL
1 cup	honey roasted peanuts	250 mL
½ cup	unsweetened cocoa powder	125 mL
2 tsp	baking powder	10 mL
1 tsp	salt	5 mL
½ tsp	baking soda	2 mL
1 cup	packed brown sugar	250 mL
3	large eggs, beaten	3
¼ cup	buttermilk	60 mL
¼ cup	unsalted butter, melted and cooled	60 mL
2 tsp	vanilla extract	10 mL
	Canola oil	

1. In food processor fitted with metal blade, combine 2 cups (500 mL) of the flour, peanuts, cocoa powder, baking powder, salt and baking soda and process for 30 seconds or until peanuts are finely ground. Set aside.

2. In mixer bowl fitted with paddle attachment, combine brown sugar, eggs, buttermilk, butter and vanilla. On low speed, mix until well combined. Add dry ingredients and mix until incorporated. Gradually mix in more of the remaining flour, as necessary, until dough starts to come together and is the consistency of biscuit dough. Cover and refrigerate for 10 minutes.

3. Meanwhile, in a large, deep pot or deep fryer, heat about 4 inches (10 cm) oil over medium heat until temperature registers 360°F (182°C).

Finishing suggestions

Icings: Milk Chocolate Glaze (page 201), Mocha Glaze (page 202), Bittersweet Chocolate Glaze (page 197) or Truffle Fudge Icing (page 196).

Topping: Sprinkle freshly glazed donuts with chopped peanuts.

4. On a floured work surface, roll out dough to slightly thicker than $\frac{1}{4}$ inch (0.5 cm). If dough is tacky, dust with additional flour. Cut dough with cutter into 18 donuts, re-rolling scraps as necessary. Place at least 1 inch (2.5 cm) apart on prepared baking sheet.

5. Deep-fry 4 donuts at a time in hot oil, turning once with wooden chopsticks, until puffy and firm, about 25 seconds per side. Using a slotted spatula, transfer to paper towels to absorb excess oil. Fry remaining donuts, adjusting heat as necessary between batches to maintain oil temperature.

6. Let donuts cool completely before icing or topping.

Espresso Buttermilk Bars

**Makes about
12 donuts**

A slight hint of coffee creates a perfect donut to savor while enjoying a cappuccino.

Finishing suggestions

Icings: Bittersweet Chocolate Glaze (page 197) or Mocha Glaze (page 202).

- Stand mixer with paddle attachment
- Digital candy/deep-fry thermometer
- 5- by 2-inch (12.5 by 5 cm) bar cutter, optional
- Baking sheet, lined with parchment paper

3 cups	all-purpose flour, divided (approx.)	750 mL
1½ tsp	baking powder	7 mL
1 tsp	salt	5 mL
½ tsp	baking soda	2 mL
¼ tsp	ground cardamom	1 mL
1 cup	granulated sugar	250 mL
2	large eggs, beaten	2
1	large egg yolk, beaten	1
¼ cup	buttermilk	60 mL
2 tbsp	unsalted butter, melted and cooled	30 mL
2 tbsp	brewed espresso	30 mL
	Canola oil	

1. In a bowl, whisk together 2½ cups (625 mL) of the flour, baking powder, salt, baking soda and cardamom. Set aside.

2. In mixer bowl fitted with paddle attachment, combine sugar, eggs, egg yolk, buttermilk, butter and espresso. On low speed, mix until well combined. Add dry ingredients and mix until incorporated. Gradually mix in more of the remaining flour, as necessary, until dough starts to come together and is the consistency of biscuit dough. Cover and refrigerate for 10 minutes.

3. Meanwhile, in a large, deep pot or deep fryer, heat about 4 inches (10 cm) oil over medium heat until temperature registers 360°F (182°C).

4. On a floured work surface, roll out dough to slightly thicker than ¼ inch (0.5 cm). If dough is tacky, dust with additional flour. Cut dough with cutter into 12 donuts (or cut with a knife or pizza cutter into 5- by 2-inch/12.5 by 5 cm rectangles), re-rolling scraps as necessary. Place at least 1 inch (2.5 cm) apart on prepared baking sheet.

5. Deep-fry 4 donuts at a time in hot oil, turning once with wooden chopsticks, until golden brown, about 25 seconds per side. Using a slotted spatula, transfer to paper towels to absorb excess oil. Fry remaining donuts, adjusting heat as necessary between batches to maintain oil temperature.

6. Let donuts cool completely prior to icing.

Pumpkin Nutmeg Spice Donuts

Makes about 18 donuts

In the cooler fall season, warm your kitchen with these cozy donuts.

Finishing suggestions

Icings: Autumn Spiced Sugar (page 204) or Maple Glaze (page 201).

- Stand mixer with paddle attachment
- Digital candy/deep-fry thermometer
- 3-inch (7.5 cm) round donut cutter
- Baking sheet, lined with parchment paper

3½ cups	all-purpose flour, divided (approx.)	875 mL
1½ tsp	baking powder	7 mL
1½ tsp	freshly ground nutmeg	7 mL
1 tsp	salt	5 mL
½ tsp	baking soda	2 mL
1 cup	granulated sugar	250 mL
2	large eggs, beaten	2
½ cup	pumpkin purée (not pie filling)	125 mL
¼ cup	whole milk	60 mL
2 tbsp	unsalted butter, melted and cooled	30 mL
	Canola oil	

1. In a bowl, whisk together 2¾ cups (675 mL) of the flour, baking powder, nutmeg, salt and baking soda. Set aside.

2. In mixer bowl fitted with paddle attachment, combine sugar, eggs, pumpkin, milk and butter. On low speed, mix until well combined. Add dry ingredients and mix until incorporated. Gradually mix in more of the remaining flour, as necessary, until dough starts to come together and is the consistency of biscuit dough. Cover and refrigerate for 10 minutes.

3. Meanwhile, in a large, deep pot or deep fryer, heat about 4 inches (10 cm) oil over medium heat until temperature registers 360°F (182°C).

4. On a floured work surface, roll out dough to slightly thicker than ¼ inch (0.5 cm). If dough is tacky, dust with additional flour. Cut dough with cutter into 18 donuts, re-rolling scraps as necessary. Place at least 1 inch (2.5 cm) apart on prepared baking sheet.

5. Deep-fry 3 to 4 donuts at a time in hot oil, turning once with wooden chopsticks, until golden brown, about 25 seconds per side. Using a slotted spatula, transfer to paper towels to absorb excess oil. Fry remaining donuts, adjusting heat as necessary between batches to maintain oil temperature.

6. Toss warm donuts with Autumn Spiced Sugar, if using, or let cool completely prior to icing.

Pumpkin Bars

● ●

**Makes about
18 donuts**

I like to slice these bars
in half and fill with
Cream Cheese Filling
(page 209).

● Stand mixer with paddle attachment
● Digital candy/deep-fry thermometer
● 5- by 2-inch (12.5 by 5 cm) bar cutter, optional
● Baking sheet, lined with parchment paper

3½ cups	all-purpose flour, divided (approx.)	875 mL
1½ tsp	baking powder	7 mL
1 tsp	salt	5 mL
1 tsp	ground cinnamon	5 mL
½ tsp	freshly ground nutmeg	2 mL
½ tsp	baking soda	2 mL
1 cup	packed brown sugar	250 mL
2	large eggs, beaten	2
½ cup	pumpkin purée (not pie filling)	125 mL
¼ cup	whole milk	60 mL
2 tbsp	unsalted butter, melted and cooled	30 mL
	Canola oil	

1. In a bowl, whisk together 3 cups (750 mL) of the flour,
   baking powder, salt, cinnamon, nutmeg and baking
   soda. Set aside.

2. In mixer bowl fitted with paddle attachment, combine
   brown sugar, eggs, pumpkin, milk and butter. On low
   speed, mix until well combined. Add dry ingredients
   and mix until incorporated. Gradually mix in more of
   the remaining flour, as necessary, until dough starts to
   come together and is the consistency of biscuit dough.
   Cover and refrigerate for 10 minutes.

3. Meanwhile, in a large, deep pot or deep fryer, heat
   about 4 inches (10 cm) oil over medium heat until
   temperature registers 360°F (182°C).

Finishing suggestions

Icings: Autumn Spiced Sugar (page 204) or Maple Glaze (page 201).

Filling (cut donuts in half): Cream Cheese Filling (page 209).

4. On a floured work surface, roll out dough to slightly thicker than ¼ inch (0.5 cm). If dough is tacky, dust with additional flour. Cut dough with cutter into 18 donuts (or cut with a knife or pizza cutter into 5- by 2-inch/12.5 by 5 cm rectangles), re-rolling scraps as necessary. Place at least 1 inch (2.5 cm) apart on prepared baking sheet.

5. Deep-fry 3 to 4 donuts at a time in hot oil, turning once with wooden chopsticks, until golden brown, about 25 seconds per side. Using a slotted spatula, transfer to paper towels to absorb excess oil. Fry remaining donuts, adjusting heat as necessary between batches to maintain oil temperature.

6. Toss warm donuts with Autumn Spiced Sugar, if using, or let cool completely prior to icing and/or filling.

Red Velvet Chip Donut Bars

**Makes about
18 donuts**

Here's a donut bar that's red in color with rich grated chocolate right in the batter.

- Stand mixer with paddle attachment
- Digital candy/deep-fry thermometer
- 5- by 2-inch (12.5 by 5 cm) bar cutter, optional
- Baking sheet, lined with parchment paper

3 cups	all-purpose flour, divided (approx.)	750 mL
1½ tsp	baking powder	7 mL
1 tsp	salt	5 mL
½ tsp	baking soda	2 mL
1 cup	granulated sugar	250 mL
2	large eggs, beaten	2
1	large egg yolk, beaten	1
¼ cup	whole milk	60 mL
¼ cup	unsalted butter, melted and cooled	60 mL
2 tbsp	brewed espresso	30 mL
¼ tsp	liquid red food coloring	1 mL
3 oz	bittersweet chocolate, finely grated	90 g
	Canola oil	

1. In a bowl, whisk together 2½ cups (625 mL) of the flour, baking powder, salt and baking soda. Set aside.

2. In mixer bowl fitted with paddle attachment, combine sugar, eggs, egg yolk, milk, butter, espresso and food coloring. On low speed, mix until well combined. Add dry ingredients and mix until incorporated. Gradually mix in more of the remaining flour, as necessary, until dough starts to come together and is the consistency of biscuit dough. Using a rubber spatula, mix in chocolate. Cover and refrigerate for 10 minutes.

3. Meanwhile, in a large, deep pot or deep fryer, heat about 4 inches (10 cm) oil over medium heat until temperature registers 360°F (182°C).

Finishing suggestions

Icing: Bittersweet
Chocolate Glaze
(page 197).

Filling (cut donut bars
horizontally creating a
"hinge"): Bavarian Cream
Custard (page 209).

4. On a floured work surface, roll out dough to about ¼-inch (0.5 cm) thickness. If dough is tacky, dust with additional flour. Cut dough with cutter into 18 donuts (or cut with a knife or pizza cutter into 5- by 2-inch/12.5 by 5 cm rectangles), re-rolling scraps as necessary. Place at least 1 inch (2.5 cm) apart on prepared baking sheet.

5. Deep-fry 4 donuts at a time in hot oil, turning once with wooden chopsticks, until puffy and firm, about 25 seconds per side. Using a slotted spatula, transfer to paper towels to absorb excess oil. Fry remaining donuts, adjusting heat as necessary between batches to maintain oil temperature.

6. Let donuts cool completely prior to icing and/or filling.

Rum Raisin Donuts

Makes about 18 donuts

Years ago rum raisin ice cream was the rage. Today you can create a raging donut with those same flavors.

- Stand mixer with paddle attachment
- Digital candy/deep-fry thermometer
- 3-inch (7.5 cm) round donut cutter
- Baking sheet, lined with parchment paper

½ cup	dark raisins	125 mL
½ cup	dark rum	125 mL
3 cups	all-purpose flour, divided (approx.)	750 mL
1½ tsp	baking powder	7 mL
1½ tsp	ground cinnamon	7 mL
1 tsp	salt	5 mL
½ tsp	baking soda	2 mL
1 cup	granulated sugar	250 mL
2	large eggs, beaten	2
¼ cup	whole milk	60 mL
2 tbsp	unsalted butter, melted and cooled	30 mL
	Canola oil	

1. In a small saucepan, combine raisins and rum and heat over medium heat until bubbling. Turn heat off. Set aside.

2. In a bowl, whisk together 2½ cups (625 mL) of the flour, baking powder, cinnamon, salt and baking soda. Set aside.

3. In mixer bowl fitted with paddle attachment, combine sugar, eggs, milk and butter. On low speed, mix until well combined. Add dry ingredients and mix until incorporated. Gradually mix in more of the remaining flour, as necessary, until dough starts to come together and is the consistency of biscuit dough.

4. Drain raisins, discarding rum or reserving for another use, and using a rubber spatula, mix into dough just until incorporated. Cover and refrigerate for 10 minutes.

Finishing suggestions

Icings: Autumn Spiced Sugar (page 204) or Maple Glaze (page 201).

5. Meanwhile, in a large, deep pot or deep fryer, heat about 4 inches (10 cm) oil over medium heat until temperature registers 360°F (182°C).

6. On a floured work surface, roll out dough to slightly thicker than ¼ inch (0.5 cm). If dough is tacky, dust with additional flour. Cut dough with cutter into 18 donuts, re-rolling scraps as necessary. Place at least 1 inch (2.5 cm) apart on prepared baking sheet.

7. Deep-fry 3 to 4 donuts at a time in hot oil, turning once with wooden chopsticks, until golden brown, about 25 seconds per side. Using a slotted spatula, transfer to paper towels to absorb excess oil. Fry remaining donuts, adjusting heat as necessary between batches to maintain oil temperature.

8. Toss warm donuts with Autumn Spiced Sugar, if using, or let cool completely prior to icing.

Dark Devil's Food Donuts

Makes about 12 donuts

This dark and rich donut will please any sinful pallet.

Finishing suggestions

Icings: Belgian Chocolate Ganache Glaze (page 197), Milk Chocolate Glaze (page 201), Mocha Glaze (page 202), Bittersweet Chocolate Glaze (page 197) or Truffle Fudge Icing (page 196).

- Stand mixer with paddle attachment
- Digital candy/deep-fry thermometer
- 3-inch (7.5 cm) round donut cutter
- Baking sheet, lined with parchment paper

2¾ cups	all-purpose flour, divided (approx.)	675 mL
½ cup	unsweetened cocoa powder	125 mL
1¼ tsp	baking powder	6 mL
1 tsp	salt	5 mL
½ tsp	baking soda	2 mL
1 cup	packed brown sugar	250 mL
3	large eggs, beaten	3
¼ cup	heavy or whipping (35%) cream	60 mL
¼ cup	unsalted butter, melted and cooled	60 mL
2 tsp	vanilla extract	10 mL
1 tsp	liquid red food coloring	5 mL
	Canola oil	

1. In a large bowl, whisk together 2 cups (500 mL) of the flour, cocoa powder, baking powder, salt and baking soda. Set aside.

2. In mixer bowl fitted with paddle attachment, combine sugar, eggs, cream, butter, vanilla and red food coloring. On low speed, mix until well combined. Add dry ingredients and mix until incorporated. Gradually mix in more of the remaining flour, as necessary, until dough starts to come together and is the consistency of biscuit dough. Cover and refrigerate for 10 minutes.

3. Meanwhile, in a large, deep pot or deep fryer, heat about 4 inches (10 cm) oil over medium heat until temperature registers 360°F (182°C).

4. On a floured work surface, roll out dough to slightly thicker than ¼ inch (0.5 cm). If dough is tacky, dust with additional flour. Cut dough with cutter into 12 donuts, re-rolling scraps as necessary. Place at least 1 inch (2.5 cm) apart on prepared baking sheet.

5. Deep-fry 4 donuts at a time in hot oil, turning once with wooden chopsticks, until puffy and firm, about 25 seconds per side. Using a slotted spatula, transfer to paper towels to absorb excess oil. Fry remaining donuts, adjusting heat as necessary between batches to maintain oil temperature.

6. Let donuts cool completely prior to icing.

Baked Donuts

• •

With **the help** of a simple donut pan you can create flavorful light donuts without getting your fryer out. Also, all of the donut batters can be whipped up by hand without using your mixer.

Almond Apricot Donuts.............................92

Apple Cream Donuts..............................93

Banana Bran Donuts 94

Banana Pecan Donuts 95

Blueberry Donuts.................................96

Cherry Blossom Donuts..........................97

Chocolate Donuts 98

Chocolate Rum Cream Donuts....................99

Coconut Marshmallow Donuts 100

Double Chocolate Raspberry Donuts............101

Framboise-Glazed Donuts.......................102

Green Tea Donuts 103

Honey Bran–Glazed Donuts 104

Lemon Crème Donuts 105

Maple Cinnamon Donuts.......................106

Orange Donuts................................107

Orange Honey Donuts.........................108

Pineapple Macadamia Nut Donuts..............109

Red Devil Donuts 110

Simple Spice Donuts 111

Sour Cream Blackberry Donuts.................112

Strawberry Donuts 113

Tangerine Donuts.............................114

Roasted Peanut Donuts.......................115

Vanilla Bean Donuts..........................116

White Chocolate Crème Donuts...............117

Baked Whole Wheat Pecan Donuts 118

Almond Apricot Donuts

**Makes about
18 donuts**

Rich flavor with nutty
almonds make this
a perfect donut for
breakfast or brunch.

Tip

If you only have one 6-well
donut pan, use one-third
of the batter to fill pan as
directed and bake, then
remove donuts and let
the pan cool completely.
Spray again, fill with
remaining batter and bake
as directed. It's important
to let the pan cool before
refilling so you get the
right texture for your next
batch of donuts.

Finishing suggestions

Icings: Simple Sugar Glaze
(page 205) or Honey Glaze
(page 200).

- Preheat oven to 325°F (160°C)
- Two 6-well donut pans, sprayed with nonstick spray

2½ cups	cake flour	625 mL
1 cup	granulated sugar	250 mL
2½ tsp	baking powder	12 mL
½ tsp	salt	2 mL
½ tsp	ground cardamom	2 mL
2	large eggs, beaten	2
¾ cup	heavy or whipping (35%) cream	175 mL
2 tbsp	unsalted butter, melted and cooled	30 mL
1 tsp	vanilla extract	5 mL
½ tsp	almond extract	2 mL
½ cup	finely chopped fresh apricots	125 mL
½ cup	almonds, chopped	125 mL

1. In a large bowl, whisk together flour, sugar, baking powder, salt and cardamom. Set aside.

2. In another bowl, whisk together eggs, cream, butter and vanilla and almond extracts. Add to flour mixture and mix with a rubber spatula just until incorporated. Fold in apricots and almonds.

3. Spoon batter into resealable freezer bag or pastry bag (see page 8) and fill each prepared well two-thirds full, using two-thirds of the batter.

4. Bake in preheated oven until donut springs back when lightly touched, 10 to 14 minutes.

5. Let donuts cool in pans on a rack for 5 minutes. Turn out of pans onto rack and let cool completely prior to icing. Let pan cool, then spray again and repeat to bake remaining batter.

Apple Cream Donuts

● ●

Makes about 12 donuts

Fall harvest would not be the same without the aroma of apples and spices, and they go together perfectly in this cream donut.

● ● ● ● ● ● ● ● ● ● ● ● ● ● ● ● ●

Finishing suggestions

Icings: Honey Glaze (page 200) or Simple Sugar Glaze (page 205).

Fillings (cut donuts in half): Bavarian Cream Custard (page 209) or Banana Cream Filling (page 208).

● Preheat oven to 325°F (160°C)
● Two 6-well donut pans, sprayed with nonstick spray (see Tip, page 94)

2 cups	all-purpose flour	500 mL
¾ cup	packed brown sugar	175 mL
2 tsp	baking powder	10 mL
1 tsp	salt	5 mL
1 tsp	ground cinnamon	5 mL
2	large eggs, beaten	2
¾ cup	heavy or whipping (35%) cream	175 mL
1 tbsp	unsalted butter, melted	15 mL
1 tsp	vanilla extract	5 mL
1½ cups	finely chopped apples	375 mL

1. In a large bowl, whisk together flour, brown sugar, baking powder, salt and cinnamon. Set aside.

2. In another bowl, whisk together eggs, cream, butter and vanilla. Add to flour mixture and mix with a rubber spatula just until incorporated. Fold in apples.

3. Spoon batter into resealable freezer bag or pastry bag (see page 8) and fill each prepared well two-thirds full.

4. Bake in preheated oven until donut springs back when lightly touched, 10 to 14 minutes.

5. Let donuts cool in pans on a rack for 5 minutes. Turn out of pans onto rack and let cool completely prior to icing and/or filling.

Banana Bran Donuts

These donuts are full of flavor and the bananas make them very moist.

Tip

If you only have one 6-well donut pan, use half of the batter to fill pan as directed and bake. Remove donuts and let the pan cool completely, spray again and fill with remaining batter and bake as directed. It's important to let the pan cool before refilling so you get the right texture for your second batch of donuts.

Finishing suggestions

Icing: Simple Sugar Glaze (page 205).

- Preheat oven to 325°F (160°C)
- Two 6-well donut pans, sprayed with nonstick spray (see Tip, left)

1 cup	all-purpose flour	250 mL
1/3 cup	granulated sugar	75 mL
2 tsp	baking powder	10 mL
1/2 tsp	salt	2 mL
1/2 tsp	ground cinnamon	2 mL
1 cup	oat bran	250 mL
1	large egg, beaten	1
1 cup	whole milk	250 mL
1 cup	mashed ripe banana	250 mL
3 tbsp	canola oil	45 mL
1 cup	pecans, chopped	250 mL

1. In a bowl, whisk together flour, sugar, baking powder, salt and cinnamon. Set aside.

2. In a large bowl, whisk together oat bran, egg, milk, banana and oil. Let stand for 5 minutes. Add flour mixture and mix with a rubber spatula just until incorporated. Fold in pecans.

3. Spoon batter into resealable freezer bag or pastry bag (see page 8) and fill each prepared well two-thirds full.

4. Bake in preheated oven until donut springs back when lightly touched, 10 to 14 minutes.

5. Let donuts cool in pans on a rack for 5 minutes. Turn out of pans onto rack and let cool completely prior to icing.

Banana Pecan Donuts

Makes about 12 donuts

These fruity and nutty donuts make a perfect brunch pastry.

• • • • • • • • • • • • • • • • •

Finishing suggestions

Icing: Simple Sugar Glaze (page 205).

- Preheat oven to 325°F (160°C)
- Two 6-well donut pans, sprayed with nonstick spray (see Tip, page 94)

1 cup	all-purpose flour	250 mL
1 cup	whole wheat flour	250 mL
¾ cup	packed brown sugar	175 mL
2 tsp	baking powder	10 mL
1 tsp	salt	5 mL
1 tsp	ground cinnamon	5 mL
½ tsp	freshly ground nutmeg	2 mL
1	large egg, beaten	1
¾ cup	whole milk	175 mL
1 tbsp	unsalted butter, melted	15 mL
⅔ cup	mashed ripe banana	150 mL
1 cup	chopped pecans	250 mL

1. In a large bowl, whisk together all-purpose flour, whole wheat flour, brown sugar, baking powder, salt, cinnamon and nutmeg. Set aside.

2. In another bowl, whisk together egg, milk and butter. Add to flour mixture and mix with a rubber spatula just until incorporated. Fold in bananas and pecans.

3. Spoon batter into resealable freezer bag or pastry bag (see page 8) and fill each prepared well two-thirds full.

4. Bake in preheated oven until donut springs back when lightly touched, 10 to 14 minutes.

5. Let donuts cool in pans on a rack for 5 minutes. Turn out of pans onto rack and let cool completely prior to icing.

Blueberry Donuts

**Makes about
12 donuts**

Making blueberry
donuts for a brunch
instead of muffins sure
will get your guests
talking.

Finishing suggestions
Icing: Simple Sugar Glaze
(page 205).

• Preheat oven to 325°F (160°C)
• Two 6-well donut pans, sprayed with nonstick spray
  (see Tip, page 94)

2½ cups	cake flour	625 mL
1 cup	granulated sugar	250 mL
2½ tsp	baking powder	12 mL
½ tsp	salt	2 mL
2	large eggs, beaten	2
¾ cup	whole milk	175 mL
2 tbsp	unsalted butter, melted	30 mL
1 tsp	vanilla extract	5 mL
1 tsp	almond extract	5 mL
1 cup	fresh or frozen blueberries	250 mL

1. In a large bowl, whisk together flour, sugar, baking
   powder and salt. Set aside.

2. In another bowl, whisk together eggs, milk, butter and
   vanilla and almond extracts. Add to flour mixture and
   mix with a rubber spatula just until incorporated. Fold
   in blueberries.

3. Spoon batter into resealable freezer bag or pastry bag
   (see page 8) and fill each prepared well two-thirds full.

4. Bake in preheated oven until donut springs back when
   lightly touched, 10 to 14 minutes.

5. Let donuts cool in pans on a rack for 5 minutes. Turn
   out of pans onto rack and let cool completely prior
   to icing.

Light-As-Air Glazed Donuts (page 46)

Fresh Jelly Donuts (page 22)

Applesauce Donuts (page 62)

Mandarin Orange Donuts (page 48)

Perfect Chocolate–Glazed Donuts (page 52)

Blackout Donuts (page 64)

White Chocolate Crème Donuts (page 117)

Chocolate Cake Donuts (page 70)

Cherry Blossom Donuts

● ●

Makes about 12 donuts

Serve these during cherry blossom festival time in the spring. Light pink in color just like the blossoms.

● ● ● ● ● ● ● ● ● ● ● ● ● ● ● ● ● ●

Finishing suggestions

Icings: Cherry Glaze (page 198), Simple Sugar Glaze (page 205) or Rose Petal Dust (page 206).

● Preheat oven to 325°F (160°C)
● Two 6-well donut pans, sprayed with nonstick spray (see Tip, page 94)

2¼ cups	all-purpose flour	550 mL
¾ cup	granulated sugar	175 mL
2 tsp	baking powder	10 mL
1 tsp	salt	5 mL
2	large eggs, beaten	2
¾ cup	whole milk	175 mL
1 tbsp	unsalted butter, melted	15 mL
1 tsp	vanilla extract	5 mL
1 tsp	almond extract	5 mL
½ cup	finely chopped cherries	125 mL

1. In a large bowl, whisk together flour, sugar, baking powder and salt. Set aside.

2. In another bowl, whisk together eggs, milk, butter and vanilla and almond extracts. Add to flour mixture and mix with a rubber spatula just until incorporated. Fold in cherries.

3. Spoon batter into resealable freezer bag or pastry bag (see page 8) and fill each prepared well two-thirds full.

4. Bake in preheated oven until donut springs back when lightly touched, 10 to 14 minutes.

5. Let donuts cool in pans on a rack for 5 minutes. Turn out of pans and toss with Rose Petal Dust, if using, or let cool completely on racks prior to icing.

Chocolate Donuts

**Makes about
12 donuts**

These rich and flavorful
chocolate donuts can
be iced with an array
of toppings.

Finishing suggestions

Icings: Belgian Chocolate
Ganache Glaze (page 197),
Bittersweet Chocolate
Glaze (page 197),
Honey Glaze (page 200),
Milk Chocolate Glaze
(page 201) or Mocha Glaze
(page 202).

Topping: Sprinkle freshly
glazed donuts with
crushed peanuts.

- Preheat oven to 325°F (160°C)
- Two 6-well donut pans, sprayed with nonstick spray
  (see Tip, page 94)

1½ cups	all-purpose flour	375 mL
⅔ cup	granulated sugar	150 mL
⅓ cup	unsweetened cocoa powder	75 mL
1 tsp	baking powder	5 mL
¼ tsp	salt	1 mL
2	large eggs, beaten	2
¼ cup	heavy or whipping (35%) cream	60 mL
¼ cup	whole milk	60 mL
2 tbsp	canola oil	30 mL
1 tsp	vanilla extract	5 mL

1. In a large bowl, whisk together flour, sugar, cocoa,
   baking powder and salt. Set aside.

2. In another bowl, whisk together eggs, cream, milk, oil
   and vanilla. Add to flour mixture and mix with a rubber
   spatula just until incorporated.

3. Spoon batter into resealable freezer bag or pastry bag
   (see page 8) and fill each prepared well two-thirds full.

4. Bake in preheated oven until donut springs back when
   lightly touched, 10 to 14 minutes.

5. Let donuts cool in pans on a rack for 5 minutes. Turn
   out of pans onto rack and let cool completely prior
   to icing or topping.

Chocolate Rum Cream Donuts

Makes about 12 donuts

These rich chocolate donuts have a hint of rum.

Finishing suggestions

Icings: Belgian Chocolate Ganache Glaze (page 197), Bittersweet Chocolate Glaze (page 197), Honey Glaze (page 200) or Milk Chocolate Glaze (page 201).

- Preheat oven to 325°F (160°C)
- Two 6-well donut pans, sprayed with nonstick spray (see Tip, page 94)

1½ cups	all-purpose flour	375 mL
⅔ cup	packed brown sugar	150 mL
⅓ cup	unsweetened cocoa powder	75 mL
1 tsp	baking powder	5 mL
¼ tsp	salt	1 mL
2	large eggs, beaten	2
1	large egg white	1
½ cup	heavy or whipping (35%) cream	125 mL
2 tbsp	canola oil	30 mL
1 tsp	rum extract	5 mL

1. In a large bowl, whisk together flour, brown sugar, cocoa, baking powder and salt. Set aside.

2. In another bowl, whisk together eggs, egg white, cream, oil and rum extract. Add to flour mixture and mix with a rubber spatula just until incorporated.

3. Spoon batter into resealable freezer bag or pastry bag (see page 8) and fill each prepared well two-thirds full.

4. Bake in preheated oven until donut springs back when lightly touched, 10 to 14 minutes.

5. Let donuts cool in pans on a rack for 5 minutes. Turn out of pans onto rack and let cool completely prior to icing.

Coconut Marshmallow Donuts

Makes about 12 donuts

Creamy marshmallow with the tropical coconut favor makes this a donut perfect for a spring brunch.

Finishing suggestions

Icing: Honey Glaze (page 200).

Topping: Sprinkle freshly glazed donuts with toasted flaked coconut.

- Preheat oven to 325°F (160°C)
- Two 6-well donut pans, sprayed with nonstick spray (see Tip, page 102)

1½ cups	all-purpose flour	375 mL
½ cup	sweetened flaked coconut	125 mL
¾ cup	granulated sugar	175 mL
2 tsp	baking powder	10 mL
1 tsp	salt	5 mL
2	large eggs, beaten	2
¾ cup	whole milk	175 mL
1 tbsp	canola oil	15 mL
1 tsp	rum extract	5 mL
	Marshmallow Filling (page 210)	

1. In a large bowl, whisk together flour, coconut, sugar, baking powder and salt. Set aside.

2. In another bowl, whisk together eggs, milk, oil and rum extract. Add to flour mixture and mix with a rubber spatula just until incorporated.

3. Spoon batter into resealable freezer bag or pastry bag (see page 8) and fill each prepared well two-thirds full.

4. Bake in preheated oven until donut springs back when lightly touched, 10 to 14 minutes.

5. Let donuts cool in pans on a rack for 5 minutes. Turn out of pans onto rack and let cool completely prior to icing or topping.

6. Cut donuts in half horizontally and fill with marshmallow filling.

Double Chocolate Raspberry Donuts

Makes 24 donuts

Two chocolates with sweet fresh raspberries make a rich breakfast donut that anyone would be proud to serve. This is a big batch perfect to serve a crowd.

Finishing suggestions

Icings: Truffle Fudge Icing (page 196) or Milk Chocolate Glaze (page 201).

- Preheat oven to 325°F (160°C)
- Two 6-well donut pans, sprayed with nonstick spray

3½ cups	all-purpose flour	875 mL
½ cup	unsweetened cocoa powder	125 mL
¾ cup	granulated sugar	175 mL
1 tbsp	baking soda	15 mL
2 tsp	salt	10 mL
4	large eggs, beaten	4
2 cups	whole milk	500 mL
¼ cup	unsalted butter, melted	60 mL
2 tsp	vanilla extract	10 mL
1 cup	semisweet chocolate chips	250 mL
1 cup	raspberries	250 mL

1. In a large bowl, whisk together flour, cocoa, sugar, baking soda and salt. Set aside.

2. In another bowl, whisk together eggs, milk, butter and vanilla. Add to flour mixture and mix with a rubber spatula just until incorporated. Fold in chocolate chips and raspberries.

3. Spoon batter into resealable freezer bag or pastry bag (see page 8) and fill each prepared well two-thirds full, using half the batter.

4. Bake in preheated oven until donut springs back when lightly touched, 10 to 14 minutes.

5. Let donuts cool in pans on a rack for 5 minutes. Turn out of pans onto rack and let cool completely prior to icing. Let pans cool completely, then spray again and repeat with remaining batter.

Framboise-Glazed Donuts

**Makes about
12 donuts**

Sweet raspberries
are encased in a rich
vanilla-based donut.

Tip

If you only have one
6-well donut pan, use half
of the batter to fill pan
as directed and bake.
Remove donuts and let
the pan cool completely,
spray again and fill with
remaining batter and bake
as directed. It's important
to let the pan cool before
refilling so you get the
right texture for your
second batch of donuts.

Finishing suggestions

Icings: Simple Sugar Glaze
(page 205) or Raspberry
Glaze (page 203).

- Preheat oven to 325°F (160°C)
- Two 6-well donut pans, sprayed with nonstick spray
  (see Tip, left)

2¼ cups	all-purpose flour	550 mL
¾ cup	granulated sugar	175 mL
2 tsp	baking powder	10 mL
1 tsp	salt	5 mL
2	large eggs, beaten	2
½ cup	whole milk	125 mL
¼ cup	heavy or whipping (35%) cream	60 mL
1 tbsp	unsalted butter, melted	15 mL
1 tsp	vanilla extract	5 mL
¼ cup	raspberries, lightly mashed	60 mL

1. In a large bowl, whisk together flour, sugar, baking
   powder and salt. Set aside.

2. In another bowl, whisk together eggs, milk, cream,
   butter and vanilla. Add to flour mixture and mix
   with a rubber spatula just until incorporated. Fold in
   raspberries.

3. Spoon batter into resealable freezer bag or pastry bag
   (see page 8) and fill each prepared well two-thirds full.

4. Bake in preheated oven until donut springs back when
   lightly touched, 10 to 14 minutes.

5. Let donuts cool in pans on a rack for 5 minutes. Turn
   out of pans onto rack and let cool completely prior
   to icing.

Green Tea Donuts

**Makes about
12 donuts**

Infusing this donut with green tea gives it a hint of Asian flavors.

● ● ● ● ● ● ● ● ● ● ● ● ● ● ●

Finishing suggestions

Icings: Green Tea Glaze (page 199), Honey Glaze (page 200) or Simple Sugar Glaze (page 205).

- Preheat oven to 325°F (160°C)
- Two 6-well donut pans, sprayed with nonstick spray (see Tip, page 102)

¾ cup	whole milk	175 mL
1	green tea bag	1
1½ cups	all-purpose flour	375 mL
½ cup	cake flour	125 mL
¾ cup	granulated sugar	175 mL
2 tsp	baking powder	10 mL
1 tsp	salt	5 mL
2	large eggs, beaten	2
1 tbsp	unsalted butter, melted	15 mL
1 tsp	vanilla extract	5 mL

1. In a small saucepan over medium heat, bring milk to a simmer. Turn off heat. Add tea bag and let infuse for 20 minutes. Discard tea bag.

2. In a large bowl, whisk together all-purpose flour, cake flour, sugar, baking powder and salt. Set aside.

3. In a medium bowl, whisk together infused milk, eggs, butter and vanilla. Add to flour mixture and mix with a rubber spatula just until incorporated.

4. Spoon batter into resealable freezer bag or pastry bag (see page 8) and fill each prepared well two-thirds full.

5. Bake in preheated oven until donut springs back when lightly touched, 10 to 14 minutes.

6. Let donuts cool in pans on a rack for 5 minutes. Turn out of pans onto rack and let cool completely prior to icing.

Honey Bran–Glazed Donuts

**Makes about
18 donuts**

Just like a bran muffin
but more fun to eat!

Tip

Make sure that you let
the mixture stand for the
10 minutes so that the
bran can soak up the
liquid.

Finishing suggestions

Icing: Honey Glaze
(page 200).

- Preheat oven to 375°F (190°C)
- Two 6-well donut pans, sprayed with nonstick spray
(see Tip, page 92)

4 cups	oat bran	1 L
1/2 cup	packed brown sugar	125 mL
1 tbsp	baking powder	15 mL
1 tsp	salt	5 mL
4	large eggs, beaten	4
2 cups	whole milk	500 mL
1/2 cup	liquid honey	125 mL
1/4 cup	canola oil	60 mL

1. In a large bowl, whisk together oat bran, brown sugar,
baking powder and salt. Set aside.

2. In another bowl, whisk together eggs, milk, honey and
oil. Add to bran mixture and mix with a rubber spatula
just until incorporated. Let stand for 10 minutes.

3. Spoon batter into resealable freezer bag or pastry bag
(see page 8) and fill each prepared well two-thirds full,
using two-thirds of the batter.

4. Bake in preheated oven until donut springs back when
lightly touched, 18 to 22 minutes.

5. Let donuts cool in pans on a rack for 5 minutes. Turn
out of pans onto rack and let cool completely prior to
icing. Let pan cool completely, then spray again and
repeat with remaining batter.

Lemon Crème Donuts

This donut has all
the flavor of rich, tart
lemon.

Finishing suggestions

Icings: Honey Glaze
(page 200), Simple Sugar
Glaze (page 205), Rose
Petal Dust (page 206)
or Lavender Sugar Dust
(page 206).

- Preheat oven to 325°F (160°C)
- Two 6-well donut pans, sprayed with nonstick spray
  (see Tip, page 102)

2 cups	all-purpose flour	500 mL
¾ cup	granulated sugar	175 mL
2 tsp	baking powder	10 mL
1 tsp	salt	5 mL
2	large eggs, beaten	2
½ cup	heavy or whipping (35%) cream	125 mL
1 tbsp	canola oil	15 mL
1 tbsp	grated lemon zest	15 mL
¼ cup	freshly squeezed lemon juice	60 mL
1 tsp	vanilla extract	5 mL

1. In a large bowl, whisk together flour, sugar, baking
   powder and salt. Set aside.

2. In another bowl, whisk together eggs, cream, oil, lemon
   zest, lemon juice and vanilla. Add to flour mixture and
   mix with a rubber spatula just until incorporated.

3. Spoon batter into resealable freezer bag or pastry bag
   (see page 8) and fill each prepared well two-thirds full.

4. Bake in preheated oven until donut springs back when
   lightly touched, 10 to 14 minutes.

5. Let donuts cool in pans on a rack for 5 minutes. Turn
   out of pans and toss with Rose Petal Dust or Lavender
   Sugar Dust, if using, or let cool completely on racks
   prior to icing.

Maple Cinnamon Donuts

Makes about 12 donuts

Rich maple flavor can only be produced by using real maple syrup.

Finishing suggestions

Icings: Honey Glaze (page 200) or Maple Glaze (page 201).

- Preheat oven to 325°F (160°C)
- Two 6-well donut pans, sprayed with nonstick spray (see Tip, page 102)

2 cups	all-purpose flour	500 mL
1/4 cup	packed brown sugar	60 mL
1/4 cup	granulated sugar	60 mL
2 tsp	baking powder	10 mL
1 tsp	salt	5 mL
1 tsp	ground cinnamon	5 mL
2	large eggs, beaten	2
1/2 cup	pure maple syrup	125 mL
1/4 cup	whole milk	60 mL
1 tbsp	unsalted butter, melted	15 mL
1 tsp	vanilla extract	5 mL

1. In a large bowl, whisk together flour, brown sugar, granulated sugar, baking powder, salt and cinnamon. Set aside.

2. In another bowl, whisk together eggs, maple syrup, milk, butter and vanilla. Add to flour mixture and mix with a rubber spatula just until incorporated.

3. Spoon batter into resealable freezer bag or pastry bag (see page 8) and fill each prepared well two-thirds full.

4. Bake in preheated oven until donut springs back when lightly touched, 10 to 14 minutes.

5. Let donuts cool in pans on a rack for 5 minutes. Turn out of pans onto rack and let cool completely prior to icing.

Orange Donuts

Tart orange flavor with
a nice citrus glaze
makes a sunny donut
for any breakfast.

Finishing suggestions

Icings: Orange Glaze
(page 202) or Milk
Chocolate Glaze
(page 201).

- Preheat oven to 325°F (160°C)
- Two 6-well donut pans, sprayed with nonstick spray
  (see Tip, page 102)

2½ cups	cake flour	625 mL
1 cup	granulated sugar	250 mL
2½ tsp	baking powder	12 mL
½ tsp	salt	2 mL
2	large eggs, beaten	2
¾ cup	whole milk	175 mL
1½ tbsp	canola oil	22 mL
1 tbsp	grated orange zest	15 mL
1 tsp	vanilla extract	5 mL
1 tsp	orange extract	5 mL

1. In a large bowl, whisk together flour, sugar, baking
   powder and salt. Set aside.

2. In another bowl, whisk together eggs, milk, oil,
   orange zest, and vanilla and orange extracts. Add to
   flour mixture and mix with a rubber spatula just until
   incorporated.

3. Spoon batter into resealable freezer bag or pastry bag
   (see page 8) and fill each prepared well two-thirds full.

4. Bake in preheated oven until donut springs back when
   lightly touched, 10 to 14 minutes.

5. Let donuts cool in pans on a rack for 5 minutes. Turn
   out of pans onto rack and let cool completely prior
   to icing.

Orange Honey Donuts

Flavorful orange essence combines with the natural sweetness of honey — an array of spring flavors that brings the sunny weather into your baking.

Finishing suggestions

Icings: Honey Glaze (page 200), Autumn Spiced Sugar (page 204) or Sunset Orange Glaze (page 204).

Fillings (cut donuts in half): Blood Orange Filling (Variation, page 211) or Sunset Orange Filling (page 211).

- Preheat oven to 325°F (160°C)
- Two 6-well donut pans, sprayed with nonstick spray (see Tip, page 102)

2¼ cups	all-purpose flour	550 mL
¾ cup	granulated sugar	175 mL
2 tsp	baking powder	10 mL
1 tsp	salt	5 mL
2	large eggs, beaten	2
½ cup	whole milk	125 mL
¼ cup	frozen orange juice concentrate, thawed	60 mL
2 tbsp	liquid honey	30 mL
1 tbsp	unsalted butter, melted	15 mL
1 tsp	vanilla extract	5 mL
1 tsp	grated orange zest	5 mL

1. In a large bowl, whisk together flour, sugar, baking powder and salt. Set aside.

2. In another bowl, whisk together eggs, milk, orange juice concentrate, honey, butter, vanilla and orange zest. Add to flour mixture and mix with a rubber spatula just until incorporated.

3. Spoon batter into resealable freezer bag or pastry bag (see page 8) and fill each prepared well two-thirds full.

4. Bake in preheated oven until donut springs back when lightly touched, 10 to 14 minutes.

5. Let donuts cool in pans on a rack for 5 minutes. Turn out of pans and toss with Autumn Spiced Sugar, if using, or let cool completely on racks prior to icing and/or filling.

Pineapple Macadamia Nut Donuts

Makes about 12 donuts

Pacific islands have so many great flavors, from pineapples to macadamia nuts. Try these island delight donuts.

Finishing suggestions

Icings: Honey Glaze (page 200) or Simple Sugar Glaze (page 205).

- Preheat oven to 325°F (160°C)
- Two 6-well donut pans, sprayed with nonstick spray (see Tip, page 102)

1 cup	all-purpose flour	250 mL
1 cup	large-flake (old-fashioned) rolled oats	250 mL
¾ cup	packed brown sugar	175 mL
1 tbsp	baking powder	15 mL
1½ tsp	ground cinnamon	7 mL
½ tsp	freshly ground nutmeg	2 mL
½ tsp	ground allspice	2 mL
½ tsp	salt	2 mL
1	large egg, beaten	1
1 cup	buttermilk	250 mL
½ cup	canned crushed pineapple	125 mL
½ cup	macadamia nuts, chopped	125 mL

1. In a large bowl, whisk together flour, oats, brown sugar, baking powder, cinnamon, nutmeg, allspice and salt. Set aside.

2. In another bowl, whisk together egg and buttermilk. Add to flour mixture and mix with a rubber spatula just until incorporated. Fold in pineapple and macadamia nuts.

3. Spoon batter into resealable freezer bag or pastry bag (see page 8) and fill each prepared well two-thirds full.

4. Bake in preheated oven until donut springs back when lightly touched, 10 to 14 minutes.

5. Let donuts cool in pans on a rack for 5 minutes. Turn out of pans onto rack and let cool completely prior to icing.

Red Devil Donuts

Makes about 12 donuts

I always envision these donuts being served at an eight-year-old's birthday party instead of cake. Try these for your little ones.

Tip

If you only have one 6-well donut pan, use half of the batter to fill pan as directed and bake. Remove donuts and let the pan cool completely, spray again and fill with remaining batter and bake as directed. It's important to let the pan cool before refilling so you get the right texture for your second batch of donuts.

Finishing suggestions

Icings: Belgian Chocolate Ganache Glaze (page 197), Bittersweet Chocolate Glaze (page 197) or Milk Chocolate Glaze (page 201).

- Preheat oven to 325°F (160°C)
- Two 6-well donut pans, sprayed with nonstick spray (see Tip, left)

1 cup	all-purpose flour	250 mL
½ cup	cake flour	125 mL
⅔ cup	granulated sugar	150 mL
⅓ cup	unsweetened cocoa powder	75 mL
1 tsp	baking powder	5 mL
¼ tsp	salt	1 mL
2	large eggs, beaten	2
½ cup	heavy or whipping (35%) cream	125 mL
2 tbsp	unsalted butter, melted	30 mL
1 tsp	vanilla extract	5 mL
1 tsp	liquid red food coloring	5 mL

1. In a large bowl, whisk together all-purpose flour, cake flour, sugar, cocoa, baking powder and salt. Set aside.

2. In another bowl, whisk together eggs, cream, butter, vanilla and red food coloring. Add to flour mixture and mix with a rubber spatula just until incorporated.

3. Spoon batter into resealable freezer bag or pastry bag (see page 8) and fill each prepared well two-thirds full.

4. Bake in preheated oven until donut springs back when lightly touched, 10 to 14 minutes.

5. Let donuts cool in pans on a rack for 5 minutes. Turn out of pans onto rack and let cool completely prior to icing.

Simple Spice Donuts

**Makes about
12 donuts**

An array of spicy fall flavors brings the autumn weather into your baking.

Finishing suggestions

Icing: Autumn Spiced Sugar (page 204).

Variation

Spiced Chai Donuts: Use cream instead of milk and reduce it to ¼ cup (60 mL). In a small saucepan over medium heat, bring ½ cup (125 mL) water to a simmer. Turn off heat. Add 1 chai tea bag and let infuse for 20 minutes. Discard tea bag and combine tea with cream. Replace cinnamon, nutmeg, allspice and ginger with ½ tsp (2 mL) Chinese five-spice powder. Finish with Green Tea Glaze (page 199), Honey Glaze (page 200) or Simple Sugar Glaze (page 205).

- Preheat oven to 325°F (160°C)
- Two 6-well donut pans, sprayed with nonstick spray (see Tip, page 110)

2 cups	all-purpose flour	500 mL
¾ cup	granulated sugar	175 mL
2 tsp	baking powder	10 mL
1 tsp	salt	5 mL
1 tsp	ground cinnamon	5 mL
½ tsp	freshly ground nutmeg	2 mL
¼ tsp	ground allspice	1 mL
⅛ tsp	ground ginger	0.5 mL
2	large eggs, beaten	2
¾ cup	whole milk	175 mL
1 tbsp	unsalted butter, melted	15 mL
1 tsp	vanilla extract	5 mL

1. In a large bowl, whisk together flour, sugar, baking powder, salt, cinnamon, nutmeg, allspice and ginger. Set aside.

2. In another bowl, whisk together eggs, milk, butter and vanilla. Add to flour mixture and mix with a rubber spatula just until incorporated.

3. Spoon batter into resealable freezer bag or pastry bag (see page 8) and fill each prepared well two-thirds full.

4. Bake in preheated oven until donut springs back when lightly touched, 10 to 14 minutes.

5. Let donuts cool in pans on a rack for 5 minutes. Turn out of pans and toss with Autumn Spiced Sugar.

Sour Cream Blackberry Donuts

●●

Makes about 12 donuts

Sour cream adds a special tang to this donut.

●●●●●●●●●●●●●●●●●●●●●

Tip

If the blackberries are large, they should be chopped to the size of peas.

Finishing suggestions

Icings: Honey Glaze (page 200) or Simple Sugar Glaze (page 205).

- Preheat oven to 325°F (160°C)
- Two 6-well donut pans, sprayed with nonstick spray (see Tip, page 110)

2½ cups	cake flour	625 mL
1 cup	granulated sugar	250 mL
2½ tsp	baking powder	12 mL
½ tsp	salt	2 mL
2	large eggs, beaten	2
½ cup	whole milk	125 mL
2 tbsp	unsalted butter, melted	30 mL
¼ cup	sour cream	60 mL
1 tsp	vanilla extract	5 mL
1 cup	fresh or frozen blackberries, chopped if large (see Tip, left)	250 mL

1. In a large bowl, whisk together flour, sugar, baking powder and salt. Set aside.

2. In another bowl, whisk together eggs, milk, butter, sour cream and vanilla. Add to flour mixture and mix with a rubber spatula just until incorporated. Fold in blackberries.

3. Spoon batter into resealable freezer bag or pastry bag (see page 8) and fill each prepared well two-thirds full.

4. Bake in preheated oven until donut springs back when lightly touched, 10 to 14 minutes.

5. Let donuts cool in pans on a rack for 5 minutes. Turn out of pans onto rack and let cool completely prior to icing.

Strawberry Donuts

Makes about 12 donuts

Fresh bites of sweet strawberries make a wonderful donut. Pair with some blackberry or raspberry donuts for a brunch.

Finishing suggestions

Icings: Honey Glaze (page 200), Simple Sugar Glaze (page 205) or Strawberry Glaze (Variation, page 203).

Filling (cut donuts in half): Strawberry Filling (page 214).

- Preheat oven to 325°F (160°C)
- Two 6-well donut pans, sprayed with nonstick spray (see Tip, page 110)

2 cups	all-purpose flour	500 mL
1 cup	granulated sugar	250 mL
2½ tsp	baking powder	12 mL
½ tsp	salt	2 mL
2	large eggs, beaten	2
¾ cup	heavy or whipping (35%) cream	175 mL
3 tbsp	unsalted butter, melted	45 mL
1 tsp	vanilla extract	5 mL
1 cup	finely chopped strawberries	250 mL

1. In a large bowl, whisk together flour, sugar, baking powder and salt. Set aside.

2. In another bowl, whisk together eggs, cream, butter and vanilla. Add to flour mixture and mix with a rubber spatula just until incorporated. Fold in strawberries.

3. Spoon batter into resealable freezer bag or pastry bag (see page 8) and fill each prepared well two-thirds full.

4. Bake in preheated oven until donut springs back when lightly touched, 10 to 14 minutes.

5. Let donuts cool in pans on a rack for 5 minutes. Turn out of pans onto rack and let cool completely prior to icing and/or filling.

Tangerine Donuts

**Makes about
12 donuts**

This simple citrus donut packed with flavor will remind you of a sunny day.

Finishing suggestions

Icings: Citrus Sugar (page 205) or Sunset Orange Glaze (page 204).

Filling (cut donuts in half): Sunset Orange Filling (page 211).

- Preheat oven to 325°F (160°C)
- Two 6-well donut pans, sprayed with nonstick spray (see Tip, page 110)

2 cups	all-purpose flour	500 mL
¾ cup	granulated sugar	175 mL
2 tsp	baking powder	10 mL
1 tsp	salt	5 mL
2	large eggs, beaten	2
½ cup	whole milk	125 mL
1 tbsp	grated tangerine zest	15 mL
¼ cup	freshly squeezed tangerine juice	60 mL
1 tbsp	canola oil	15 mL

1. In a large bowl, whisk together flour, sugar, baking powder and salt. Set aside.

2. In another bowl, whisk together eggs, milk, tangerine zest and juice and oil. Add to flour mixture and mix with a rubber spatula just until incorporated.

3. Spoon batter into resealable freezer bag or pastry bag (see page 8) and fill each prepared well two-thirds full.

4. Bake in preheated oven until donut springs back when lightly touched, 10 to 14 minutes.

5. Let donuts cool in pans on a rack for 5 minutes. Turn out of pans and toss with Citrus Sugar, if using, or let cool completely on racks prior to icing and/or filling.

Roasted Peanut Donuts

**Makes about
12 donuts**

I enjoy topping this
donut with a bittersweet
glaze and chopped
peanuts.

Finishing suggestions

Icing: Bittersweet
Chocolate Glaze
(page 197).

Topping: Sprinkle freshly
glazed donuts with
crushed peanuts.

- Preheat oven to 325°F (160°C)
- Two 6-well donut pans, sprayed with nonstick spray
  (see Tip, page 110)

1 cup	all-purpose flour	250 mL
¾ cup	packed brown sugar	175 mL
½ cup	whole wheat flour	125 mL
½ cup	finely chopped roasted peanuts	125 mL
2 tsp	baking powder	10 mL
1 tsp	salt	5 mL
2	large eggs, beaten	2
¾ cup	whole milk	175 mL
1 tbsp	canola oil	15 mL
1 tsp	vanilla extract	5 mL

1. In a large bowl, whisk together all-purpose flour, brown
   sugar, whole wheat flour, peanuts, baking powder and
   salt. Set aside.

2. In another bowl, whisk together eggs, milk, oil and
   vanilla. Add to flour mixture and mix with a rubber
   spatula just until incorporated.

3. Spoon batter into resealable freezer bag or pastry bag
   (see page 8) and fill each prepared well two-thirds full.

4. Bake in preheated oven until donut springs back when
   lightly touched, 10 to 14 minutes.

5. Let donuts cool in pans on a rack for 5 minutes. Turn
   out of pans onto rack and let cool completely prior to
   icing or topping.

Vanilla Bean Donuts

**Makes about
12 donuts**

Rich flavors of vanilla
make this a perfect
simple baked donut.

Finishing suggestions
Icings: Honey Glaze
(page 200), Bittersweet
Chocolate Glaze
(page 197) or Strawberry
Glaze (Variation,
page 203).

- Preheat oven to 325°F (160°C)
- Two 6-well donut pans, sprayed with nonstick spray
  (see Tip, page 110)

2 cups	all-purpose flour	500 mL
¾ cup	granulated sugar	175 mL
2 tsp	baking powder	10 mL
1 tsp	salt	5 mL
2	large eggs, beaten	2
¾ cup	heavy or whipping (35%) cream	175 mL
1 tbsp	unsalted butter, melted	15 mL
1 tbsp	vanilla bean paste	15 mL

1. In a large bowl, whisk together flour, sugar, baking
   powder and salt. Set aside.

2. In another bowl, whisk together eggs, cream, butter
   and vanilla paste. Add to flour mixture and mix with a
   rubber spatula just until incorporated.

3. Spoon batter into resealable freezer bag or pastry bag
   (see page 8) and fill each prepared well two-thirds full.

4. Bake in preheated oven until donut springs back when
   lightly touched, 10 to 14 minutes.

5. Let donuts cool in pans on a rack for 5 minutes. Turn
   out of pans onto rack and let cool completely prior
   to icing.

White Chocolate Crème Donuts

Makes about 12 donuts

Here's a rich donut with flavors of white chocolate and macadamia nuts.

Finishing suggestions

Icings: Honey Glaze (page 200), Simple Sugar Glaze (page 205), Rose Petal Dust (page 206), or Lavender Sugar Dust (page 206).

Topping: Roll donuts in confectioner's (icing) sugar).

Variation

White Chocolate Key Lime Donuts: Omit vanilla and macadamia nuts. Add 1½ tsp (7 mL) grated Key lime zest and 1 tbsp (15 mL) freshly squeezed Key lime juice with cream. Finish with Simple Sugar Glaze (page 205) or Citrus Sugar (page 205).

- Preheat oven to 325°F (160°C)
- Two 6-well donut pans, sprayed with nonstick spray (see Tip, page 110)

2 cups	all-purpose flour	500 mL
¾ cup	granulated sugar	175 mL
2 tsp	baking powder	10 mL
1 tsp	salt	5 mL
2	large eggs, beaten	2
¾ cup	heavy or whipping (35%) cream	175 mL
1 tbsp	canola oil	15 mL
1 tbsp	vanilla extract	15 mL
6 oz	white chocolate, finely chopped	175 g
¼ cup	macadamia nuts, chopped	60 mL

1. In a large bowl, whisk together flour, sugar, baking powder and salt. Set aside.

2. In another bowl, whisk together eggs, cream, oil and vanilla. Add to flour mixture and mix with a rubber spatula just until incorporated. Fold in white chocolate and macadamia nuts.

3. Spoon batter into resealable freezer bag or pastry bag (see page 8) and fill each prepared well two-thirds full.

4. Bake in preheated oven until donut springs back when lightly touched, 10 to 14 minutes.

5. Let donuts cool in pans on a rack for 5 minutes. Turn out of pans and toss with Rose Petal Dust or Lavender Sugar Dust, if using, or let cool completely on racks prior to icing. Or instead, you can roll donuts in confectioner's (icing) sugar. Place confectioner's sugar in a bowl and roll donuts in the sugar. Serve promptly.

Baked Whole Wheat Pecan Donuts

Makes about 12 donuts

This nutty whole wheat donut can be topped with a simple glaze.

Finishing suggestions

Icings: Maple Glaze (page 201) or Simple Sugar Glaze (page 205).

Topping: Sprinkle freshly glazed donuts with crushed pecans.

- Preheat oven to 325°F (160°C)
- Two 6-well donut pans, sprayed with nonstick spray (see Tip, page 110)

1 cup	all-purpose flour	250 mL
1 cup	whole wheat flour	250 mL
½ cup	granulated sugar	125 mL
¼ cup	packed brown sugar	60 mL
2 tsp	baking powder	10 mL
1 tsp	salt	5 mL
½ tsp	ground cinnamon	2 mL
¼ tsp	freshly ground nutmeg	1 mL
2	large eggs, beaten	2
¾ cup	whole milk	175 mL
1 tbsp	canola oil	15 mL
1 tsp	vanilla extract	5 mL
½ cup	pecans, chopped	125 mL

1. In a large bowl, whisk together all-purpose flour, whole wheat flour, granulated sugar, brown sugar, baking powder, salt, cinnamon and nutmeg. Set aside.

2. In another bowl, whisk together eggs, milk, oil and vanilla. Add to flour mixture and mix with a rubber spatula just until incorporated. Fold in pecans.

3. Spoon batter into resealable freezer bag or pastry bag (see page 8) and fill each prepared well two-thirds full.

4. Bake in preheated oven until donut springs back when lightly touched, 10 to 14 minutes.

5. Let donuts cool in pans on a rack for 5 minutes. Turn out of pans onto rack and let cool completely prior to icing or topping.

Holiday Donuts

• •

You can create donuts to celebrate any holiday or event. Try making donuts for a birthday party or even dessert on New Year's Day. Make new memories.

Christmas Swirl Donuts 120

Father's Day Tie Donuts. 122

Candied Fruit Donuts 124

Minty Chocolate Donut Bars 126

Mother's Day Crown Donuts 128

New Year's Champagne Donuts 130

Thanksgiving Maple Donuts 132

Holiday Eggnog Donuts 134

Red Valentine Heart Donuts 135

Peppermint Chocolate Squares 136

Strawberry Rose Donuts 138

Cranberry Orange Donuts. 140

Christmas Swirl Donuts

Makes about 18 donuts

Here's a donut with a little mint and cinnamon for holiday cheer.

- Stand mixer with paddle attachment
- Baking sheet, lined with parchment paper
- Digital candy/deep-fry thermometer

¾ cup + 1 tbsp	whole milk, warmed to 110°F (43°C)	190 mL
1	package (¼ oz/8 g) quick-rising (instant) yeast	1
1	large egg	1
2 tbsp	unsalted butter, melted	30 mL
1 tsp	vanilla extract	5 mL
2¾ cups	all-purpose flour, divided (approx.)	675 mL
2 tbsp	granulated sugar, divided	30 mL
⅛ tsp	salt	0.5 mL
¼ cup	mint-flavored chocolate chips	60 mL
2 tsp	ground cinnamon	10 mL
	Canola oil	

1. In mixer bowl, sprinkle yeast over milk and stir with a fork. Let stand until foamy, about 5 minutes.

2. Attach bowl to mixer fitted with paddle attachment and add egg, butter, vanilla, 1 cup (250 mL) of the flour, 1 tbsp (15 mL) of the sugar and salt to yeast mixture. Let stand in bowl for 10 minutes. On low speed, mix just until blended, then add just enough of the remaining flour until dough starts to pull away from sides of bowl. Increase speed to medium and beat for 1 minute.

3. Transfer dough to a large oiled bowl and cover with plastic wrap. Let rise in a warm, draft-free place until doubled in volume, about 30 minutes.

4. Meanwhile, in a small bowl, combine chocolate chips, remaining 1 tbsp (15 mL) of sugar and cinnamon. Set aside.

5. Turn dough out onto a floured work surface. Roll out dough to about 24 by 18 inches (60 by 45 cm) and about ¼ inch (0.5 cm) thick. If dough is tacky, dust with additional flour.

Finishing suggestions

Icing: Honey Glaze
(page 200).

6. Sprinkle chocolate chip mixture on top. Starting at one long side, roll up dough jelly-roll style to create a long rolled log. Cut roll crosswise into 18 equal pieces. Place, cut side up, at least 1 inch (2.5 cm) apart on prepared baking sheet. Cover with a clean kitchen towel and let rise for 20 minutes.

7. Meanwhile, in a large, deep pot or deep fryer, heat about 4 inches (10 cm) oil over medium heat until temperature registers 360°F (182°C). Deep-fry 3 donuts at a time in hot oil, turning once with wooden chopsticks, until golden brown, 15 to 20 seconds per side. Using a slotted spatula, transfer to paper towels to absorb excess oil. Fry remaining donuts, adjusting heat as necessary between batches to maintain oil temperature.

8. Let donuts cool completely prior to icing.

Father's Day Tie Donuts

Makes about 12 donuts

Dads will love this donut in the shape of a tie for his special day.

Tip

Most cookware stores carry cookie cutters in the shape of men's bow ties around father's day. If you like, you can also just make this recipe into the twist (see page 31).

- Stand mixer with paddle attachment
- 3-inch (7.5 cm) cookie cutter in shape of a tie (see Tip, left)
- Baking sheet, lined with parchment paper
- Digital candy/deep-fry thermometer

¾ cup + 1 tbsp	whole milk, warmed to 110°F (43°C)	190 mL
1	package (¼ oz/8 g) quick-rising (instant) yeast	1
1	large egg	1
2 tbsp	canola oil	30 mL
1 tsp	vanilla extract	5 mL
2¾ cups	all-purpose flour, divided (approx.)	675 mL
1 tbsp	granulated sugar	15 mL
⅛ tsp	salt	0.5 mL
	Canola oil	

1. In mixer bowl, sprinkle yeast over milk and stir with a fork. Let stand until foamy, about 5 minutes.

2. Attach bowl to mixer fitted with paddle attachment and add egg, oil, vanilla, 1 cup (250 mL) of the flour, sugar and salt to yeast mixture. Let stand in bowl for 10 minutes. On low speed, mix just until blended, then add just enough of the remaining flour until dough starts to pull away from sides of bowl. Increase speed to medium and beat for 1 minute.

3. Transfer dough to a large oiled bowl and cover with plastic wrap. Let rise in a warm, draft-free place until doubled in volume, about 30 minutes.

Finishing suggestions

Icings: Honey Glaze
(page 200), Maple Glaze
(page 201), Milk Chocolate
Glaze (page 201) or Sunset
Orange Glaze (page 204).

4. Turn dough out onto a floured work surface. Roll out dough to slightly thicker than $\frac{1}{4}$ inch (0.5 cm). If dough is tacky, dust with additional flour. Cut dough with tie cutter into 12 donuts, re-rolling scraps as necessary. Place at least 1 inch (2.5 cm) apart on prepared baking sheet. Cover with a clean kitchen towel and let rise for 20 minutes.

5. Meanwhile, in a large, deep pot or deep fryer, heat about 4 inches (10 cm) oil over medium heat until temperature registers 360°F (182°C). Deep-fry 4 donuts at a time in hot oil, turning once with wooden chopsticks, until golden brown, about 15 seconds per side. Using a slotted spatula, transfer to paper towels to absorb excess oil. Fry remaining donuts, adjusting heat as necessary between batches to maintain oil temperature.

6. Let donuts cool completely prior to icing.

Candied Fruit Donuts

These colorful donuts contain the glazed fruit of cherries and pineapple.

Tip

When you are making ring-shaped donuts you may like to fry up the center holes for a treat. Depending on the size of the hole, your frying time will have to be adjusted since they tend to fry faster. I sometimes like to test a donut hole just to see how the flavor of the donut is and what icing I will want to dress it with.

- Stand mixer with paddle attachment
- 3-inch (7.5 cm) round donut cutter
- Baking sheet, lined with parchment paper
- Digital candy/deep-fry thermometer

¾ cup	whole milk, warmed to 110°F (43°C)	175 mL
1	package (¼ oz/8 g) quick-rising (instant) yeast	1
1	large egg	1
2 tbsp	unsalted butter, melted	30 mL
1 tsp	vanilla extract	5 mL
2¾ cups	all-purpose flour, divided (approx.)	675 mL
2 tbsp	granulated sugar	30 mL
⅛ tsp	salt	0.5 mL
½ cup	mixed candied cherries and pineapple, finely chopped	125 mL
	Canola oil	

1. In mixer bowl, sprinkle yeast over milk and stir with a fork. Let stand until foamy, about 5 minutes.

2. Attach bowl to mixer fitted with paddle attachment and add egg, butter, vanilla, 1 cup (250 mL) of the flour, sugar and salt to yeast mixture. Let stand in bowl for 10 minutes. On low speed, mix just until blended, then add just enough of the remaining flour until dough starts to pull away from sides of bowl. Increase speed to medium and beat for 1 minute.

3. Transfer dough to a floured work surface. Knead in candied fruit with your hands until evenly distributed. (Additional flour may be needed, depending on the stickiness of the fruit.)

Finishing suggestions

Icings: Honey Glaze
(page 200) or Simple
Sugar Glaze (page 205).

4. Transfer dough to a large oiled bowl and cover with plastic wrap. Let rise in a warm, draft-free place until doubled in volume, about 30 minutes.

5. Turn dough out onto a floured work surface. Roll out dough to slightly thicker than $\frac{1}{4}$ inch (0.5 cm). If dough is tacky, dust with additional flour. Cut dough with cutter into 12 pieces, re-rolling scraps as necessary. Place at least 1 inch (2.5 cm) apart on prepared baking sheet. Cover with a clean kitchen towel and let rise for 20 minutes.

6. Meanwhile, in a large, deep pot or deep fryer, heat about 4 inches (10 cm) oil over medium heat until temperature registers 360°F (182°C). Deep-fry 4 donuts at a time in hot oil, turning once with wooden chopsticks, until golden brown, about 15 seconds per side. Using a slotted spatula, transfer to paper towels to absorb excess oil. Fry remaining donuts, adjusting heat as necessary between batches to maintain oil temperature.

7. Let donuts cool completely prior to icing.

Minty Chocolate Donut Bars

● ●

**Makes about
18 donuts**

Mint and chocolate
have always reminded
me of Christmas Eve —
the fragrance of the
tree with the cold chill
outside.

● Stand mixer with paddle attachment
● 5- by 2-inch (12.5 cm by 5 cm) bar cutter, optional
● Baking sheet, lined with parchment paper
● Digital candy/deep-fry thermometer

¾ cup + 1 tbsp	whole milk, warmed to 110°F (43°C)	190 mL
1	package (¼ oz/8 g) quick-rising (instant) yeast	1
1	large egg	1
2 tbsp	canola oil	30 mL
½ tsp	peppermint extract	2 mL
2¾ cups	all-purpose flour, divided (approx.)	675 mL
1 tbsp	granulated sugar	15 mL
⅛ tsp	salt	0.5 mL
½ cup	mint-flavored chocolate chips	125 mL
	Canola oil	

1. In mixer bowl, sprinkle yeast over milk and stir with a fork. Let stand until foamy, about 5 minutes.

2. Attach bowl to mixer fitted with paddle attachment and add egg, oil, extract, 1 cup (250 mL) of the flour, sugar and salt to yeast mixture. Let stand in bowl for 10 minutes. On low speed, mix just until blended, then add just enough of the remaining flour until dough starts to pull away from sides of bowl. Increase speed to medium and beat for 1 minute. On low speed, mix in chocolate chips.

3. Transfer dough to a large oiled bowl and cover with plastic wrap. Let rise in a warm, draft-free place until doubled in volume, about 30 minutes.

Finishing suggestions

Icing: Simple Sugar Glaze (page 205).

4. Turn dough out onto a floured work surface. Roll out dough to slightly thicker than ¼ inch (0.5 cm). If dough is tacky, dust with additional flour. Cut dough with cutter into 18 donuts (or cut with a knife or pizza cutter into 5- by 2-inch/12.5 by 5 cm rectangles), re-rolling scraps as necessary. Place at least 1 inch (2.5 cm) apart on prepared baking sheet. Cover with a clean kitchen towel and let rise for 20 minutes.

5. Meanwhile, in a large, deep pot or deep fryer, heat about 4 inches (10 cm) oil over medium heat until temperature registers 360°F (182°C). Deep-fry 3 to 4 donuts at a time in hot oil, turning once with wooden chopsticks, until puffy, about 20 seconds per side. Using a slotted spatula, transfer to paper towels to absorb excess oil. Fry remaining donuts, adjusting heat as necessary between batches to maintain oil temperature.

6. Let donuts cool completely prior to icing.

Mother's Day Crown Donuts

Makes about 12 donuts

As a kid I always thought that on Mother's Day my mom should have a crown on for the day, thus creating a special day just for her.

Tip

If you do not have a cutter in the shape of a crown, you can also use a 3-inch (7.5 cm) star cutter as mom is also a star!

- Stand mixer with paddle attachment
- 3-inch (7.5 cm) cookie cutter in shape of a crown (see Tip, left)
- Baking sheet, lined with parchment paper
- Digital candy/deep-fry thermometer

¾ cup + 1 tbsp	heavy or whipping (35%) cream, warmed to 110°F (43°C)	190 mL
1	package (¼ oz/8 g) quick-rising (instant) yeast	1
1	large egg	1
2 tbsp	unsalted butter, melted	30 mL
1 tsp	vanilla extract	5 mL
1 tsp	grated lemon zest	5 mL
1 tsp	grated orange zest	5 mL
2¾ cups	all-purpose flour, divided (approx.)	675 mL
1 tbsp	granulated sugar	15 mL
⅛ tsp	salt	0.5 mL
	Canola oil	

1. In mixer bowl, sprinkle yeast over milk and stir with a fork. Let stand until foamy, about 5 minutes.

2. Attach bowl to mixer fitted with paddle attachment and add egg, butter, vanilla, lemon zest, orange zest, 1 cup (250 mL) of the flour, sugar and salt to yeast mixture. Let stand in bowl for 10 minutes. On low speed, mix just until blended, then add just enough of the remaining flour until dough starts to pull away from sides of bowl. Increase speed to medium and beat for 1 minute.

3. Transfer dough to a large oiled bowl and cover with plastic wrap. Let rise in a warm, draft-free place until doubled in volume, about 30 minutes.

Finishing suggestions

Icings: Honey Glaze
(page 200), Simple Sugar
Glaze (page 205) or Sunset
Orange Glaze (page 204).

4. Turn dough out onto a floured work surface. Roll out dough to slightly thicker than $\frac{1}{4}$ inch (0.5 cm). If dough is tacky, dust with additional flour. Cut dough with crown cutter into 12 donuts, re-rolling scraps as necessary. Place at least 1 inch (2.5 cm) apart on prepared baking sheet. Cover with a clean kitchen towel and let rise for 20 minutes.

5. Meanwhile, in a large, deep pot or deep fryer, heat about 4 inches (10 cm) oil over medium heat until temperature registers 360°F (182°C). Deep-fry 4 donuts at a time in hot oil, turning once with wooden chopsticks, until golden brown, about 15 seconds per side. Using a slotted spatula, transfer to paper towels to absorb excess oil. Fry remaining donuts, adjusting heat as necessary between batches to maintain oil temperature.

6. Let donuts cool completely prior to icing.

New Year's Champagne Donuts

**Makes about
12 donuts**

When you have a little
Champagne leftover use
it to add a special touch
to these donuts.

- Stand mixer with paddle attachment
- 3-inch (7.5 cm) round donut cutter
- Baking sheet, lined with parchment paper
- Digital candy/deep-fry thermometer

½ cup + 1 tbsp	whole milk, warmed to 110°F (43°C)	140 mL
1	package (¼ oz/8 g) quick-rising (instant) yeast	1
¼ cup	dry Champagne	60 mL
2	large egg whites	2
2 tbsp	unsalted butter, softened	30 mL
1 tsp	vanilla extract	5 mL
2¾ cups	all-purpose flour, divided (approx.)	675 mL
1 tbsp	granulated sugar	15 mL
⅛ tsp	salt	0.5 mL
	Canola oil	

1. In mixer bowl, sprinkle yeast over milk and stir with a fork. Let stand until foamy, about 5 minutes.

2. Attach bowl to mixer fitted with paddle attachment and add Champagne, egg whites, butter, vanilla, 1 cup (250 mL) of the flour, sugar and salt to yeast mixture. Let stand in bowl for 10 minutes. On low speed, mix just until blended, then add just enough of the remaining flour until dough starts to pull away from sides of bowl. Increase speed to medium and beat for 1 minute.

3. Transfer dough to a large oiled bowl and cover with plastic wrap. Let rise in a warm, draft-free place until doubled in volume, about 30 minutes.

Finishing suggestions

Icings: Honey Glaze
(page 200) or Simple
Sugar Glaze (page 205).

4. Turn dough out onto a floured work surface. Roll out dough to slightly thicker than $\frac{1}{4}$ inch (0.5 cm). If dough is tacky, dust with additional flour. Cut dough with cutter into 12 donuts, re-rolling scraps as necessary. Place at least 1 inch (2.5 cm) apart on prepared baking sheet. Cover with a clean kitchen towel and let rise for 20 minutes.

5. Meanwhile, in a large, deep pot or deep fryer, heat about 4 inches (10 cm) oil over medium heat until temperature registers 360°F (182°C). Deep-fry 4 donuts at a time in hot oil, turning once with wooden chopsticks, until golden brown, about 15 seconds per side. Using a slotted spatula, transfer to paper towels to absorb excess oil. Fry remaining donuts, adjusting heat as necessary between batches to maintain oil temperature.

6. Let donuts cool completely prior to icing.

Thanksgiving Maple Donuts

**Makes about
16 donuts**

A perfect donut for a
Thanksgiving morning.

- Stand mixer with paddle attachment
- 3-inch (7.5 cm) round donut cutter
- Baking sheet, lined with parchment paper
- Digital candy/deep-fry thermometer

¾ cup	whole milk, warmed to 110°F (43°C)	175 mL
1	package (¼ oz/8 g) quick-rising (instant) yeast	1
1	large egg	1
3 tbsp	pure maple syrup	45 mL
2 tbsp	unsalted butter, melted	30 mL
½ tsp	maple extract	2 mL
2¾ cups	all-purpose flour, divided (approx.)	675 mL
½ tsp	ground cinnamon	2 mL
½ tsp	salt	2 mL
¼ tsp	freshly ground nutmeg	1 mL
¼ tsp	ground allspice	1 mL
	Canola oil	

1. In mixer bowl, sprinkle yeast over milk and stir with a fork. Let stand until foamy, about 5 minutes.

2. Attach bowl to mixer fitted with paddle attachment and add egg, maple syrup, butter, maple extract, 1 cup (250 mL) of the flour, cinnamon, salt, nutmeg and allspice to yeast mixture. Let stand in bowl for 10 minutes. On low speed, mix just until blended, then add just enough of the remaining flour until dough starts to pull away from sides of bowl. Increase speed to medium and beat for 1 minute.

3. Transfer dough to a large oiled bowl and cover with plastic wrap. Let rise in a warm, draft-free place until doubled in volume, about 30 minutes.

Finishing suggestions

Icing: Maple Glaze
(page 201).

4. Turn dough out onto a floured work surface. Roll out dough to slightly thicker than $\frac{1}{4}$ inch (0.5 cm). If dough is tacky, dust with additional flour. Cut dough with cutter into 16 donuts, re-rolling scraps as necessary. Place at least 1 inch (2.5 cm) apart on prepared baking sheet. Cover with a clean kitchen towel and let rise for 20 minutes.

5. Meanwhile, in a large, deep pot or deep fryer, heat about 4 inches (10 cm) oil over medium heat until temperature registers 360°F (182°C). Deep-fry 4 donuts at a time in hot oil, turning once with wooden chopsticks, until puffy, about 20 seconds per side. Using a slotted spatula, transfer to paper towels to absorb excess oil. Fry remaining donuts, adjusting heat as necessary between batches to maintain oil temperature.

6. Let donuts cool completely prior to icing.

Holiday Eggnog Donuts

**Makes about
18 donuts**

Besides drinking
eggnog, you can make
these flavorful donuts
for Christmas morning.

Finishing suggestions

Icing: Autumn Spiced
Sugar (page 204).

- Stand mixer with paddle attachment
- Digital candy/deep-fry thermometer
- 3-inch (7.5 cm) round donut cutter
- Baking sheet, lined with parchment paper

3½ cups	all-purpose flour, divided	875 mL
1½ tsp	baking powder	7 mL
1½ tsp	freshly ground nutmeg	7 mL
1 tsp	salt	5 mL
½ tsp	baking soda	2 mL
1 cup	granulated sugar	250 mL
3	large eggs	3
¼ cup	prepared eggnog	60 mL
¼ cup	unsalted butter, melted and cooled	60 mL
	Canola oil	

1. In a bowl, whisk together 2½ cups (625 mL) of the flour, baking powder, nutmeg, salt and baking soda. Set aside.

2. In mixer bowl fitted with paddle attachment, combine sugar, eggs, eggnog and butter. On low speed, mix until well combined. Add dry ingredients and mix until incorporated. Gradually mix in more of the remaining flour, as necessary, until dough starts to come together and is the consistency of biscuit dough. Cover and refrigerate for 10 minutes.

3. Meanwhile, in a large, deep pot or deep fryer, heat about 4 inches (10 cm) oil over medium heat until temperature registers 360°F (182°C).

4. On a floured work surface, roll out dough to slightly thicker than ¼ inch (0.5 cm). If dough is tacky, dust with additional flour. Cut dough with cutter into 18 donuts, re-rolling scraps as necessary. Place at least 1 inch (2.5 cm) apart on prepared baking sheet. Cover with a clean kitchen towel until ready to fry.

5. Deep-fry 3 to 4 donuts at a time in hot oil, turning once with wooden chopsticks, until golden brown, about 15 seconds per side. Using a slotted spatula, transfer to paper towels to absorb excess oil. Fry remaining donuts, adjusting heat as necessary between batches to maintain oil temperature.

6. Toss warm donuts with Autumn Spiced Sugar, if using.

Red Valentine Heart Donuts

Make these red love donuts for your special Valentine.

Finishing suggestions

Icings: Belgian Chocolate Ganache Glaze (page 197), Milk Chocolate Glaze (page 201), Mocha Glaze (page 202), Bittersweet Chocolate Glaze (page 197) or Truffle Fudge Icing (page 196).

Filling (injected): Raspberry Filling (Variation, page 214).

Filling (cut donuts in half): Fresh Cherry Filling (page 211) or Strawberry Filling (page 214).

- Stand mixer with paddle attachment
- Digital candy/deep-fry thermometer
- 4-inch (10 cm) heart cookie cutter
- Baking sheet, lined with parchment paper

2¾ cups	all-purpose flour, divided	675 mL
1¼ tsp	baking powder	6 mL
1 tsp	salt	5 mL
½ tsp	baking soda	2 mL
1 cup	packed brown sugar	250 mL
3	large eggs	3
¼ cup	heavy or whipping (35%) cream	60 mL
¼ cup	unsalted butter, melted and cooled	60 mL
2 tsp	vanilla extract	10 mL
1 tsp	liquid red food coloring	5 mL
	Canola oil	

1. In a bowl, whisk together 2 cups (500 mL) of the flour, baking powder, salt and baking soda. Set aside.

2. In mixer bowl fitted with paddle attachment, combine sugar, eggs, cream, butter, vanilla and food coloring. On low speed, mix until well combined. Add dry ingredients and mix until incorporated. Gradually mix in more of the remaining flour, as necessary, until dough starts to come together and is the consistency of biscuit dough. Cover and refrigerate for 10 minutes.

3. Meanwhile, in a large, deep pot or deep fryer, heat about 4 inches (10 cm) oil over medium heat until temperature registers 360°F (182°C) (see Tip, page 136).

4. On a floured work surface, roll out dough to slightly thicker than ¼ inch (0.5 cm). If dough is tacky, dust with additional flour. Cut dough with cutter into 18 donuts, re-rolling scraps as necessary. Place at least 1 inch (2.5 cm) apart on prepared baking sheet.

5. Deep-fry 3 to 4 donuts at a time in hot oil, turning once with wooden chopsticks, until golden brown, about 15 seconds per side. Using a slotted spatula, transfer to paper towels to absorb excess oil. Fry remaining donuts, adjusting heat as necessary between batches to maintain oil temperature.

6. Let donuts cool completely prior to icing and/or filling.

Peppermint Chocolate Squares

**Makes about
12 donuts**

These are in the shape
of little presents.
Something to enjoy
while opening yours
during the holiday
season.

Tip

When heating the oil
for deep-frying, keep a
close eye on it to be sure
it doesn't overheat, and
never leave the room
while the oil is on the
heat. Reduce the heat or
carefully remove the pot
from the burner when the
oil reaches the desired
temperature. Always keep
a metal lid that tightly fits
the pot handy to quickly
place on the pot should
the oil start to smoke or
burn.

- Stand mixer with paddle attachment
- Digital candy/deep-fry thermometer
- 3-inch (7.5 cm) square donut cutter, optional
- Baking sheet, lined with parchment paper

3 cups	all-purpose flour, divided	750 mL
½ cup	unsweetened cocoa powder	125 mL
1¼ tsp	baking powder	6 mL
1 tsp	baking soda	5 mL
½ tsp	salt	2 mL
1 cup	granulated sugar	250 mL
3	large eggs	3
¼ cup	whole milk	60 mL
¼ cup	unsalted butter, melted	60 mL
1½ tsp	vanilla extract	7 mL
½ tsp	peppermint extract	2 mL
	Canola oil	

1. In a large bowl, whisk together 2 cups (500 mL) of the
   flour, cocoa powder, baking powder, baking soda and
   salt. Set aside.

2. In mixer bowl fitted with paddle attachment, combine
   sugar, eggs, milk, butter, and vanilla and peppermint
   extracts. On low speed, mix until well combined. Add
   dry ingredients and mix until incorporated. Gradually
   mix in more of the remaining flour, as necessary, until
   dough starts to come together and is the consistency of
   biscuit dough. Cover and refrigerate for 10 minutes.

3. Meanwhile, in a large, deep pot or deep fryer, heat
   about 4 inches (10 cm) oil over medium heat until
   temperature registers 360°F (182°C) (see Tip, left).

Finishing suggestions

Icings: Belgian Chocolate Ganache Glaze (page 197), Milk Chocolate Glaze (page 201), Mocha Glaze (page 202) or Truffle Fudge Icing (page 196).

Topping: Sprinkle freshly glazed donuts with crushed hard-candy mints.

4. On a floured work surface, roll out dough to slightly thicker than ¼ inch (0.5 cm). If dough is tacky, dust with additional flour. Cut dough with cutter into 12 donuts, re-rolling scraps as necessary (or use a knife or pizza cutter to cut 3-inch/7.5 cm squares). Place at least 1 inch (2.5 cm) apart on prepared baking sheet.

5. Deep-fry 4 donuts at a time in hot oil, turning once with wooden chopsticks, until puffy and firm, about 15 seconds per side. Using a slotted spatula, transfer to paper towels to absorb excess oil. Fry remaining donuts, adjusting heat as necessary between batches to maintain oil temperature.

6. Let donuts cool completely prior to icing or topping.

Strawberry Rose Donuts

**Makes about
36 donuts**

Valentine's Day or
anniversaries are
times for roses and
strawberries.

- Stand mixer with paddle attachment
- Digital candy/deep-fry thermometer
- 2-inch (5 cm) round cutter
- Baking sheet, lined with parchment paper

3¼ cups	all-purpose flour, divided	800 mL
1¼ tsp	baking powder	6 mL
1 tsp	salt	5 mL
½ tsp	baking soda	2 mL
1 cup	granulated sugar	250 mL
2	large eggs	2
3 tbsp	heavy or whipping (35%) cream	45 mL
2 tbsp	canola oil	30 mL
1 tbsp	rose water	15 mL
½ cup	finely chopped fresh strawberries	125 mL
	Canola oil	

1. In a bowl, whisk together 2 cups (500 mL) of the flour, baking powder, salt and baking soda. Set aside.

2. In mixer bowl fitted with paddle attachment, combine sugar, eggs, cream, oil and rose water. On low speed, mix until well combined. Add dry ingredients and mix until incorporated. Gradually mix in more of the remaining flour, as necessary, until dough starts to come together and is the consistency of biscuit dough. Using a rubber spatula, stir in strawberries. Cover and refrigerate for 10 minutes.

3. Meanwhile, in a large, deep pot or deep fryer, heat about 4 inches (10 cm) oil over medium heat until temperature registers 360°F (182°C) (see Tip, page 136).

Finishing suggestions

Icings: Rose Petal Dust (page 206), Honey Glaze (page 200) or Strawberry Glaze (Variation, page 203).

4. On a floured work surface, roll out dough to slightly thicker than $1/4$ inch (0.5 cm). If dough is tacky, dust with additional flour. Cut dough with cutter into 36 donuts, re-rolling scraps as necessary. Place at least 1 inch (2.5 cm) apart on prepared baking sheet.

5. Deep-fry 4 to 6 donuts at a time in hot oil, turning once with wooden chopsticks, until golden brown, about 15 seconds per side. Using a slotted spatula, transfer to paper towels to absorb excess oil. Fry remaining donuts, adjusting heat as necessary between batches to maintain oil temperature.

6. Toss warm donuts with Rose Petal Dust, if using, or let cool completely prior to icing.

Cranberry Orange Donuts

Makes about 12 donuts

Tart cranberries with sweet orange flavors create a flavorful fall donut.

Finishing suggestions
Icings: Honey Glaze (page 200) or Simple Sugar Glaze (page 205).

- Preheat oven to 325°F (160°C)
- Two 6-well donut pans, sprayed with nonstick cooking spray

2½ cups	cake flour	625 mL
1 cup	granulated sugar	250 mL
2½ tsp	baking powder	12 mL
½ tsp	salt	2 mL
2	large eggs	2
¾ cup	whole milk	175 mL
2 tbsp	unsalted butter, melted	30 mL
1 tbsp	grated orange zest	15 mL
1 tsp	orange extract	5 mL
1 cup	fresh or frozen cranberries	250 mL
½ cup	almonds, chopped	125 mL

1. In a large bowl, whisk together flour, sugar, baking powder and salt. Set aside.

2. In a medium bowl, whisk together eggs, milk, butter, orange zest and orange extract. Add to flour mixture and mix with a rubber spatula just until incorporated. Fold in cranberries and almonds.

3. Spoon batter into resealable freezer bag or pastry bag (see page 8) and fill each prepared well two-thirds full.

4. Bake in preheated oven until donut springs back when lightly touched, 10 to 14 minutes.

5. Let donuts cool in pans on a rack for 5 minutes. Turn out of pans onto rack and let cool completely prior to icing.

One-Bite Donuts

● ●

From that first time when I was in first grade seeing the mini donuts being manufactured, I knew I wanted to be a pastry chef. The tour of the Hostess factory changed my life. Here you can create one-bite donuts that are perfect for the little ones or just for an afternoon tea.

Aztec Donut Bites 142

Bavarian Crème Bites 144

Blackberry Bites 146

Delicate Dainty Donut Bites 148

French Bites 150

Triple Chocolate Bites 152

Chocolate Donut Holes 154

Coffee Bites 155

Pistachio Bites 156

Spicy Donut Balls 157

All Spiced-Up Bites 158

Baked Maple Mini Donuts 159

Blueberry Bites 160

Citrus Donut Bites 161

Cranberry Almond Donut Bites 162

Green Tea Bites 163

Mini Pumpkin Donuts 164

Oat Berry Mini Donuts 165

Strawberry Cream Bites 166

Aztec Donut Bites

Here's a little spicy donut with chocolate bursts of flavor.

Tip

McCormick makes a cocoa chile spice blend. Look for it in your grocery store in the spice section. The chipotle powder is a fine substitute.

- Stand mixer with paddle attachment
- 2-inch (5 cm) round cutter
- Baking sheet, lined with parchment paper
- Digital candy/deep-fry thermometer

¾ cup + 1 tbsp	whole milk, warmed to 110°F (43°C)	190 mL
1	package (¼ oz/8 g) quick-rising (instant) yeast	1
1	large egg	1
2 tbsp	unsalted butter, melted	30 mL
1 tsp	vanilla extract	5 mL
2 cups	all-purpose flour, divided (approx.)	500 mL
½ cup	unsweetened cocoa powder	125 mL
⅓ cup	packed brown sugar	75 mL
½ tsp	cocoa chile blend spice (see Tip, left) or ¼ tsp (1 mL) chipotle powder	2 mL
⅛ tsp	salt	0.5 mL
	Canola oil	

1. In mixer bowl, sprinkle yeast over milk and stir with a fork. Let stand until foamy, about 5 minutes.

2. Attach bowl to mixer fitted with paddle attachment and add egg, butter, vanilla, ½ cup (125 mL) of the flour, cocoa powder, brown sugar, cocoa chile spice and salt to yeast mixture. Let stand in bowl for 10 minutes. On low speed, mix just until blended, then gradually add just enough of the remaining flour until dough starts to pull away from sides of bowl. Increase speed to medium and beat for 1 minute.

3. Transfer dough to a large oiled bowl and cover with plastic wrap. Let rise in a warm, draft-free place until doubled in volume, about 30 minutes.

Finishing suggestions

Icings: Dulce de Leche Glaze (page 199), Honey Glaze (page 200) Milk Chocolate Glaze (page 201) Mocha Glaze (page 202) Truffle Fudge Icing (page 196) or Bittersweet Chocolate Glaze (page 197).

4. Turn dough out onto a floured work surface. Roll out dough to slightly thicker than ¼ inch (0.5 cm). If dough is tacky, dust with additional flour. Cut dough with cutter into 36 donuts, re-rolling scraps as necessary. Place at least 1 inch (2.5 cm) apart on prepared baking sheet. Cover with a clean kitchen towel and let rise for 20 minutes.

5. Meanwhile, in a large, deep pot or deep fryer, heat about 4 inches (10 cm) oil over medium heat until temperature registers 360°F (182°C). Deep-fry 6 to 8 donuts at a time in hot oil, turning once with wooden chopsticks, until puffy, about 20 seconds per side. Using a slotted spoon, transfer to paper towels to absorb excess oil. Fry remaining donuts, adjusting heat as necessary between batches to maintain oil temperature.

6. Let donuts cool completely prior to dipping in icing.

Bavarian Crème Bites

Rich crème filling packs
these one-bite donuts
with a punch.

- Stand mixer with paddle attachment
- 2-inch (5 cm) round cutter
- Baking sheet, lined with parchment paper
- Digital candy/deep-fry thermometer

¾ cup + 1 tbsp	whole milk, warmed to 110°F (43°C)	190 mL
1	package (¼ oz/8 g) quick-rising (instant) yeast	1
2	large eggs	2
2 tbsp	unsalted butter, softened	30 mL
1 tsp	vanilla extract	5 mL
2¾ cups	all-purpose flour, divided (approx.)	675 mL
1 tbsp	granulated sugar	15 mL
½ tsp	ground cinnamon	2 mL
¼ tsp	ground cardamom	1 mL
⅛ tsp	salt	0.5 mL
	Canola oil	
	Bavarian Cream Custard (page 209)	

1. In mixer bowl, sprinkle yeast over milk and stir with a fork. Let stand until foamy, about 5 minutes.

2. Attach bowl to mixer fitted with paddle attachment and add eggs, butter, vanilla, 1 cup (250 mL) of the flour, sugar, cinnamon, cardamom and salt to yeast mixture. Let stand in bowl for 10 minutes. On low speed, mix just until blended, then gradually add just enough of the remaining flour until dough starts to pull away from sides of bowl. Increase speed to medium and beat for 1 minute.

3. Transfer dough to a large oiled bowl and cover with plastic wrap. Let rise in a warm, draft-free place until doubled in volume, about 30 minutes.

Finishing suggestions

Icings: Honey Glaze
(page 200) or Simple
Sugar Glaze (page 205).

4. Turn dough out onto a floured work surface. Roll out dough to slightly thicker than $\frac{1}{4}$ inch (0.5 cm). If dough is tacky, dust with additional flour. Cut dough with cutter into 36 donuts, re-rolling scraps as necessary. Place at least 1 inch (2.5 cm) apart on prepared baking sheet. Cover with a clean kitchen towel and let rise for 20 minutes.

5. Meanwhile, in a large, deep pot or deep fryer, heat about 4 inches (10 cm) oil over medium heat until temperature registers 360°F (182°C). Deep-fry 6 to 8 donuts at a time in hot oil, turning once with wooden chopsticks, until golden brown, about 15 seconds per side. Using a slotted spoon, transfer to paper towels to absorb excess oil. Fry remaining donuts, adjusting heat as necessary between batches to maintain oil temperature.

6. Let donuts cool completely before injecting with Bavarian Cream Custard (see page 23).

Blackberry Bites

Every bite of this
donut has a blackberry
encased around yeasty
dough.

- Stand mixer with paddle attachment
- 2-inch (5 cm) round cutter
- Baking sheet, lined with parchment paper
- Digital candy/deep-fry thermometer

¾ cup + 1 tbsp	whole milk, warmed to 110°F (43°C)	190 mL
1	package (¼ oz/8 g) quick-rising (instant) yeast	1
1	large egg	1
2 tbsp	unsalted butter, melted	30 mL
1 tsp	vanilla extract	5 mL
2¾ cups	all-purpose flour, divided (approx.)	675 mL
1 tbsp	packed brown sugar	15 mL
⅛ tsp	salt	0.5 mL
24	whole fresh blackberries	24
	Canola oil	

1. In mixer bowl, sprinkle yeast over milk and stir with a fork. Let stand until foamy, about 5 minutes.

2. Attach bowl to mixer fitted with paddle attachment and add egg, butter, vanilla, 1 cup (250 mL) of the flour, brown sugar and salt to yeast mixture. Let stand in bowl for 10 minutes. On low speed, mix just until blended, then gradually add just enough of the remaining flour until dough starts to pull away from sides of bowl. Increase speed to medium and beat for 1 minute.

3. Transfer dough to a large oiled bowl and cover with plastic wrap. Let rise in a warm, draft-free place until doubled in volume, about 30 minutes.

Finishing suggestions

Icings: Honey Glaze (page 200), Maple Glaze (page 201), Milk Chocolate Glaze (page 201), Sunset Orange Glaze (page 202) or Rose Petal Dust (page 206).

4. Turn dough out onto a floured work surface. Roll out dough to slightly thicker than $\frac{1}{4}$ inch (0.5 cm). If dough is tacky, dust with additional flour. Cut dough with cutter into 24 rounds, re-rolling scraps as necessary. Place a whole blackberry on top of each round, wrap dough around each berry to enclose, and pinch the dough to seal it completely. Place at least 1 inch (2.5 cm) apart on prepared baking sheet. Cover with a clean kitchen towel and let rise for 20 minutes.

5. Meanwhile, in a large, deep pot or deep fryer, heat about 4 inches (10 cm) oil over medium heat until temperature registers 360°F (182°C). Deep-fry 4 donuts at a time in hot oil, turning once with wooden chopsticks, until golden brown, about 15 seconds per side. Using a slotted spoon, transfer to paper towels to absorb excess oil. Fry remaining donuts, adjusting heat as necessary between batches to maintain oil temperature.

6. Toss warm donuts with Rose Petal Dust, if using, or let cool completely prior to icing.

Delicate Dainty Donut Bites

Makes about 36 donut bites

This is a light-tasting bite that you can glaze or roll in any flavor to suit your tastes.

- Stand mixer with paddle attachment
- 2-inch (5 cm) scalloped cookie cutter
- Baking sheet, lined with parchment paper
- Digital candy/deep-fry thermometer

¾ cup	heavy or whipping (35%) cream, warmed to 110°F (43°C)	175 mL
1	package (¼ oz/8 g) quick-rising (instant) yeast	1
1	large egg	1
2 tbsp	canola oil	30 mL
1 tsp	vanilla extract	5 mL
2¾ cups	cake flour (approx.)	675 mL
1 tbsp	granulated sugar	15 mL
½ tsp	ground allspice	2 mL
⅛ tsp	salt	0.5 mL
	Canola oil	

1. In mixer bowl, sprinkle yeast over cream, stir with a fork. Let stand until foamy, about 5 minutes.

2. Attach bowl to mixer fitted with paddle attachment and add egg, oil, vanilla, 1 cup (250 mL) of the flour, sugar, allspice and salt to yeast mixture. Let stand in bowl for 10 minutes. On low speed, mix just until blended, then gradually add just enough of the remaining flour until dough starts to pull away from sides of bowl. Increase speed to medium and beat for 1 minute.

3. Transfer dough to a large oiled bowl and cover with plastic wrap. Let rise in a warm, draft-free place until doubled in volume, about 30 minutes.

Finishing suggestions

Icings: Belgian Chocolate Ganache Glaze (page 197), Maple Glaze (page 201), Raspberry Glaze (page 203) or Strawberry Glaze (Variation, page 203).

4. Turn dough out onto a floured work surface. Roll out dough to slightly thicker than $\frac{1}{4}$ inch (0.5 cm). If dough is tacky, dust with additional flour. Cut dough with cutter into 36 donuts, re-rolling scraps as necessary. Place at least 1 inch (2.5 cm) apart on prepared baking sheet. Cover with a clean kitchen towel and let rise for 20 minutes.

5. Meanwhile, in a large, deep pot or deep fryer, heat about 4 inches (10 cm) oil over medium heat until temperature registers 360°F (182°C). Deep-fry 6 donuts at a time in hot oil, turning once with wooden chopsticks, until golden brown, about 15 seconds per side. Using a slotted spoon, transfer to paper towels to absorb excess oil. Fry remaining donuts, adjusting heat as necessary between batches to maintain oil temperature.

6. Let donuts cool completely prior to icing.

French Bites

**Makes about
18 donut bites**

While in Paris, I was walking close to the Louvre and found a small patisserie that created these light and skinny fried bites. Serve them with an array of glazes that your family can use as dipping sauces.

- Stand mixer with paddle attachment
- 2- by 1-inch (5 by 2.5 cm) bar cutter, optional
- Baking sheet, lined with parchment paper
- Digital candy/deep-fry thermometer

¾ cup	heavy or whipping (35%) cream, warmed to 110°F (43°C)	175 mL
1	package (¼ oz/8 g) quick-rising (instant) yeast	1
2	large egg whites	2
2 tbsp	canola oil	30 mL
1 tsp	vanilla extract	5 mL
2¾ cups	cake flour, divided (approx.)	675 mL
1 tbsp	granulated sugar	15 mL
⅛ tsp	salt	0.5 mL
	Canola oil	

1. In mixer bowl, sprinkle yeast over cream and stir with a fork. Let stand until foamy, about 5 minutes.

2. Attach bowl to mixer fitted with paddle attachment and add egg whites, oil, vanilla, 1 cup (250 mL) of the flour, sugar and salt to yeast mixture. Let stand in bowl for 10 minutes. On low speed, mix just until blended, then gradually add just enough of the remaining flour until dough starts to pull away from sides of bowl. Increase speed to medium and beat for 1 minute.

3. Transfer dough to a large oiled bowl and cover with plastic wrap. Let rise in a warm, draft-free place until doubled in volume, about 30 minutes.

4. Turn dough out onto a floured work surface. Roll out dough to slightly thicker than ¼ inch (0.5 cm). If dough is tacky, dust with additional flour. Cut dough with cutter into 18 donuts (or cut with a knife or pizza cutter into 2- by 1-inch/5 by 2.5 cm rectangles), re-rolling scraps as necessary. Place at least 1 inch (2.5 cm) apart on prepared baking sheet. Cover with a clean kitchen towel and let rise for 20 minutes.

Finishing suggestions

Icings: Belgian Chocolate Ganache Glaze (page 197), Maple Glaze (page 201), Raspberry Glaze (page 203) or Strawberry Glaze (Variation, page 203).

5. Meanwhile, in a large, deep pot or deep fryer, heat about 4 inches (10 cm) oil over medium heat until temperature registers 360°F (182°C). Deep-fry 6 donuts at a time in hot oil, turning once with wooden chopsticks, until golden brown, about 15 seconds per side. Using a slotted spoon, transfer to paper towels to absorb excess oil. Fry remaining donuts, adjusting heat as necessary between batches to maintain oil temperature.

6. Let donuts cool completely prior to icing.

Triple Chocolate Bites

Makes about 36 donut bites

Small yet packed with three different types of chocolate, these donuts will fulfill any chocoholics dream.

- Stand mixer with paddle attachment
- 2- by 1-inch (5 by 2.5 cm) cutter, optional
- Baking sheet, lined with parchment paper
- Digital candy/deep-fry thermometer

¾ cup + 1 tbsp	whole milk, warmed to 110°F (43°C)	190 mL
1	package (¼ oz/8 g) quick-rising (instant) yeast	1
1	large egg	1
2 tbsp	canola oil	30 mL
2 cups	all-purpose flour, divided (approx.)	500 mL
¾ cup	unsweetened cocoa powder	175 mL
1 tbsp	granulated sugar	15 mL
⅛ tsp	salt	0.5 mL
¼ cup	semisweet chocolate chips	60 mL
¼ cup	milk chocolate chips	60 mL
	Canola oil	

1. In mixer bowl, sprinkle yeast over milk and stir with a fork. Let stand until foamy, about 5 minutes.

2. Attach bowl to mixer fitted with paddle attachment and add egg, oil, ½ cup (125 mL) of the flour, cocoa powder, sugar and salt to yeast mixture. Let stand in bowl for 10 minutes. On low speed, mix just until blended, then gradually add just enough of the remaining flour until dough starts to pull away from sides of bowl. Increase speed to medium and beat for 1 minute. On low speed, mix in semisweet and milk chocolate chips.

3. Transfer dough to a large oiled bowl and cover with plastic wrap. Let rise in a warm, draft-free place until doubled in volume, about 30 minutes.

Finishing suggestions

Icings: Belgian Chocolate Ganache Glaze (page 197), Milk Chocolate Glaze (page 201) or Mocha Glaze (page 202).

4. Turn dough out onto a floured work surface. Roll out dough to slightly thicker than $\frac{1}{4}$ inch (0.5 cm). If dough is tacky, dust with additional flour. Cut dough with cutter into 36 donuts (or cut with a knife or pizza cutter into 2- by 1-inch/5 by 2.5 cm rectangles), re-rolling scraps as necessary. Place at least 1 inch (2.5 cm) apart on prepared baking sheet. Cover with a clean kitchen towel and let rise for 20 minutes.

5. Meanwhile, in a large, deep pot or deep fryer, heat about 4 inches (10 cm) oil over medium heat until temperature registers 360°F (182°C). Deep-fry 6 donuts at a time in hot oil, turning once with wooden chopsticks, until puffy, about 20 seconds per side. Using a slotted spoon, transfer to paper towels to absorb excess oil. Fry remaining donuts, adjusting heat as necessary between batches to maintain oil temperature.

6. Let donuts cool completely prior to icing.

Chocolate Donut Holes

**Makes about
36 donut holes**

I love just popping a few of these at a time into my mouth.

Finishing suggestions

Icings: Belgian Chocolate Ganache Glaze (page 197), Milk Chocolate Glaze (page 201), Mocha Glaze (page 202), Bittersweet Chocolate Glaze (page 197) or Truffle Fudge Icing (page 196).

- Stand mixer with paddle attachment
- Digital candy/deep-fry thermometer
- 2-inch (5 cm) round cutter
- Baking sheet, lined with parchment paper

3 cups	all-purpose flour	750 mL
½ cup	unsweetened cocoa powder	125 mL
1¼ tsp	baking powder	6 mL
1 tsp	salt	5 mL
½ tsp	baking soda	2 mL
1 cup	packed brown sugar	250 mL
3	large eggs, beaten	3
¼ cup	buttermilk	60 mL
¼ cup	canola oil	60 mL
2 tsp	vanilla extract	10 mL
1 tsp	rum extract	5 mL
	Canola oil	

1. In a large bowl, whisk together 2 cups (500 mL) of the flour, cocoa powder, baking powder, salt and baking soda. Set aside.

2. In mixer bowl fitted with paddle attachment, combine sugar, eggs, buttermilk, oil, vanilla and rum extracts. On low speed, mix until well combined. Add dry ingredients and mix until incorporated. Gradually mix in more of the remaining flour, as necessary, until dough starts to come together and is the consistency of biscuit dough. Cover and refrigerate for 10 minutes.

3. Meanwhile, in a large, deep pot or deep fryer, heat about 4 inches (10 cm) oil over medium heat until temperature registers 375°F (190°C) (see Tip, page 136).

4. On a floured work surface, roll out dough to slightly thicker than ¼ inch (0.5 cm). If dough is tacky, dust with additional flour. Cut dough with cutter into 36 donuts, re-rolling scraps as necessary. Place on baking sheet.

5. Deep-fry 6 donuts at a time in hot oil, turning once with wooden chopsticks, until puffed and firm, about 15 seconds per side. Using a slotted spoon, transfer to paper towels to absorb excess oil. Adjust heat as necessary between batches to maintain oil temperature.

6. Let donuts cool completely prior to icing.

Coffee Bites

Makes about 36 donut bites

A slight hint of coffee creates a perfect donut bite while enjoying an espresso.

Tip

You can use instant espresso powder. Check the packaging for the amounts so you do not have to brew an espresso for the recipe.

Finishing suggestions

Icings: Bittersweet Chocolate Glaze (page 197) or Mocha Glaze (page 202).

- Stand mixer with paddle attachment
- Digital candy/deep-fry thermometer
- 2-inch (5 cm) round cutter
- Baking sheet, lined with parchment paper

2 cups	all-purpose flour, divided	500 mL
1 tsp	baking powder	5 mL
1/4 tsp	salt	1 mL
1/4 tsp	baking soda	1 mL
1/4 tsp	ground cardamom	1 mL
1/2 cup	granulated sugar	125 mL
1	large egg, beaten	1
1	large egg yolk, beaten	1
2 tbsp	buttermilk	30 mL
1 tbsp	unsalted butter, melted and cooled	15 mL
1 tbsp	brewed espresso (see Tip, left)	15 mL
	Canola oil	

1. In a bowl, whisk together 1 1/4 cups (300 mL) of the flour, baking powder, salt, baking soda and cardamom. Set aside.

2. In mixer bowl fitted with paddle attachment, combine sugar, egg, egg yolk, buttermilk, butter and espresso. On low speed, mix until well combined. Add dry ingredients and mix until incorporated. Gradually mix in more of the remaining flour, as necessary, until dough starts to come together and is the consistency of biscuit dough. Cover and refrigerate for 10 minutes.

3. Meanwhile, in a large, deep pot or deep fryer, heat about 4 inches (10 cm) oil over medium heat until temperature registers 360°F (182°C) (see Tip, page 136).

4. On a floured work surface, roll out dough to slightly thicker than 1/4 inch (0.5 cm). If dough is tacky, dust with additional flour. Cut dough with cutter into 36 donut bites, re-rolling scraps as necessary. Place on prepared baking sheet.

5. Deep-fry 6 donuts at a time in hot oil, turning once with wooden chopsticks, until puffed and firm, about 15 seconds per side. Using a slotted spoon, transfer to paper towels to absorb excess oil. Adjust heat as necessary between batches to maintain oil temperature.

6. Let donuts cool completely prior to icing.

Pistachio Bites

Ground pistachio nuts make these donuts a nice light green color. Perfect for St. Patty's Day or Christmas.

Tip

If you only can purchase salted pistachio nuts, place them in a damp towel and rub as much salt off as possible.

Finishing suggestions

Icings: Simple Sugar Glaze (page 205) or Lemon Zest Glaze (page 200).

- Food processor
- Stand mixer with paddle attachment
- Digital candy/deep-fry thermometer
- 2-inch (5 cm) round cutter

2½ cups	all-purpose flour, divided	625 mL
1 cup	shelled unsalted pistachios (see Tip, left)	250 mL
1½ tsp	baking powder	7 mL
1 tsp	baking soda	5 mL
¾ cup	granulated sugar	175 mL
2	large eggs, beaten	2
2 tbsp	buttermilk	30 mL
¼ cup	unsalted butter, melted	60 mL
1½ tsp	vanilla extract	7 mL
	Canola oil	

1. In food processor fitted with metal blade, combine 2 cups (500 mL) of the flour, pistachios, baking powder and soda and process for 30 seconds or until nuts are finely chopped. Set aside.

2. In mixer bowl fitted with paddle attachment, combine sugar, eggs, buttermilk, butter and vanilla. On low speed, mix until well combined. Add dry ingredients and mix until incorporated. Gradually mix in more of the remaining flour, as necessary, until dough starts to come together and is the consistency of biscuit dough. Cover and refrigerate for 10 minutes.

3. Meanwhile, in a large, deep pot or deep fryer, heat about 4 inches (10 cm) oil over medium heat until temperature registers 360°F (182°C) (see Tip, page 136).

4. On a floured work surface, roll out dough to slightly thicker than ¼ inch (0.5 cm). If dough is tacky, dust with additional flour. Cut dough with cutter into 48 donuts, re-rolling scraps as necessary. Place on prepared baking sheet.

5. Deep-fry 6 donuts at a time in hot oil, turning once with wooden chopsticks, until golden brown, about 15 seconds per side. Using a slotted spoon, transfer to paper towels to absorb excess oil. Fry remaining donuts, adjusting heat as necessary between batches to maintain oil temperature.

6. Let donuts cool completely prior to icing.

Spicy Donut Balls

Makes about 36 donut bites

Makes about 36 donut bites

A slightly spicy tang from these donuts will leave your taste buds wanting more.

Finishing suggestions

Icing: Autumn Spiced Sugar (page 204).

- Stand mixer with paddle attachment
- Digital candy/deep-fry thermometer
- 2-inch (5 cm) round cutter
- Baking sheet, lined with parchment paper

2 cups	all-purpose flour, divided	500 mL
1 tsp	baking powder	5 mL
1/4 tsp	salt	1 mL
1/4 tsp	baking soda	1 mL
1/4 tsp	ground cardamom	1 mL
1/4 tsp	freshly ground nutmeg	1 mL
1/4 tsp	Chinese five-spice powder	1 mL
1/2 cup	packed brown sugar	125 mL
2	large eggs, beaten	2
2 tbsp	buttermilk	30 mL
	Canola oil	

1. In a large bowl, whisk together 1 1/4 cups (300 mL) of the flour, baking powder, salt, baking soda, cardamom, nutmeg and five-spice powder. Set aside.

2. In mixer bowl fitted with paddle attachment, combine sugar, eggs, buttermilk and 2 tbsp (30 mL) oil. On low speed, mix until well combined. Add dry ingredients and mix until incorporated. Gradually mix in more of the remaining flour, as necessary, until dough starts to come together and is the consistency of biscuit dough. Cover and refrigerate for 10 minutes.

3. Meanwhile, in a large, deep pot or deep fryer, heat about 4 inches (10 cm) oil over medium heat until temperature registers 360°F (182°C) (see Tip, page 136).

4. On a floured work surface, roll out dough to slightly thicker than 1/4 inch (0.5 cm). If dough is tacky, dust with additional flour. Cut dough with cutter into 36 donut bites, re-rolling scraps as necessary. Place on prepared baking sheet.

5. Deep-fry 6 donuts at a time in hot oil, turning once with wooden chopsticks, until puffed and firm, about 15 seconds per side. Using a slotted spoon, transfer to paper towels to absorb excess oil. Adjust heat as necessary between batches to maintain oil temperature.

6. Toss warm donuts with Autumn Spiced Sugar, if using.

All Spiced-Up Bites

● ●

**Makes about
24 mini donuts**

Sometimes you will find
spiced little donuts at
a carnival or a fair. Try
this easy, baked version
for your kid's next
party.

Finishing suggestions

Icing: Autumn Spiced
Sugar (page 204).

- Preheat oven to 325°F (160°C)
- Two 12-well mini-donut pans, sprayed with nonstick spray

2 cups	all-purpose flour	500 mL
¾ cup	packed brown sugar	175 mL
2 tsp	baking powder	10 mL
1 tsp	salt	5 mL
1 tsp	ground cinnamon	5 mL
½ tsp	freshly ground nutmeg	2 mL
¼ tsp	ground allspice	1 mL
⅛ tsp	ground ginger	0.5 mL
2	large eggs, beaten	2
¾ cup	whole milk	175 mL
1 tbsp	unsalted butter, melted	15 mL
1 tsp	vanilla extract	5 mL

1. In a large bowl, whisk together flour, brown sugar, baking powder, salt, cinnamon, nutmeg, allspice and ginger. Set aside.

2. In a medium bowl, whisk together eggs, milk, butter and vanilla. Add to flour mixture and mix with a rubber spatula just until incorporated.

3. Spoon batter into a resealable freezer bag or pastry bag (see page 8) and fill each prepared well two-thirds full.

4. Bake in preheated oven until donut springs back when lightly touched, 8 to 12 minutes.

5. Let donuts cool in pans on a rack for 5 minutes. Turn out of pans onto rack and toss with Autumn Spiced Sugar, if using.

Baked Maple Mini Donuts

● ●

**Makes about
24 mini donuts**

Rich pure maple syrup
makes these donuts full
of flavor.

● ● ● ● ● ● ● ● ● ● ● ● ● ● ● ● ● ●

Finishing suggestions
Icings: Simple Sugar Glaze
(page 205), Maple Glaze
(page 201) or Brown Butter
Glaze (page 198).

● Preheat oven to 350°F (180°C)
● Two 12-well mini-donut pans, sprayed with nonstick
  spray

3 cups	all-purpose flour	750 mL
½ cup	large-flake (old-fashioned) rolled oats	125 mL
½ cup	packed light brown sugar	125 mL
1 tbsp	baking powder	15 mL
1 tsp	salt	5 mL
2	large eggs, beaten	2
1 cup	whole milk	250 mL
¼ cup	pure maple syrup	60 mL
2 tbsp	unsalted butter, melted	30 mL
1 tsp	vanilla extract	5 mL

1. In a large bowl, whisk together flour, oats, brown sugar,
   baking powder and salt. Set aside.

2. In a medium bowl, whisk together eggs, milk, maple
   syrup, butter and vanilla. Add to flour mixture and mix
   with a rubber spatula just until incorporated.

3. Place batter into a resealable freezer bag or pastry bag
   (see page 8) and fill each prepared well two-thirds full.

4. Bake in preheated oven until donut springs back when
   lightly touched, 10 to 14 minutes.

5. Let donuts cool in pans on a rack for 5 minutes. Turn
   out of pans onto rack and let cool completely prior
   to icing.

Blueberry Bites

**Makes about
24 mini donuts**

A basket full of
blueberry mini donuts
will complete your
brunch table.

Finishing suggestions

Icings: Simple Sugar Glaze
(page 205), Lavender
Sugar Dust (page 206)
or Rose Petal Dust
(page 206).

- Preheat oven to 325°F (160°C)
- Two 12-well mini-donut pans, sprayed with nonstick spray

2½ cups	all-purpose flour	625 mL
½ cup	granulated sugar	125 mL
½ cup	packed brown sugar	125 mL
2½ tsp	baking powder	12 mL
½ tsp	salt	2 mL
2	large eggs, beaten	2
½ cup	heavy or whipping (35%) cream	125 mL
¼ cup	water	60 mL
2 tbsp	unsalted butter, melted	30 mL
1 tsp	vanilla extract	5 mL
1 tsp	almond extract	5 mL
1 cup	fresh or frozen blueberries	250 mL

1. In a large bowl, whisk together flour, granulated sugar, brown sugar, baking powder and salt. Set aside.

2. In a medium bowl, whisk together eggs, cream, water, butter and vanilla and almond extracts. Add to flour mixture and mix with a rubber spatula just until incorporated. Fold in blueberries.

3. Place batter into a resealable freezer bag or pastry bag (see page 8) and fill each prepared well two-thirds full.

4. Bake in preheated oven until donut springs back when lightly touched, 8 to 10 minutes.

5. Let donuts cool in pans on a rack for 5 minutes. Turn out of pans onto rack and toss with either Lavender Dust Sugar or Rose Petal Dust, if using, or let cool completely prior to icing.

Delicate Dainty Donut Bites (page 148)
with Chocolate Fudge Filling (page 215)

Boules de Berlin Donuts (page 172)

Rum-Glazed Donuts (page 192)

All Spiced-Up Bites (page 158)

Hanukkah Sufganiyot Donuts (page 180)

Italian Crème–Filled Donuts (page 182)

French Crullers (page 187)

New Orleans
Beignets (page 188)

Citrus Donut Bites

**Makes about
24 mini donuts**

Here's a mixture of orange and lemon flavors to brighten up your morning.

Finishing suggestions

Icings: Simple Sugar Glaze (page 205), Lemon Zest Glaze (page 200) or Citrus Sugar (page 205).

Variation

Lemon Poppy Seed Mini Donuts: Omit orange zest and increase lemon zest to 2 tbsp (30 mL). Add 1 tbsp (15 mL) poppy seeds with the zest. Finish with Lemon Zest Glaze (page 200), Honey Glaze (page 200) or Simple Sugar Glaze (page 205).

- Preheat oven to 325°F (160°C)
- Two 12-well mini-donut pans, sprayed with nonstick spray

2½ cups	cake flour	625 mL
1 cup	granulated sugar	250 mL
2½ tsp	baking powder	12 mL
½ tsp	salt	2 mL
2	large eggs, beaten	2
¾ cup	whole milk	175 mL
2 tbsp	canola oil	30 mL
1 tbsp	grated orange zest	15 mL
1 tbsp	grated lemon zest	15 mL
1 tsp	vanilla extract	5 mL

1. In a large bowl, whisk together flour, sugar, baking powder and salt. Set aside.

2. In a medium bowl, whisk together eggs, milk, oil, orange zest, lemon zest and vanilla. Add to flour mixture and mix with a rubber spatula just until incorporated.

3. Place batter into a resealable freezer bag or pastry bag (see page 8) and fill each prepared well two-thirds full.

4. Bake in preheated oven until donut springs back when lightly touched, 10 to 14 minutes.

5. Let donuts cool in pans on a rack for 5 minutes. Turn out of pans onto rack and toss with Citrus Sugar, if using, or let cool completely prior to icing.

Cranberry Almond Donut Bites

Makes about 24 mini donuts

Tart cranberries and crunchy almonds make up this perfect donut for brunch.

Tip

Almond flour, made from ground almonds, is also known as almond meal. It can be purchased in most major grocery stores or health food stores. Watch the expiration date as it does go rancid quickly.

Finishing suggestions

Icing: Simple Sugar Glaze (page 205).

- Preheat oven to 325°F (160°C)
- Two 12-well mini-donut pans, sprayed with nonstick spray

2 cups	cake flour	500 mL
1/2 cup	almond flour (see Tip, left)	125 mL
1 cup	granulated sugar	250 mL
2 1/2 tsp	baking powder	12 mL
1/2 tsp	salt	2 mL
2	large eggs, beaten	2
3/4 cup	whole milk	175 mL
2 tbsp	unsalted butter, melted	30 mL
1 tsp	vanilla extract	5 mL
1 cup	fresh or frozen cranberries, chopped	250 mL
1/2 cup	almonds, chopped	125 mL

1. In a large bowl, whisk together cake flour, almond flour, sugar, baking powder and salt. Set aside.

2. In a medium bowl, whisk together eggs, milk, butter and vanilla. Add to flour mixture and mix with a rubber spatula just until incorporated. Fold in cranberries and almonds.

3. Place batter into a resealable freezer bag or pastry bag (see page 8) and fill each prepared well two-thirds full.

4. Bake in preheated oven until donut springs back when lightly touched, 10 to 14 minutes.

5. Let donuts cool in pans on a rack for 5 minutes. Turn out of pans onto rack and let cool completely prior to icing.

Green Tea Bites

Makes about 12 mini donuts

A hint of Asian flavors and spice combine in this one-bite donut.

Finishing suggestions

Icings: Green Tea Glaze (page 199), Honey Glaze (page 200) or Simple Sugar Glaze (page 205).

- Preheat oven to 325°F (160°C)
- One 12-well mini-donut pan, sprayed with nonstick spray

½ cup	whole milk	125 mL
1	green tea bag	1
2 cups	all-purpose flour	500 mL
⅓ cup	cake flour	75 mL
½ cup	granulated sugar	125 mL
1½ tsp	baking powder	7 mL
½ tsp	salt	2 mL
¼ tsp	Chinese five-spice powder	1 mL
1	large egg, beaten	1
2 tsp	unsalted butter, melted	10 mL
½ tsp	vanilla extract	2 mL

1. In a small saucepan over medium heat, bring milk to a simmer. Turn off heat. Add tea bag and let infuse for 20 minutes. Discard tea bag.

2. In a large bowl, whisk together all-purpose flour, cake flour, sugar, baking powder, salt and five-spice powder. Set aside.

3. In a medium bowl, whisk together infused milk, egg, butter and vanilla. Add to flour mixture and mix with a rubber spatula just until incorporated.

4. Place batter into a resealable freezer bag or pastry bag (see page 8) and fill each prepared well two-thirds full.

5. Bake in preheated oven until donut springs back when lightly touched, 10 to 14 minutes.

6. Let donuts cool in pans on a rack for 5 minutes. Turn out of pans onto rack and let cool completely prior to icing.

Mini Pumpkin Donuts

These small simple bites offer an array of fall spicy flavors to tantalize your taste buds.

Finishing suggestions

Icings: Autumn Spiced Sugar (page 204) or Milk Chocolate Glaze (page 201).

- Preheat oven to 325°F (160°C)
- Two 12-well mini-donut pans, sprayed with nonstick spray

2½ cups	all-purpose flour	625 mL
¾ cup	packed brown sugar	175 mL
2 tsp	baking powder	10 mL
1 tsp	salt	5 mL
1 tsp	ground cinnamon	5 mL
½ tsp	freshly ground nutmeg	2 mL
¼ tsp	ground allspice	1 mL
⅛ tsp	ground ginger	0.5 mL
2	large eggs, beaten	2
¾ cup	whole milk	175 mL
½ cup	pumpkin purée (not pie filling)	125 mL
1 tbsp	unsalted butter, melted	15 mL
1 tsp	vanilla extract	5 mL

1. In a large bowl, whisk together flour, brown sugar, baking powder, salt, cinnamon, nutmeg, allspice and ginger. Set aside.

2. In a medium bowl, whisk together eggs, milk, pumpkin purée, butter and vanilla. Add to flour mixture and mix with a rubber spatula just until incorporated.

3. Place batter into a resealable freezer bag or pastry bag (see page 8) and fill each prepared well two-thirds full.

4. Bake in preheated oven until donut springs back when lightly touched, 10 to 14 minutes.

5. Let donuts cool in pans on a rack for 5 minutes. Turn out of pans onto rack and toss with Autumn Spiced Sugar, if using, or let cool completely prior to icing.

Oat Berry Mini Donuts

**Makes about
24 mini donuts**

The sweetness of
berries complements
the nutty flavor of oats.

Finishing suggestions

Icings: Strawberry Glaze
(Variation, page 203) or
Milk Chocolate Glaze
(page 201).

- Preheat oven to 350°F (180°C)
- Two 12-well mini-donut pans, sprayed with nonstick
  spray

1 cup	all-purpose flour	250 mL
1 cup	large-flake (old-fashioned) rolled oats	250 mL
¾ cup	packed light brown sugar	175 mL
1 tbsp	baking powder	15 mL
½ tsp	salt	2 mL
1	large egg, beaten	1
1 cup	buttermilk	250 mL
¼ cup	unsalted butter, melted	60 mL
2 tsp	vanilla extract	10 mL
1 cup	fresh or frozen mixed berries, chopped if large	250 mL

1. In a large bowl, whisk together flour, oats, brown sugar,
   baking powder and salt. Set aside.

2. In a medium bowl, whisk together egg, buttermilk,
   butter and vanilla. Add to flour mixture and mix with
   a rubber spatula just until incorporated. Fold in berries.

3. Place batter into a resealable freezer bag or pastry bag
   (see page 8) and fill each prepared well two-thirds full.

4. Bake in preheated oven until donut springs back when
   lightly touched, 10 to 14 minutes.

5. Let donuts cool in pans on a rack for 5 minutes. Turn
   out of pans onto rack and let cool completely prior
   to icing.

Strawberry Cream Bites

Makes about 24 mini donuts

These mini donuts remind me of little bites of strawberry shortcake.

Finishing suggestions

Icings: Strawberry Glaze (Variation, page 203), Honey Glaze (page 200) or Rose Petal Dust (page 206).

- Preheat oven to 325°F (160°C)
- Two 12-well mini-donut pans, sprayed with nonstick spray

1¾ cups	all-purpose flour	425 mL
1 cup	granulated sugar	250 mL
¼ cup	white cornmeal	60 mL
2½ tsp	baking powder	12 mL
½ tsp	salt	2 mL
2	large eggs, beaten	2
¾ cup	heavy or whipping (35%) cream	175 mL
2 tbsp	unsalted butter, melted	30 mL
1 tsp	vanilla extract	5 mL
1 cup	finely chopped strawberries	250 mL

1. In a large bowl, whisk together flour, sugar, cornmeal, baking powder and salt. Set aside.

2. In a medium bowl, whisk together eggs, cream, butter and vanilla. Add to flour mixture and mix with a rubber spatula just until incorporated. Fold in strawberries.

3. Place batter into a resealable freezer bag or pastry bag (see page 8) and fill each prepared well two-thirds full.

4. Bake in preheated oven until donut springs back when lightly touched, 8 to 12 minutes.

5. Let donuts cool in pans on a rack for 5 minutes. Turn out of pans onto rack and toss with Rose Petal Dust, if using, or let cool completely prior to icing.

Specialty Donuts

• •

When **you are** looking for a donut that's a little more special for an event or party, try one of these.

Banana Crème Donuts. 168

Boston Cream Donuts 170

Boules de Berlin Donuts 172

Campfire S'more Donuts 174

Caramel Apple Fritters 176

Cinnamon Donut Sticks 178

Hanukkah Sufganiyot Donuts 180

Italian Crème–Filled Donuts 182

Maple Bacon Bars 184

Churro Bites 186

French Crullers 187

New Orleans Beignets. 188

Piña Colada Donuts 190

Rum-Glazed Donuts. 192

Elvis Memphis Donuts 194

Banana Crème Donuts

Here's a donut with a tropical banana flavor and a hint of rum.

Tip

When you are making ring-shaped donuts you may like to fry up the center holes for a treat. Depending on the size of the hole, your frying time will have to be adjusted since they tend to fry faster. I sometimes like to test a donut hole just to see how the flavor of the donut is and what icing I will want to dress it with.

- Stand mixer with paddle attachment
- 4-inch (10 cm) round cutter
- Baking sheet, lined with parchment paper
- Digital candy/deep-fry thermometer

¾ cup + 1 tbsp	whole milk, warmed to 110°F (43°C)	190 mL
1	package (¼ oz/8 g) quick-rising (instant) yeast	1
2	large eggs	2
⅔ cup	mashed ripe banana	150 mL
2 tbsp	unsalted butter, melted	30 mL
2 tsp	vanilla extract	10 mL
½ tsp	rum extract	2 mL
3 cups	all-purpose flour, divided (approx.)	750 mL
1 tbsp	granulated sugar	15 mL
⅛ tsp	salt	0.5 mL
	Canola oil	
	Banana Cream Filling (page 208)	

1. In mixer bowl, sprinkle yeast over milk and stir with a fork. Let stand until foamy, about 5 minutes.

2. Attach bowl to mixer fitted with paddle attachment and add eggs, banana, butter, vanilla and rum extracts, 1 cup (250 mL) of the flour, sugar and salt to yeast mixture. Let stand in bowl for 10 minutes. On low speed, mix just until blended, then gradually add just enough of the remaining flour until dough starts to pull away from sides of bowl. Increase speed to medium and beat for 1 minute.

3. Transfer dough to a large oiled bowl and cover with plastic wrap. Let rise in a warm, draft-free place until doubled in volume, about 30 minutes.

●●

Tip

You can make the banana cream filling 3 days prior to use. Refrigerate in a closed container and stir before using.

4. Turn dough out onto a floured work surface. Roll out dough to slightly thicker than ¼ inch (0.5 cm) thick. If dough is tacky, dust with additional flour. Cut dough with cutter into 12 donuts, re-rolling scraps as necessary. Place at least 1 inch (2.5 cm) apart on prepared baking sheet. Cover with a clean kitchen towel and let rise for 20 minutes.

5. Meanwhile, in a large, deep pot or deep fryer, heat about 4 inches (10 cm) oil over medium heat until temperature registers 360°F (182°C). Deep-fry 3 donuts at a time in hot oil, turning once with wooden chopsticks, until golden brown, about 15 seconds per side. Using a slotted spatula, transfer to paper towels to absorb excess oil. Fry remaining donuts, adjusting heat as necessary between batches to maintain oil temperature.

6. Let donuts cool completely and then fill with Banana Cream Filling, using a Bismarck tip (see page 8) or a pastry bag.

Boston Cream Donuts

**Makes about
12 donuts**

Just like the creamy
cake, these donuts
deliver.

- Stand mixer with paddle attachment
- 4-inch (10 cm) round cutter
- Baking sheet, lined with parchment paper
- Digital candy/deep-fry thermometer

¾ cup + 1 tbsp	whole milk, warmed to 110°F (43°C)	190 mL
1	package (¼ oz/8 g) quick-rising (instant) yeast	1
1	large egg	1
1	large egg white	1
2 tbsp	unsalted butter, melted	30 mL
1 tsp	vanilla extract	5 mL
2¾ cups	all-purpose flour, divided (approx.)	675 mL
1 tbsp	granulated sugar	15 mL
⅛ tsp	salt	0.5 mL
	Canola oil	
	Bavarian Cream Custard (page 209)	
	Bittersweet Chocolate Glaze (page 197)	

1. In mixer bowl, sprinkle yeast over milk and stir with a fork. Let stand until foamy, about 5 minutes.

2. Attach bowl to mixer fitted with paddle attachment and add egg, egg white, butter, vanilla, 1 cup (250 mL) of the flour, sugar and salt to yeast mixture. Let stand in bowl for 10 minutes. On low speed, mix just until blended, then gradually add just enough of the remaining flour until dough starts to pull away from sides of bowl. Increase speed to medium and beat for 1 minute.

3. Transfer dough to a large oiled bowl and cover with plastic wrap. Let rise in a warm, draft-free place until doubled in volume, about 30 minutes.

4. Turn dough out onto a floured work surface. Roll out dough to slightly thicker than ¼ inch (0.5 cm). If dough is tacky, dust with additional flour. Cut dough with cutter into 12 donuts, re-rolling scraps as necessary. Place at least 1 inch (2.5 cm) apart on prepared baking sheet. Cover with a clean kitchen towel and let rise for 20 minutes.

5. Meanwhile, in a large, deep pot or deep fryer, heat about 4 inches (10 cm) oil over medium heat until temperature registers 360°F (182°C). Deep-fry 3 donuts at a time in hot oil, turning once with wooden chopsticks, until golden brown, about 15 seconds per side. Using a slotted spatula, transfer to paper towels to absorb excess oil. Fry remaining donuts, adjusting heat as necessary between batches to maintain oil temperature.

6. Let donuts cool completely and then fill with Bavarian Cream Custard, using a Bismarck tip (see page 8) or a pastry bag. Top each donut with Bittersweet Chocolate Glaze.

Boules de Berlin Donuts

**Makes about
12 donuts**

This French donut is
yeast-based and round
and filled with jelly
while warm.

Finishing suggestions

Icing: Honey Glaze
(page 200).

- Stand mixer with paddle attachment
- 3-inch (7.5 cm) round cutter
- Baking sheet, lined with parchment paper
- Digital candy/deep-fry thermometer

¾ cup + 1 tbsp	whole milk, warmed to 110°F (43°C)	190 mL
1	package (¼ oz/8 g) quick-rising (instant) yeast	1
1	large egg	1
1	large egg white	1
2 tbsp	canola oil	30 mL
1 tsp	vanilla extract	5 mL
2¼ cups	all-purpose flour, divided (approx.)	550 mL
½ cup	hazelnut flour	125 mL
1 tbsp	granulated sugar	15 mL
⅛ tsp	salt	0.5 mL
	Canola oil	
	Raspberry Filling (Variation, page 214)	

1. In mixer bowl, sprinkle yeast over milk and stir with a fork. Let stand until foamy, about 5 minutes.

2. Attach bowl to mixer fitted with paddle attachment and add egg, egg white, oil, vanilla, ½ cup (125 mL) of the flour, hazelnut flour, sugar and salt to yeast mixture. Let stand in bowl for 10 minutes. On low speed, mix just until blended, then gradually add just enough of the remaining flour until dough starts to pull away from sides of bowl. Increase speed to medium and beat for 1 minute.

3. Transfer dough to a large oiled bowl and cover with plastic wrap. Let rise in a warm, draft-free place until doubled in volume, about 30 minutes.

Variation

Fillings (injected): Instead of Raspberry Filling, try Lemon Zest Filling (page 213) or Strawberry Filling (page 214).

Fillings (cut donuts in half): Fresh Cherry Filling (page 211).

4. Turn dough out onto a floured work surface. Roll out dough to slightly thicker than ¼ inch (0.5 cm). If dough is tacky, dust with additional flour. Cut dough with cutter into 12 donuts, re-rolling scraps as necessary. Place at least 1 inch (2.5 cm) apart on prepared baking sheet. Cover with a clean kitchen towel and let rise for 20 minutes.

5. Meanwhile, in a large, deep pot or deep fryer, heat about 4 inches (10 cm) oil over medium heat until temperature registers 360°F (182°C). Deep-fry 4 donuts at a time in hot oil, turning once with wooden chopsticks, until golden brown, about 15 seconds per side. Using a slotted spatula, transfer to paper towels to absorb excess oil. Fry remaining donuts, adjusting heat as necessary between batches to maintain oil temperature.

6. Let donut cool enough for you to hold and then fill with jelly, using a Bismarck tip or a pastry bag (see page 8). If desired, ice after filling.

Campfire S'More Donuts

Makes about 18 donuts

A little like the popular campfire dessert s'mores. Try these in the winter when you can't get to a campfire.

- Stand mixer with paddle attachment
- 3-inch (7.5 cm) square cutter, optional
- Baking sheet, lined with parchment paper
- Digital candy/deep-fry thermometer

¾ cup + 1 tbsp	whole milk, warmed to 110°F (43°C)	190 mL
1	package (¼ oz/8 g) quick-rising (instant) yeast	1
2	large eggs	2
1 tbsp	canola oil	15 mL
1 tbsp	unsalted butter, melted	15 mL
1 tsp	vanilla extract	5 mL
1 cup	all-purpose flour, divided (approx.)	250 mL
1 cup	graham cracker crumbs	250 mL
½ cup	unsweetened cocoa powder	125 mL
¼ cup	cake flour	60 mL
1 tbsp	granulated sugar	15 mL
⅛ tsp	salt	0.5 mL
	Canola oil	
	Marshmallow Filling (page 210)	

1. In mixer bowl, sprinkle yeast over milk and stir with a fork. Let stand until foamy, about 5 minutes.

2. Attach bowl to mixer fitted with paddle attachment and add eggs, oil, butter, vanilla, ½ cup (125 mL) of the all-purpose flour, graham cracker crumbs, cocoa powder, cake flour, sugar and salt to yeast mixture. Let stand in bowl for 10 minutes. On low speed, mix just until blended, then gradually add just enough of the remaining flour until dough starts to pull away from sides of bowl. Increase speed to medium and beat for 1 minute.

3. Transfer dough to a large oiled bowl and cover with plastic wrap. Let rise in a warm, draft-free place until doubled in volume, about 30 minutes.

Finishing suggestions

Icing: Simple Sugar Glaze (page 205).

4. Turn dough out onto a floured work surface. Roll out dough to slightly thicker than ¼ inch (0.5 cm). If dough is tacky, dust with additional flour. Cut dough with cutter into 18 donuts, re-rolling scraps as necessary (or cut with a knife or pizza cutter into 3-inch/7.5 cm squares). Place at least 1 inch (2.5 cm) apart on prepared baking sheet. Cover with a clean kitchen towel and let rise for 20 minutes.

5. Meanwhile, in a large, deep pot or deep fryer, heat about 4 inches (10 cm) oil over medium heat until temperature registers 360°F (182°C). Deep-fry 4 donuts at a time in hot oil, turning once with wooden chopsticks, until golden brown, about 15 seconds per side. Using a slotted spatula, transfer to paper towels to absorb excess oil. Fry remaining donuts, adjusting heat as necessary between batches to maintain oil temperature.

6. Let donuts cool completely and then slice in half and fill with Marshmallow Filling. If desired, ice after filling.

Caramel Apple Fritters

**Makes about
12 donuts**

Just like a caramel
apple but in a donut.

- Stand mixer with paddle attachment
- Baking sheet, lined with parchment paper
- Digital candy/deep-fry thermometer

¾ cup	whole milk, warmed to 110°F (43°C)	175 mL
1	package (¼ oz/8 g) quick-rising (instant) yeast	1
1	large egg	1
2 tbsp	canola oil	30 mL
1 tsp	vanilla extract	5 mL
2¾ cups	all-purpose flour, divided (approx.)	675 mL
2 tbsp	granulated sugar	30 mL
⅛ tsp	salt	0.5 mL
2	medium apples, peeled and diced	2
¾ cup	soft caramels, cut into small pieces (about 4 oz/125 g)	175 mL
	Canola oil	

1. In mixer bowl, sprinkle yeast over milk and stir with a fork. Let stand until foamy, about 5 minutes.

2. Attach bowl to mixer fitted with paddle attachment and add egg, oil, vanilla, 1 cup (250 mL) of the flour, sugar and salt to yeast mixture. Let stand in bowl for 10 minutes. On low speed, mix just until blended, then gradually add just enough of the remaining flour until dough starts to pull away from sides of bowl. Increase speed to medium and beat for 1 minute. On low speed, mix in apples and caramel pieces. (Additional flour may be needed, depending on the juice of the fresh apples. Add just enough to keep dough from getting sticky.)

3. Transfer dough to a large oiled bowl and cover with plastic wrap. Let rise in a warm, draft-free place until doubled in volume, about 30 minutes.

Finishing suggestions

Icings: Honey Glaze (page 200), Simple Sugar Glaze (page 205) or Autumn Spiced Sugar (page 204).

4. On a floured work surface, press dough out to a rectangle, about 12 by 8 inches (30 by 20 cm) and to ¾-inch (2 cm) thickness. Divide dough into 12 equal rectangles and press edges to neaten. Place at least 1 inch (2.5 cm) apart on prepared baking sheet. Cover with a clean kitchen towel and let rise for 20 minutes.

5. Meanwhile, in a large, deep pot or deep fryer, heat about 4 inches (10 cm) oil over medium heat until temperature registers 360°F (182°C). Deep-fry 4 donuts at a time in hot oil, turning once with wooden chopsticks, until golden brown, about 30 seconds per side. The donuts will sink to the bottom of the fryer and then float to the top. Using a slotted spatula, transfer to paper towels to absorb excess oil. Fry remaining donuts, adjusting heat as necessary between batches to maintain oil temperature.

6. Toss warm donuts with Autumn Spiced Sugar, if using, or let cool completely prior to icing.

Cinnamon Donut Sticks

● ●

Makes about 12 donuts

These donuts are fried right on a skewer. They are great for parties and fun.

● ● ● ● ● ● ● ● ● ● ● ● ● ● ● ● ● ●

- Stand mixer with paddle attachment
- Pizza cutter
- Twelve 9-inch (23 cm) bamboo skewers
- Baking sheet, lined with parchment paper
- Digital candy/deep-fry thermometer

¾ cup + 1 tbsp	whole milk, warmed to 110°F (43°C)	190 mL
1	package (¼ oz/8 g) quick-rising (instant) yeast	1
2	large egg whites	2
1 tbsp	canola oil	15 mL
1 tbsp	unsalted butter, melted	15 mL
1 tsp	vanilla extract	5 mL
2¾ cups	all-purpose flour, divided (approx.)	675 mL
1 tbsp	granulated sugar	15 mL
⅛ tsp	salt	0.5 mL
1 tbsp	packed brown sugar	15 mL
2 tsp	ground cinnamon	10 mL
1 tsp	freshly ground nutmeg	5 mL
	Canola oil	

1. In mixer bowl, sprinkle yeast over milk and stir with a fork. Let stand until foamy, about 5 minutes.

2. Attach bowl to mixer fitted with paddle attachment and add egg whites, oil, butter, vanilla, 1 cup (250 mL) of the flour, granulated sugar and salt to yeast mixture. Let stand in bowl for 10 minutes. On low speed, mix just until blended, then gradually add just enough of the remaining flour until dough starts to pull away from sides of bowl. Increase speed to medium and beat for 1 minute.

3. Transfer dough to a large oiled bowl and cover with plastic wrap. Let rise in a warm, draft-free place until doubled in volume, about 30 minutes.

Finishing suggestions
Icing: Honey Glaze
(page 200).

4. Meanwhile in a small bowl, combine brown sugar, cinnamon and nutmeg. Set aside.

5. Turn dough out onto a floured work surface. Roll out dough to a rectangle about 24 by 18 inches (60 by 45 cm) and about $\frac{1}{4}$ inch (0.5 cm) thick with one long side closest to you. If dough is tacky, dust with additional flour. Sprinkle cinnamon-sugar mixture on top. Starting with one short side, fold dough in half over the mixture from left to right. Cut dough lengthwise with a pizza cutter into 12 strips, about 1 inch (2.5 cm) thick. Fold each strip in half and twist. Thread each twist lengthwise onto a skewer. Place at least 1 inch (2.5 cm) apart on prepared baking sheet. Cover with a clean kitchen towel and let rise for 20 minutes.

6. Meanwhile, in a large, deep pot or deep fryer, heat about 4 inches (10 cm) oil over medium heat until temperature registers 360°F (182°C). Deep-fry 2 donut skewers at a time in hot oil, turning once with wooden chopsticks, until golden brown, about 15 seconds per side. Using a slotted spatula, transfer to paper towels to absorb excess oil. Fry remaining donuts, adjusting heat as necessary between batches to maintain oil temperature.

7. Let donuts cool completely prior to icing.

Hanukkah Sufganiyot Donuts

Makes about 18 donuts

Almost every religion and country has a special fried pastry. Sufganiyot are consumed in Israel in the weeks leading up to, and including, the Hanukkah holiday.

- Stand mixer with paddle attachment
- Baking sheet, lined with parchment paper
- Digital candy/deep-fry thermometer

¾ cup	whole milk, warmed to 110°F (43°C)	175 mL
2	packages (each ¼ oz/8 g) quick-rising (instant) yeast	2
2	large eggs	2
¼ cup	canola oil	60 mL
3 cups	all-purpose flour, divided (approx.)	750 mL
¾ cup	granulated sugar	175 mL
1 tsp	ground cinnamon	5 mL
1 tsp	salt	5 mL
	Canola Oil	
	Raspberry Filling (Variation, page 214)	

1. In mixer bowl, sprinkle yeast over milk and stir with a fork. Let stand until foamy, about 5 minutes.

2. Attach bowl to mixer fitted with paddle attachment and add eggs, oil, 1 cup (250 mL) of the flour, sugar, cinnamon and salt to yeast mixture. Let stand in bowl for 10 minutes. On low speed, mix just until blended, then gradually add just enough of the remaining flour until dough starts to pull away from sides of bowl. Increase speed to medium and beat for 1 minute.

3. Transfer dough to a large oiled bowl and cover with plastic wrap. Let rise in a warm, draft-free place until doubled in volume, about 30 minutes.

4. Turn dough out onto a floured work surface. Divide dough into 18 equal pieces. Roll dough into round balls between the palms of your hands. If dough is tacky, dust with additional flour. Place at least 1 inch (2.5 cm) apart on prepared baking sheet. Cover with a clean kitchen towel and let rise for 20 minutes.

Finishing suggestions

Icing: Simple Sugar Glaze (page 205)

Topping: Dust with confectioner's (icing) sugar

5. Meanwhile, in a large, deep pot or deep fryer, heat about 4 inches (10 cm) oil over medium heat until temperature registers 360°F (182°C). Deep-fry 4 donuts at a time in hot oil, turning once with wooden chopsticks, until golden brown, about 15 seconds per side. Using a slotted spatula, transfer to paper towels to absorb excess oil. Fry remaining donuts, adjusting heat as necessary between batches to maintain oil temperature.

6. Let donuts cool completely and then fill with Raspberry Filling, using a Bismarck tip or pastry bag (see page 8). If desired, ice with glaze and/or dust with confectioner's sugar.

Italian Crème–Filled Donuts

Makes about 12 donuts

A simple Italian cream filling makes this donut special for any occasion.

Tip

Cake spice is a combination of cinnamon, star anise, nutmeg, allspice, ginger and cloves (see Sources, page 217). If you don't have cake spice, use a total of 1 tsp (5 mL) of those same spices you have on hand, keeping in mind that star anise, allspice and cloves are quite strong so use them sparingly.

- Stand mixer with paddle attachment
- 4-inch (10 cm) round cutter
- Baking sheet, lined with parchment paper
- Digital candy/deep-fry thermometer

¾ cup + 1 tbsp	whole milk, warmed to 110°F (43°C)	190 mL
1	package (¼ oz/8 g) quick-rising (instant) yeast	1
2	large eggs	2
2 tbsp	unsalted butter, melted	30 mL
1 tsp	vanilla extract	5 mL
2¾ cups	all-purpose flour, divided (approx.)	675 mL
1 tbsp	granulated sugar	15 mL
1 tsp	cake spice (see Tip, left)	5 mL
½ tsp	ground ginger	2 mL
½ tsp	ground cinnamon	2 mL
⅛ tsp	salt	0.5 mL
	Canola oil	
	Italian Crème Filling (page 208)	

1. In mixer bowl, sprinkle yeast over milk and stir with a fork. Let stand until foamy, about 5 minutes.

2. Attach bowl to mixer fitted with paddle attachment and add eggs, butter, vanilla, 1 cup (250 mL) of the flour, sugar, cake spice, ginger, cinnamon and salt to yeast mixture. Let stand in bowl for 10 minutes. On low speed, mix just until blended, then gradually add just enough of the remaining flour until dough starts to pull away from sides of bowl. Increase speed to medium and beat for 1 minute.

3. Transfer dough to a large oiled bowl and cover with plastic wrap. Let rise in a warm, draft-free place until doubled in volume, about 30 minutes.

Finishing suggestions

Icings: Honey Glaze
(page 200) or Simple
Sugar Glaze (page 205).

4. Turn dough out onto a floured work surface. Roll out dough to slightly thicker than ¼ inch (0.5 cm). If dough is tacky, dust with additional flour. Cut dough with cutter into 12 donuts, re-rolling scraps as necessary. Place at least 1 inch (2.5 cm) apart on prepared baking sheet. Cover with a clean kitchen towel and let rise for 20 minutes.

5. Meanwhile, in a large, deep pot or deep fryer, heat about 4 inches (10 cm) oil over medium heat until temperature registers 360°F (182°C). Deep-fry 4 donuts at a time in hot oil, turning once with wooden chopsticks, until golden brown, about 15 seconds per side. Using a slotted spatula, transfer to paper towels to absorb excess oil. Fry remaining donuts, adjusting heat as necessary between batches to maintain oil temperature.

6. Let donuts cool completely and then fill with Italian Crème Filling, using a Bismarck tip or pastry bag (see page 8). If desired, ice with glaze.

Maple Bacon Bars

**Makes about
18 donuts**

I am not sure which
donut shop was the
first to have maple and
bacon together, but now
you, too, can try these
at home.

- Stand mixer with paddle attachment
- 5- by 2-inch (12.5 by 5 cm) bar cutter, optional
- Baking sheet, lined with parchment paper
- Digital candy/deep-fry thermometer

⅔ cup	whole milk, warmed to 110°F (43°C)	150 mL
1	package (¼ oz/8 g) quick-rising (instant) yeast	1
1	large egg	1
3 tbsp	pure maple syrup	45 mL
2 tbsp	unsalted butter, melted	30 mL
½ tsp	maple extract	2 mL
2¾ cups	all-purpose flour, divided (approx.)	675 mL
1 tbsp	granulated sugar	15 mL
⅛ tsp	salt	0.5 mL
3	strips maple-smoked bacon, cooked and crumbled, divided (see Tip, right)	3
	Canola oil	
	Maple Glaze (page 201)	

1. In mixer bowl, sprinkle yeast over milk and stir with a fork. Let stand until foamy, about 5 minutes.

2. Attach bowl to mixer fitted with paddle attachment and add egg, maple syrup, butter, maple extract, 1 cup (250 mL) of the flour, sugar and salt to yeast mixture. Let stand in bowl for 10 minutes. On low speed, mix just until blended, then gradually add about half of the bacon and just enough of the remaining flour until dough starts to pull away from sides of bowl. Increase speed to medium and beat for 1 minute.

3. Transfer dough to a large oiled bowl and cover with plastic wrap. Let rise in a warm, draft-free place until doubled in volume, about 30 minutes.

Tip

For ease, you can use ¼ cup (60 mL) real bacon bits that can be found close to the salad dressings in most supermarkets.

4. Turn dough out onto a floured work surface. Roll out dough to slightly thicker than ¼ inch (0.5 cm). If dough is tacky, dust with additional flour. Cut dough with cutter into 18 donuts, re-rolling scraps as necessary (or cut with a knife or pizza cutter into 5 by 2 inch/12.5 by 5 cm rectangles). Place at least 1 inch (2.5 cm) apart on prepared baking sheet. Cover with a clean kitchen towel and let rise for 20 minutes.

5. Meanwhile, in a large, deep pot or deep fryer, heat about 4 inches (10 cm) oil over medium heat until temperature registers 360°F (182°C). Deep-fry 3 or 4 donuts at a time in hot oil, turning once with wooden chopsticks, until puffy, about 20 seconds per side. Using a slotted spatula, transfer to paper towels to absorb excess oil. Fry remaining donuts, adjusting heat as necessary between batches to maintain oil temperature.

6. Let donuts cool completely and then glaze with Maple Glaze and crumble the remaining bacon on top.

Churro Bites

When I was growing up in Southern California, festivals and markets would sell large one-foot churros. To make full-size churros at home you would need a professional deep-fat fryer. Instead, I've created smaller churro bites for you as I have seen sold at many food trucks.

- Digital candy/deep-fry thermometer
- Pastry bag fitted with a large star tip

1 cup	water	250 mL
½ cup	unsalted butter, cut into pieces	125 mL
¼ tsp	ground cinnamon	1 mL
¼ tsp	salt	1 mL
1½ cups	all-purpose flour	375 mL
3	large eggs	3
2	large egg whites	2
	Canola oil	
	Autumn Spiced Sugar (page 204)	

1. In a medium saucepan over medium heat, bring water, butter, cinnamon and salt to a rolling boil. Add flour all at once, mixing with a wooden spoon to quickly incorporate. Cook, stirring constantly, until thickened, about 3 minutes. Remove from heat. Let stand to cool until steaming stops, about 5 minutes. Add eggs and egg whites, one at a time, beating thoroughly after each addition.

2. In a large saucepan, heat about 4 inches (10 cm) oil over medium heat until temperature registers 360°F (182°C).

3. Place batter into a pastry bag. Carefully hold the bag over the hot oil and squeeze a strip of dough about 1 inch (2.5 cm) long, snip with scissors close to the tip and let batter drop into the oil. Fry about a dozen bites at a time, turning once, until golden brown, about 1 minute on each side. Using a slotted spatula, transfer to paper towels to absorb excess oil. Fry remaining churros, adjusting heat as necessary between batches to maintain oil temperature.

4. Roll warm churros in Autumn Spiced Sugar.

French Crullers

● ●

**Makes about
12 donuts**

Crullers are made with
a dough similar to pâte
à choux that's used
for cream puffs. It's a
little trickier than other
donuts to make but
worth the effort.

● ● ● ● ● ● ● ● ● ● ● ● ● ● ● ● ●

Finishing suggestions

Icings: Simple Sugar
Glaze (page 205) or
Milk Chocolate Glaze
(page 201).

- Pastry bag fitted with a large star tip
- Parchment paper, cut into 4-inch (10 cm) squares
- Digital candy/deep-fry thermometer

1 cup	water	250 mL
¼ cup	granulated sugar	60 mL
¼ cup	vegetable shortening	60 mL
½ tsp	salt	2 mL
1 cup	all-purpose flour	250 mL
3	large eggs	3
1 tsp	vanilla extract	5 mL
	Canola oil	

1. In a medium saucepan over medium heat, bring water, sugar, shortening and salt to a rolling boil. Add flour all at once, mixing with a wooden spoon and cook, stirring constantly, until thickened, about 2 minutes. Remove from heat. Let stand to cool, about 5 minutes. Add eggs, one at a time, beating thoroughly after each addition. Mix in vanilla.

2. Place parchment paper squares on a baking sheet. Place batter into a pastry bag fitted with a large star tip. Pipe dough into 3-inch (7.5 cm) "rings" onto the parchment paper squares.

3. Meanwhile, in a large, deep pot or deep fryer, heat about 4 inches (10 cm) oil over medium heat until temperature registers 375°F (190°C). Carefully place a paper square with the piped batter upside down onto the hot oil so the crullers will drop into oil. When donut releases from paper, use tongs to remove paper carefully. Deep-fry 3 donuts at a time, turning once with wooden chopsticks, until golden brown, about 15 seconds per side. Using a slotted spatula, transfer to paper towels to absorb excess oil. Fry remaining donuts, adjusting heat as necessary between batches to maintain oil temperature.

4. Let donuts cool completely prior to icing.

New Orleans Beignets

Makes about 24 donuts

Café du Monde in the French quarter is alongside the French Market and makes these perfect donuts. They serve them 24 hours, 7 days a week with their café au lait, which is coffee with chicory.

- Stand mixer with paddle attachment
- 2½-inch (6 cm) square cutter, optional
- Baking sheet, lined with parchment paper
- Digital candy/deep-fry thermometer

¾ cup	water, warmed to 110°F (43°C)	175 mL
1	package (¼ oz/8 g) quick-rising (instant) yeast	1
1	large egg	1
½ cup	evaporated milk	125 mL
¼ cup	granulated sugar	60 mL
3½ cups	all-purpose flour, divided (approx.)	875 mL
½ tsp	salt	2 mL
2 tbsp	vegetable shortening	30 mL
	Canola oil	
	Confectioner's (icing) sugar	

1. In mixer bowl, sprinkle yeast over water and stir with a fork. Let stand until foamy, about 5 minutes.

2. Attach bowl to mixer fitted with paddle attachment and add egg, evaporated milk, sugar, 2 cups (500 mL) of the flour and salt to yeast mixture. Let stand in bowl for 10 minutes. On low speed, mix just until blended. Mix in shortening, then gradually add just enough of the remaining flour until dough starts to pull away from sides of bowl. Increase speed to medium and beat for 1 minute.

3. Transfer dough to a large oiled bowl and cover with plastic wrap. Place in the refrigerator and let chill overnight.

Tip

This dough can be kept for up to 1 week in the refrigerator and actually improves with age; just punch down when it rises. Dough can also be frozen; simply thaw, cut and roll, or shape donuts before freezing.

4. Turn dough out onto a floured work surface. Roll out dough to slightly thicker than $\frac{1}{4}$ inch (0.5 cm). If dough is tacky, dust with additional flour. Cut dough with cutter into 24 donuts, re-rolling scraps as necessary (or cut with a knife or pizza cutter into $2\frac{1}{2}$-inch/6 cm squares). Place at least 1 inch (2.5 cm) apart on prepared baking sheet. Cover with a clean kitchen towel and let rise for 20 minutes.

5. Meanwhile, in a large, deep pot or deep fryer, heat about 4 inches (10 cm) oil over medium heat until temperature registers 360°F (182°C). Deep-fry 6 to 8 donuts at a time in hot oil, turning once with wooden chopsticks, until golden brown, about 40 seconds per side. Using a slotted spatula, transfer to paper towels to absorb excess oil. Fry remaining donuts, adjusting heat as necessary between batches to maintain oil temperature.

6. Dust with a good helping of confectioner's sugar. Serve warm.

Piña Colada Donuts

Filled with a creamy mousse filling of macadamia nuts and white chocolate, you will think you are in the South Pacific.

Tip

When heating the oil for deep-frying, keep a close eye on it to be sure it doesn't overheat, and never leave the room while the oil is on the heat. Reduce the heat or carefully remove the pot from the burner when the oil reaches the desired temperature. Always keep a metal lid that tightly fits the pot handy to quickly place on the pot should the oil start to smoke or burn.

- Food processor
- Stand mixer with paddle attachment
- Digital candy/deep-fry thermometer
- 3-inch (7.5 cm) round donut cutter
- Baking sheet, lined with parchment paper

2¾ cups	all-purpose flour, divided	675 mL
1 cup	sweetened flaked coconut	250 mL
1¼ tsp	baking powder	6 mL
1 tsp	freshly ground nutmeg	5 mL
1 tsp	salt	5 mL
½ tsp	baking soda	2 mL
¾ cup	granulated sugar	175 mL
2	large eggs, beaten	2
½ cup	canned crushed pineapple	125 mL
¼ cup	whole milk	60 mL
2 tbsp	unsalted butter, melted and cooled	30 mL
¼ tsp	rum extract	1 mL
	Canola oil	
	White Chocolate and Macadamia Mousse Filling (page 216)	

1. In a food processor fitted with metal blade, combine 2 cups (500 mL) of the flour, coconut, baking powder, nutmeg, salt and baking soda and process for 20 seconds or until coconut is no longer visible. Set aside.

2. In mixer bowl fitted with paddle attachment, combine sugar, eggs, pineapple, milk, butter and rum extract. On low speed, mix until well combined. Add dry ingredients and mix until incorporated. Gradually mix in more of the remaining flour, as necessary, until dough starts to come together and is the consistency of biscuit dough. Cover and refrigerate for 10 minutes.

3. Meanwhile, in a large, deep pot or deep fryer, heat about 4 inches (10 cm) oil over medium heat until temperature registers 360°F (182°C) (see Tip, left).

Finishing Suggestions

Icing: Pineapple Topping
(page 196)

4. On a floured work surface, roll out dough to slightly thicker than ¼ inch (0.5 cm). If dough is tacky, dust with additional flour. Cut dough with cutter into 18 donuts, re-rolling scraps as necessary. Place at least 1 inch (2.5 cm) apart on prepared baking sheet.

5. Deep-fry 3 to 4 donuts at a time in hot oil, turning once with wooden chopsticks, until golden brown, about 25 seconds per side. Using a slotted spatula, transfer to paper towels to absorb excess oil. Fry remaining donuts, adjusting heat as necessary between batches to maintain oil temperature.

6. Let donuts cool completely and then split in half and fill with White Chocolate and Macadamia Mousse Filling. If desired, ice with Pineapple Topping.

Rum-Glazed Donuts

If you are looking for an adult-flavored donut, try these.

• Stand mixer with paddle attachment
• Digital candy/deep-fry thermometer
• 3-inch (7.5 cm) round donut cutter
• Baking sheet, lined with parchment paper

1 cup	cake flour, divided	250 mL
1 cup	whole wheat flour	250 mL
½ cup	pecan flour	125 mL
1¼ tsp	baking powder	6 mL
1 tsp	ground cinnamon	5 mL
1 tsp	salt	5 mL
½ tsp	freshly ground nutmeg	2 mL
½ tsp	baking soda	2 mL
¼ tsp	ground allspice	1 mL
1 cup	granulated sugar	250 mL
3	large eggs, beaten	3
¼ cup	whole milk	60 mL
	Canola oil	
	Rum Glaze (page 203)	

1. In a bowl, whisk together ½ cup (125 mL) of the cake flour, whole wheat flour, pecan flour, baking powder, cinnamon, salt, nutmeg, baking soda and allspice. Set aside.

2. In mixer bowl fitted with paddle attachment, combine sugar, eggs, milk and ¼ cup (60 mL) canola oil. On low speed, mix until well combined. Add dry ingredients and mix until incorporated. Gradually mix in more of the remaining flour, as necessary, until dough starts to come together and is the consistency of biscuit dough. Cover and refrigerate for 10 minutes.

3. Meanwhile, in a large, deep pot or deep fryer, heat about 4 inches (10 cm) of oil over medium heat until temperature registers 360°F (182°C) (see Tip, page 190).

Finishing suggestions

Topping: Sprinkle freshly glazed donuts with chopped pecans.

4. On a floured work surface, roll out dough to slightly thicker than $\frac{1}{4}$ inch (0.5 cm) thick. If dough is tacky, dust with additional flour. Cut dough with cutter into 18 donuts, re-rolling scraps as necessary. Place at least 1 inch (2.5 cm) apart on prepared baking sheet.

5. Deep-fry 4 donuts at a time in hot oil, turning once with wooden chopsticks, until puffed and firm, about 15 seconds per side. Using a slotted spatula, transfer to paper towels to absorb excess oil. Fry remaining donuts, adjusting heat as necessary between batches to maintain oil temperature.

6. Dip each warm donut into Rum Glaze, making sure to coat all sides of the donut. If desired, top with pecans.

Elvis Memphis Donuts

A trip to Memphis, Tennessee, is not complete without a tour of Graceland, where Elvis lived. His favorite sandwich was made with fried bananas and peanut butter. Here is a baked donut with the same great flavor combination for you.

Finishing suggestions
Icing: Simple Sugar Glaze (page 205).

- Preheat oven to 325°F (160°C)
- Two 6-well donut pans, sprayed with nonstick spray

2½ cups	all-purpose flour	625 mL
¾ cup	packed brown sugar	175 mL
2 tsp	baking powder	10 mL
1 tsp	salt	5 mL
1 tsp	ground cinnamon	5 mL
1	large egg, beaten	1
¾ cup	whole milk	175 mL
1 tbsp	unsalted butter, melted	15 mL
⅔ cup	mashed ripe banana	150 mL
1 cup	Peanut Butter Filling (page 215)	250 mL

1. In a large bowl, whisk together flour, brown sugar, baking powder, salt and cinnamon. Set aside.

2. In a medium bowl, whisk together egg, milk and butter. Add to flour mixture and mix with a rubber spatula just until incorporated. Fold in bananas.

3. Place batter into a resealable freezer bag or pastry bag (see page 8) and fill each prepared well two-thirds full, using two-thirds of the batter.

4. Bake in preheated oven until donut springs back when lightly touched, 10 to 14 minutes.

5. Let donuts cool in pans on a rack for 5 minutes. Turn out of pans onto rack and let cool completely. Let pan cool completely, then spray again and repeat with remaining batter.

6. Slice each in half and fill each with Peanut Butter Filling. If desired, ice with glaze.

Icings, Glazes and Sugars

• •

A donut without a sugary glaze or a fine dusting of confectioner's sugar is like a cupcake without frosting. It completes the package! Plus you can make one donut base and a few different glazes and sugars to create an array of possibilities.

Pineapple Topping. 196

Truffle Fudge Icing. 196

Belgian Chocolate
    Ganache Glaze. 197

Bittersweet Chocolate
    Glaze. 197

Brown Butter Glaze 198

Cherry Glaze. 198

Dulce de Leche Glaze 199

Green Tea Glaze. 199

Honey Glaze. 200

Lemon Zest Glaze 200

Maple Glaze 201

Milk Chocolate Glaze. 201

Mocha Glaze. 202

Orange Glaze 202

Raspberry Glaze 203

Rum Glaze 203

Sunset Orange Glaze. 204

Autumn Spiced Sugar 204

Simple Sugar Glaze 205

Citrus Sugar 205

Lavender Sugar Dust 206

Rose Petal Dust 206

Pineapple Topping

Makes about 2 cups (500 mL)

This topping is a sweet and thick island treat.

2	cans (each 8 oz/227 mL) crushed pineapple, drained with juice reserved	2
½ cup	granulated sugar	125 mL
¼ cup	cornstarch	60 mL
½ cup	cold water	125 mL

1. Place reserved pineapple juice in a measuring cup. Add additional water to equal ½ cup (125 mL) of liquid.

2. In a saucepan, heat juice and sugar over medium heat until it begins to boil. Add pineapple and bring back to a boil.

3. Meanwhile, in a small bowl, slowly whisk together cornstarch and cold water to make a milky substance. Slowly whisk mixture into boiling pineapple. Cook, whisking, until no longer cloudy and mixture is thickened, about 3 minutes. (If the mixture starts to thicken without adding all of the cornstarch mixture you can stop adding the thickener.) Let cool prior to use or cover and refrigerate for up to 7 days.

Truffle Fudge Icing

Makes about 2 cups (500 mL)

This icing is rich just like its French candy namesake. You can use any leftovers as an ice cream topping.

Tip

If chocolate does not melt after adding hot cream, place bowl over a saucepan of hot, not boiling, water and heat, stirring until melted.

8 oz	bittersweet chocolate, finely chopped	250 g
1 tbsp	light rum	15 mL
1½ tsp	unsalted butter	7 mL
1 tsp	vanilla extract	5 mL
1 cup	heavy or whipping (35%) cream	250 mL

1. In a large heatproof bowl, combine chocolate, rum, butter and vanilla. Set aside.

2. In a saucepan over medium heat, bring cream to a full boil, without stirring. Once it starts to climb up sides of pan, remove from heat and pour over chocolate mixture. Let stand for 2 minutes, undisturbed. Whisk mixture until chocolate is melted and smooth. Use immediately or cover and refrigerate for up to 7 days.

Belgian Chocolate Ganache Glaze

Makes about 2 cups (500 mL)

This rich chocolate glaze is shiny even after it's on the donut.

Tip

If chocolate does not melt after adding hot cream, place bowl over a saucepan of hot, not boiling, water and heat, stirring until melted.

8 oz	semisweet Belgian chocolate, finely chopped	250 g
1½ tsp	unsalted butter	7 mL
1 tsp	vanilla extract	5 mL
1 cup	heavy or whipping (35%) cream	250 mL

1. In a large heatproof bowl, combine chocolate, butter and vanilla. Set aside

2. In a saucepan over medium heat, bring cream to a full rolling boil, without stirring. Once it starts to climb up sides of pan, remove from heat and pour over chocolate. Let stand for 2 minutes, undisturbed. Whisk mixture until chocolate has fully melted and ganache is smooth. Use immediately or cover and refrigerate for up to 7 days.

Bittersweet Chocolate Glaze

Makes about 2½ cups (625 mL)

Topping a donut with bittersweet glaze is pure decadence.

Tip

If chocolate does not melt completely after adding hot cream, place bowl over a saucepan of hot, not boiling water and heat, stirring until fully melted.

12 oz	bittersweet chocolate, finely chopped	375 g
1 cup	heavy or whipping (35%) cream	250 mL
2 tbsp	light (white or golden) corn syrup	30 mL

1. Place chocolate in a heatproof bowl. Set aside.

2. In a saucepan over medium heat, bring cream and corn syrup to a boil, without stirring. Pour on top of chocolate. Let stand for 2 minutes, undisturbed. Whisk mixture until chocolate is completely melted and smooth. Let cool down to the consistency you need to dip your donuts. Use immediately or cover and refrigerate for up to 7 days.

Brown Butter Glaze

Makes about 2 cups (500 mL)

The color of this glaze will make any cake donut look tempting for everyone.

Tip

If your glaze cools completely, it may be too difficult to glaze the donuts. Reheat on low heat, carefully stirring, until the correct consistency is achieved.

½ cup	unsalted butter, softened	125 mL
1 cup	packed light brown sugar	250 mL
½ cup	evaporated milk	125 mL
2½ cups	confectioner's (icing) sugar	625 mL
1 tsp	vanilla extract	5 mL

1. In a saucepan over medium heat, melt butter. Add brown sugar, stirring until well combined. Add milk and bring to a gentle boil, stirring. Whisk in confectioner's sugar and vanilla until smooth. Bring to a boil to thicken. Let cool for about 5 minutes prior to using (see Tip, left).

Cherry Glaze

Makes about 1½ cups (375 mL)

The glaze will give donuts a great color of light pink — simple yet elegant for any cherry donut.

Tip

Don't throw away the syrup that maraschino cherries are packed in; now you can save it to use in this glaze.

Variation

If you don't have maraschino cherries to use the syrup for this recipe, you can use grenadine instead and it will still give a pink color, perfect for cherry donuts, though a slightly different flavor.

2 cups	confectioner's (icing) sugar	500 mL
3 tbsp	maraschino cherry syrup, heated (see Tip, left)	45 mL
1 tsp	light (white or golden) corn syrup	5 mL
1 to 2 tsp	hot water	5 to 10 mL

1. In a bowl, whisk together sugar, cherry syrup and corn syrup until smooth. Stir in hot water if needed, 1 tsp (5 mL) at a time, to make a smooth glaze that is just thick enough to cling to donuts.

2. Dip donuts into glaze as soon as it is mixed or it will harden.

Dulce de Leche Glaze

Makes about 1 cup (250 mL)

With just the one ingredient, this looks like an easy recipe. The hardest part is stirring the mixture for the length of time required. With the long cooking, the milk changes in color to a golden brown, perfect to glaze any donut.

| 1 | can (14 oz or 300 mL) sweetened condensed milk | 1 |

1. In a heatproof bowl set over a saucepan of lightly simmering water, heat sweetened condensed milk, stirring occasionally, until light caramel in color and thickened, 60 to 70 minutes. Check water periodically and add more as necessary to keep the level of water just below the bottom of the bowl. Remove from heat. Use immediately or cover and refrigerate for up to 7 days. Reheat before using.

Green Tea Glaze

Makes about 1½ cups (375 mL)

Here's a green glaze that is perfect for a St. Patty's Day donut.

2 cups	confectioner's (icing) sugar	500 mL
3 tbsp	Matcha green tea powder	45 mL
¼ cup	hot water (approx.)	60 mL

1. In a bowl, whisk together sugar, green tea and hot water until smooth. Stir in 1 to 2 tsp (5 to 10 mL) of additional hot water if needed to make a smooth glaze that is just thick enough to cling on donuts.

2. Dip donuts into glaze as soon as it is mixed or it will harden.

Honey Glaze

**Makes about
1½ cups (375 mL)**

This staple of any donut shop provides a light glaze for any donut to shine.

Tip

If the honey is thick, microwave it for 10 seconds to heat up.

2 cups	confectioner's (icing) sugar	500 mL
2 tbsp	hot water (approx.)	30 mL
1 tbsp	liquid honey	15 mL
1 tsp	light (white or golden) corn syrup	5 mL

1. In a bowl, whisk together sugar, hot water, honey and corn syrup until smooth. Stir in additional hot water if needed, 1 tsp (5 mL) at a time, to make a smooth glaze that is just thick enough to cling to donuts.

2. Dip donuts into glaze as soon as it is mixed or it will harden.

Lemon Zest Glaze

**Makes 1½ cups
(375 mL)**

This tart and flavorful glaze is a great addition to any citrus donut. I like how the little pieces of lemon show through on the finished donuts.

2 cups	confectioner's (icing) sugar	500 mL
1 tbsp	grated lemon zest	15 mL
3 tbsp	freshly squeezed lemon juice, heated	45 mL
1 tsp	light (white or golden) corn syrup	5 mL
	Hot water	

1. In a bowl, whisk together sugar, lemon zest, lemon juice and corn syrup until smooth. Stir in hot water if needed, 1 tsp (5 mL) at a time, to make a smooth glaze that is just thick enough to cling to donuts.

2. Dip donuts into glaze as soon as it is mixed or it will harden.

Maple Glaze

Makes about 1½ cups (375 mL)

This sweet light brown glaze goes well with anything from maple bars to pumpkin donuts.

2 cups	confectioner's (icing) sugar	500 mL
3 tbsp	pure maple syrup, heated	45 mL
2 tbsp	heavy or whipping (35%) cream	30 mL
1 tsp	light (white or golden) corn syrup	5 mL
	Hot water	

1. In a bowl, whisk together sugar, maple syrup, cream and corn syrup until smooth. Stir in hot water if needed, 1 tsp (5 mL) at a time, to make a smooth glaze that is just thick enough to cling to donuts.

2. Dip donuts into glaze as soon as it is mixed or it will harden.

Milk Chocolate Glaze

Makes about 2 cups (500 mL)

Topping a donut in a milky glaze like this one and then with a sprinkle of chopped nuts is pure decadence.

Tip

If chocolate does not melt completely after adding hot cream, place bowl over a saucepan of hot, not boiling, water and heat, stirring until fully melted.

10 oz	milk chocolate, finely chopped	300 g
1 cup	heavy or whipping (35%) cream	250 mL
1 tbsp	light (white or golden) corn syrup	15 mL
1 tbsp	liquid honey	15 mL

1. Place chocolate in a heatproof bowl. Set aside.

2. In a saucepan over medium heat, combine cream, corn syrup and honey and bring to a boil, without stirring. Pour on top of chocolate. Let stand for 2 minutes, undisturbed. Whisk mixture until chocolate is completely melted and smooth. Let cool until easy to handle and slightly thickened for dipping donuts.

Mocha Glaze

**Makes about 2 cups
(500 mL)**

This rich chocolate
coffee glaze is perfect
for a dark chocolate
cake donut.

Tip

Use a high-quality milk
chocolate that contains at
least 10% chocolate liquor
and 12% milk solids.

¾ cup	heavy or whipping (35%) cream	175 mL
3 tbsp	instant espresso powder	45 mL
1 tbsp	light (white or golden) corn syrup	15 mL
10 oz	milk chocolate, chopped (see Tip, left)	300 g

1. In a saucepan, heat cream over medium heat until it starts to boil.

2. Remove from heat. Add espresso powder, corn syrup and chocolate and whisk until well blended.

Orange Glaze

**Makes about
1½ cups (375 mL)**

A light orange color
with the zest of orange
highlight this glaze.

2 cups	confectioner's (icing) sugar	500 mL
2 tbsp	frozen orange juice concentrate, heated	30 mL
1 tsp	light (white or golden) corn syrup	5 mL
1 tsp	grated orange zest	5 mL
	Hot water	

1. In a bowl, whisk together sugar, orange juice concentrate, corn syrup and zest until smooth. Stir in hot water if needed, 1 tsp (5 mL) at a time, to make a smooth glaze that is just thick enough to cling to donuts.

2. Dip donuts into glaze as soon as it is mixed or it will harden.

Raspberry Glaze

**Makes about
1½ cups (375 mL)**

A nice thin coating of
raspberry glaze on a
raised donut adds a
beautiful light pink hue
to your donut.

Variation

Strawberry Glaze: Replace
the fresh raspberries with
fresh strawberries. Follow
the recipe but in Step 1
before adding the hot
water, stir in 1 to 2 drops
of red food coloring to
desired shade of red.

2 cups	confectioner's (icing) sugar	500 mL
⅓ cup	fresh raspberries, mashed with a fork	75 mL
1 tsp	light (white or golden) corn syrup	5 mL
	Hot water	

1. In a bowl, whisk together sugar, raspberries and corn syrup until smooth. Stir in hot water if needed, 1 tsp (15 mL) at a time, to make a smooth glaze that is just thick enough to cling to donuts.

2. Dip donuts into glaze as soon as it is mixed or it will harden.

Rum Glaze

**Makes about
1½ cups (375 mL)**

Here's a little kick of
rum to top your donuts.

2 cups	confectioner's (icing) sugar	500 mL
3 tbsp	light rum	45 mL
1 tsp	light (white or golden) corn syrup	5 mL
	Hot water	

1. In a bowl, whisk together sugar, rum and corn syrup until smooth. Stir in hot water if needed, 1 tsp (5 mL) at a time, to make a smooth glaze that is just thick enough to cling to donuts.

2. Dip donuts into glaze as soon as it is mixed or it will harden.

Sunset Orange Glaze

Makes about 1½ cups (375 mL)		
2 cups	confectioner's (icing) sugar	500 mL
1 tsp	grated blood orange zest (see Tip, left)	5 mL
3 tbsp	freshly squeezed blood orange juice, heated	45 mL
1 tsp	light (white or golden) corn syrup	5 mL
	Hot water	

A light orange color with the zest of oranges highlight this glaze.

Tip

If blood oranges aren't available use regular oranges instead.

1. In a bowl, whisk together sugar, blood orange zest and juice and corn syrup until smooth. Stir in hot water if needed, 1 tsp (5 mL) at a time, to make a smooth glaze that is just thick enough to cling to donuts.

2. Dip donuts into glaze as soon as it is mixed or it will harden.

Autumn Spiced Sugar

Makes about 2 cups (500 mL)

Toss any fall-flavored donut into this spicy sugar for a kick. You can even sprinkle a little into your coffee or tea for an added dimension.

Tip

To store unused sugar, place in a resealable bag and store like you would any sugar.

● Food processor

2 cups	granulated sugar	500 mL
1 tbsp	ground cinnamon	15 mL
1 tsp	freshly ground nutmeg	5 mL
½ tsp	ground cloves	2 mL
¼ tsp	sea salt	1 mL

1. In a food processor fitted with metal blade, combine sugar, cinnamon, nutmeg, cloves and salt and process until fine, about 90 seconds.

2. Toss warm donuts into sugar to coat completely.

Simple Sugar Glaze

**Makes about
1½ cups (375 mL)**

This simple sugar glaze
is perfect for all donuts.

2 cups	confectioner's (icing) sugar	500 mL
1 to	hot water	15 to
3 tbsp		45 mL
1 tsp	light (white or golden) corn syrup	5 mL

1. In a bowl, whisk together sugar, 1 tbsp (15 mL) hot water and corn syrup until smooth. Stir in more hot water if needed, 1 tsp (5 mL) at a time, to make a smooth glaze that is just thick enough to cling to donuts.

2. Dip donuts into glaze as soon as it is mixed or it will harden.

Citrus Sugar

**Makes about 2 cups
(500 mL)**

This light flavorful
sugar with three zests
is a great coating to add
just a little flavor to
your donuts.

Tip
To store unused sugar,
place in a resealable bag
and store like you would
any sugar.

● Food processor

2 cups	granulated sugar	500 mL
2 tbsp	confectioner's (icing) sugar	30 mL
2 tbsp	grated lemon zest	30 mL
1 tbsp	grated orange zest	15 mL
1 tsp	grated lime zest	5 mL
½ tsp	cornstarch	2 mL

1. In a food processor fitted with metal blade, combine granulated and confectioner's sugars, lemon zest, orange zest, lime zest and cornstarch and process for 45 seconds.

2. Toss warm donuts into sugar to coat completely.

Lavender Sugar Dust

**Makes 2 cups
(500 mL)**

This light purple floral dusting of sugar brings out the simple flavors of the donut.

Tip

Make sure the lavender is the edible variety and has not been treated with pesticides and not used for soap making or aromas. Check out Sources, page 217.

• Food processor

2 cups	granulated sugar	500 mL
2 tbsp	dried edible lavender buds (see Tip, left)	30 mL
½ tsp	sea salt	2 mL

1. In a food processor fitted with metal blade, combine sugar, lavender and salt and process for 90 seconds.

2. Toss warm donuts into sugar to coat completely. To store unused sugar, place in a resealable bag and store like you would any sugar.

Rose Petal Dust

**Makes 2 cups
(500 mL)**

Dust half your donuts with Lavender Sugar Dust (above) and the other half with this rose one to create a floral buffet!

Tip

Use organic rose petals that are pesticide-free, not those from florist shops. You can also use rose petals from your garden as long as they have not been sprayed with insecticides. Any color is good but red is best.

• Food processor

2 cups	granulated sugar	500 mL
2 tbsp	edible red rose petals (see Tip, left)	30 mL
1 tbsp	confectioner's (icing) sugar	15 mL
½ tsp	sea salt	2 mL

1. In a food processor fitted with metal blade, combine granulated sugar, rose petals, confectioner's sugar and salt and process for 90 seconds.

2. Toss warm donuts into sugar to coat completely. To store unused sugar, place in a resealable bag and store like you would any sugar.

Fresh Fillings

● ●

Most donut shops purchase ready-made fillings but made-from-scratch fillings are so much better. Fillings enhance your donuts and take them to a new level. Here is a chapter to create your own fillings.

Banana Cream Filling. 208
Italian Crème Filling. 208
Bavarian Cream Custard 209
Cream Cheese Filling. 209
Marshmallow Filling. 210
Fresh Cherry Filling 211
Sunset Orange Filling 211
Crisp Apple Filling. 212
Blueberry Filling. 212
Lemon Zest Filling 213
Meyer Lemon Curd 213
Strawberry Filling 214
Chocolate Fudge Filling 215
Peanut Butter Filling 215
White Chocolate Macadamia Mousse Filling. 216

Banana Cream Filling

Makes about 2 cups (500 mL)

Tasty island bananas make this filling perfect for any tropical donut.

Tip

If you don't have a stand mixer, you can use a hand-held electric mixer for this recipe.

1 cup	heavy or whipping (35%) cream	250 mL
2 tbsp	light rum	30 mL
1	package (8 oz/250 g) cream cheese, softened	1
¼ cup	confectioner's (icing) sugar	60 mL
1½ cups	mashed ripe bananas	375 mL

1. In a chilled stand mixer bowl fitted with whip attachment, whip cream until soft peaks form. Fold in rum. Transfer to a separate bowl, if necessary.

2. In mixer bowl fitted with paddle attachment, blend together cream cheese and confectioner's sugar until smooth. Fold in bananas and whipped cream. Use immediately or cover and refrigerate for up to 2 hours prior to use.

Italian Crème Filling

Makes about 2⅓ cups (575 mL)

This creamy filling is perfect for donuts or cannoli.

Tip

You can make this filling ahead. Place plastic wrap directly on the surface of custard and refrigerate for up to 1 day.

½ cup	granulated sugar	125 mL
½ cup	all-purpose flour	125 mL
2 cups	whole milk	500 mL
3	large eggs	3
1 tbsp	unsalted butter	15 mL
1 tsp	almond extract	5 mL
1 tsp	vanilla extract	5 mL

1. In a saucepan, whisk together sugar and flour until blended. Gradually pour in milk, while whisking, then whisk in eggs. Cook over medium heat, stirring constantly, until thick, about 4 minutes. Remove from heat. Whisk in butter and almond and vanilla extracts until smooth.

2. Let cool completely prior to filling donuts.

Bavarian Cream Custard

Makes about 4 cups (1 L)

This custard is light yet rich, making it perfect to fill any donut.

Tip

To store custard, place in an airtight container and refrigerate for up to 3 days.

1¾ cup + 2 tbsp	whole milk, divided	455 mL
1 cup	granulated sugar	250 mL
2 tbsp	cornstarch	30 mL
5	large eggs	5
1 tsp	vanilla extract	5 mL
½ cup	heavy or whipping (35%) cream	125 mL

1. In a heavy saucepan over medium heat, bring 1½ cups (375 mL) of the milk to a boil.

2. In a large bowl, whisk together sugar and cornstarch. Set aside.

3. In another bowl, whisk together remaining milk, eggs and vanilla. Gradually pour into sugar mixture, whisking until fully blended. Gradually pour egg mixture into boiling milk, whisking until blended. Cook over medium heat, whisking constantly, until mixture is thickened to pudding consistency. Transfer to a bowl, cover surface directly with plastic wrap and let refrigerate until chilled before adding cream.

4. In a chilled bowl, whip cream to soft peaks. Gently fold whipped cream into mixture creating a creamy, mousse-like custard.

Cream Cheese Filling

Makes about 2 cups (500 mL)

You will think you are biting into a cheesecake when you taste this filling in your donuts.

2	packages (each 8 oz/250 g) cream cheese, softened	2
¼ cup	confectioner's (icing) sugar	60 mL
1 tsp	vanilla extract	5 mL
½ tsp	almond extract	2 mL

1. In a bowl, using a wooden spoon, blend together cream cheese, sugar and vanilla and almond extracts until creamy. Use immediately.

Marshmallow Filling

Makes about 5 cups (1.25 L)

The freshness of this marshmallow cream is so much different than using the kind you buy in a jar.

- Digital candy/deep-fry thermometer
- Stand mixer with whip attachment

6 tbsp	water	90 mL
1¼ cups	light corn syrup	300 mL
¾ cup +1 tbsp	granulated sugar, divided	190 mL
4	large egg whites	4
Pinch	sea salt	Pinch
Pinch	cream of tartar	Pinch
2 tbsp	vanilla extract	30 mL

1. Clip thermometer to the side of a small saucepan. Add water, corn syrup and ¾ cup (175 mL) of the sugar to the saucepan and bring to a boil over medium heat, stirring just until sugar is dissolved. Boil, without stirring, until thermometer registers 246°F (119°C).

2. Meanwhile, in stand mixer with whip attachment, combine egg whites, salt and cream of tartar. Whip on medium speed until creamy and foamy, about 2 minutes. While beating, sprinkle in remaining 1 tbsp (15 mL) of sugar and beat until egg whites form very soft peaks, about 2 minutes.

3. Reduce mixer speed to low and carefully drizzle the hot syrup into the egg white mixture until incorporated. Increase mixer speed to high and whip until thick, fluffy and just warm, about 7 minutes. Reduce speed to low and whisk in vanilla.

4. Cover with a wet paper towel and let cool completely prior to filling donuts.

Fresh Cherry Filling

Makes about 2 cups (500 mL)		

When cherries are in season, make this fresh filling instead of buying the prepared version.

3 cups	sweet cherries, pitted	750 mL
1/2 cup	granulated sugar	125 mL
3 tbsp	cornstarch	45 mL
1/2 cup	cold water	125 mL
2 tsp	freshly squeezed lemon juice	10 mL

1. In a heavy saucepan, heat cherries and sugar over medium heat, stirring constantly, until juices are released and begin to boil and cherries break down into smaller pieces, about 4 minutes.

2. Meanwhile, in a small bowl, whisk together cornstarch and cold water to make a milky substance. Pour into boiling cherries, whisking to incorporate. Cook, whisking, until no longer cloudy, the color is ruby red and mixture is thickened, about 3 minutes. Remove from heat. Whisk in lemon juice.

3. Transfer to a bowl and let cool. Cover and refrigerate until chilled prior to using.

Sunset Orange Filling

Makes about 2 cups (500 mL)		

Blending oranges and lemons together for this filling will make you pucker up!

Variation

Blood Orange Filling: When blood oranges appear in winter, substitute 2 cups (500 mL) freshly squeezed blood orange juice for the 1 cup (250 mL) each orange and lemon juices and continue with Step 1. Omit nutmeg.

1 cup	orange juice	250 mL
1 cup	freshly squeezed lemon juice	250 mL
1/2 cup	granulated sugar	125 mL
3 tbsp	cornstarch	45 mL
1/2 cup	cold water	125 mL
1/2 tsp	freshly ground nutmeg	2 mL

1. In a heavy saucepan, heat orange juice, lemon juice and sugar over medium heat, stirring constantly, until boiling.

2. Meanwhile, in a small bowl, whisk together cornstarch and cold water to make a milky substance. Pour into boiling juice, whisking to incorporate. Cook, whisking, until no longer cloudy, the color is vibrant orange and mixture is thickened, about 2 minutes. Remove from heat. Stir in nutmeg.

3. Transfer to a bowl and let cool completely prior to filling donuts.

Crisp Apple Filling

Makes about 2 cups (500 mL)

Using fresh apples for your donuts will elevate your homemade pastry.

4	baking apples, such as McIntosh, Rome or Granny Smith, peeled and diced (about 6 cups/1.5 L)	4
½ cup	granulated sugar	125 mL
1 tsp	ground cinnamon	5 mL
½ tsp	freshly ground nutmeg	2 mL
¼ tsp	ground allspice	1 mL
3 tbsp	cornstarch	45 mL
½ cup	cold water	125 mL
2 tsp	freshly squeezed lemon juice	10 mL

1. In a heavy saucepan, combine apples, sugar, cinnamon, nutmeg and allspice. Cook over medium heat, stirring constantly, until juices are released and begin to boil, about 4 minutes.

2. Meanwhile, in a small bowl, whisk together cornstarch and cold water to make a milky substance. Pour into boiling apples, whisking to incorporate. Cook, stirring, until no longer cloudy and mixture is thickened, about 3 minutes. Remove from heat. Whisk in lemon juice.

3. Transfer to a bowl and let cool. Cover and refrigerate until chilled prior to using.

Blueberry Filling

Makes about 2 cups (500 mL)

This tart filling will balance out a sweet donut. Try this one in the winter for a quick taste of summer.

¼ cup	granulated sugar	60 mL
1½ tbsp	cornstarch	22 mL
1 cup	water	250 mL
1½ cups	frozen blueberries	375 mL

1. In a saucepan, whisk together sugar and cornstarch. While whisking, pour in water in a steady stream. Cook over medium heat, whisking until mixture is thickened, about 3 minutes.

2. Remove from heat. Stir in blueberries.

3. Transfer to a bowl and let cool. Cover and refrigerate until chilled prior to using.

Lemon Zest Filling

Makes about 2 cups (500 mL)

This tart puckering lemon filling will tickle your taste buds.

Variation

Lemon Cream Custard: Combine equal parts whipped cream and Lemon Zest Filling and fold together.

10	large egg yolks	10
¾ cup	granulated sugar	175 mL
1 tbsp	grated lemon zest	15 mL
¾ cup	freshly squeezed lemon juice	175 mL
½ cup	unsalted butter, softened	125 mL

1. In a large heatproof glass bowl, whisk egg yolks until blended. While whisking, gradually sprinkle sugar over egg yolks until incorporated. Whisk in lemon juice. Place on top of a saucepan of simmering water, making sure bowl does not touch the water. Cook, whisking constantly, until mixture is thickened to pudding consistency, 3 to 5 minutes.

2. Remove bowl from saucepan and whisk in butter and zest. Place plastic wrap directly on the surface. Let cool completely at room temperature.

3. Refrigerate until cold, about 1 hour, before using to fill donuts.

Meyer Lemon Curd

Makes about 1 cup (250 mL)

Meyer lemons are a cross between an orange and a lemon and are a little more fruity and less tangy than a lemon.

Variation

Meyer Lemon Cream Custard: Combine equal parts whipped cream and Meyer Lemon Curd and fold together.

5	large egg yolks	5
6 tbsp	granulated sugar	90 mL
1 tsp	Meyer lemon zest	5 mL
6 tbsp	freshly squeezed Meyer lemon juice	90 mL
¼ cup	unsalted butter, softened	60 mL

1. In a large heatproof glass bowl, whisk egg yolks until blended. While whisking, gradually sprinkle sugar over egg yolks until incorporated. Whisk in lemon juice. Place on top of a saucepan of simmering water, making sure bowl does not touch the water. Cook, whisking constantly, until mixture is thickened to pudding consistency, 3 to 5 minutes.

2. Remove bowl from saucepan and whisk in butter and zest. Place plastic wrap directly on the surface. Let cool completely at room temperature.

3. Refrigerate until cold, about 1 hour, before using to fill donuts.

Strawberry Filling

Makes about 2 cups (500 mL)

Fresh strawberry filling makes all donuts seem like a strawberry shortcake in summer.

Variation

Raspberry Filling: Instead of strawberries, use fresh or frozen raspberries. Continue with Step 1 and decrease the sugar to ½ cup (125 mL). Delete 3 drops red food coloring in Step 3.

3 cups	fresh or frozen strawberries (thawed if frozen), mashed with a fork	750 mL
¾ cup	granulated sugar	175 mL
3 tbsp	cornstarch	45 mL
½ cup	cold water	125 mL
3	drops red food coloring	3
2 tsp	freshly squeezed lemon juice	10 mL

1. In a heavy saucepan, heat strawberries and sugar over medium heat, stirring constantly, until juices are released and begin to boil.

2. Remove from heat and, using a fine-mesh strainer set over a bowl, press pulp through to strain seeds from mixture. Return juice to saucepan and bring to a boil over medium heat.

3. Meanwhile, in a small bowl, whisk together cornstarch and cold water to make a milky substance. Pour into boiling juice, whisking to incorporate. Cook, whisking, until no longer cloudy. Add food coloring and cook, whisking, until mixture is thickened, about 3 minutes. Remove from heat. Whisk in lemon juice.

4. Transfer to a bowl and let cool. Cover and refrigerate until chilled prior to using.

Chocolate Fudge Filling

Makes about 2 cups (500 mL)

This rich chocolate filling will please all chocoholics.

Tip

If chocolate does not melt after adding hot cream, place bowl over a saucepan of hot, not boiling, water and heat, stirring until melted.

12 oz	semisweet chocolate, finely chopped	375 g
1½ tsp	unsalted butter	7 mL
1 tsp	vanilla extract	5 mL
1 cup	heavy or whipping (35%) cream	250 mL

1. Place chocolate, butter and vanilla in a large heatproof bowl. Set aside.

2. In a saucepan over medium heat, bring cream to a full boil without stirring. Once cream starts to climb up sides of pan, remove from heat and pour over chocolate. Let stand, undisturbed, for 2 minutes. Whisk mixture until chocolate has fully melted and ganache is smooth.

3. Let cool completely prior to filling donuts.

Peanut Butter Filling

Makes about 2 cups (500 mL)

You can pair this peanut butter filling with any chocolate donut to make a blissful marriage.

1	package (8 oz/250 g) cream cheese, softened	1
1 cup	creamy peanut butter	250 mL
¼ cup	confectioner's (icing) sugar	60 mL
2 tsp	vanilla extract	10 mL

1. In a bowl, using a wooden spoon, blend together cream cheese, peanut butter, sugar and vanilla until creamy.

2. Use immediately or cover and refrigerate for up to 7 days.

White Chocolate Macadamia Mousse Filling

Makes about 3 cups (750 mL)

When I was on the island of Fiji, I ran across a donut shop that filled cream donuts with this flavorful filling.

Tip

To store custard, place in an airtight container and refrigerate for up to 3 days.

1¾ cup + 2 tbsp	whole milk, divided	455 mL
1 tsp	vanilla extract	5 mL
1 cup	granulated sugar	250 mL
2 tbsp	cornstarch	30 mL
5	large eggs	5
4 oz	white chocolate, chopped	125 g
1 cup	macadamia nuts, chopped	250 mL

1. In a heavy saucepan over medium heat, bring 1½ cups (375 mL) of the milk and vanilla to a boil.

2. In a large bowl, whisk together sugar and cornstarch. Set aside.

3. In another bowl, whisk together remaining milk and eggs. Gradually pour into sugar mixture, whisking until fully blended. Gradually pour egg mixture into boiling milk, whisking until blended. Cook over medium heat, whisking constantly, until mixture is thickened and coats the back of a metal spoon or thickened to pudding consistency, 3 to 5 minutes. Remove from heat. Stir in white chocolate until melted completely. Stir in macadamia nuts.

4. Transfer to a bowl, cover surface directly with plastic wrap and refrigerate, until chilled, prior to filling donuts.

Sources

Equipment and Services

Bakery.com
www.bakery.com
For the industry but also sells to home bakers. Tools include donut cutters and ingredients such as sprinkles, nuts and flour mixes.

George Geary, CCP
www.georgegeary.com
Author's website, full of recipes, tips, culinary tour information and teaching locations. Magic Line baking pans are sold here.

King Arthur Flour
800-827-6836 (Ships to Canada)
www.kingarthurflour.com
Donut pans, cutters, sugars and more.

Parrish's Cake Decorating Supplies
310-324-2253 (Ships to Canada)
800-736-8443 (U.S. only)
Magic Line baking pans, cheesecake pans, small hand tools.

Wilton Cake Supplies
www.wilton.com
Available at major craft stores. Pans, donut pans, tips and spatulas.

Ingredients
Vanilla Beans
Nielsen-Massey
847-578-1550 (Ships to Canada)
800-525-7873
www.nielsenmassey.com
Fine producer of high-quality vanilla beans, pastes, extracts and more.

Extracts and Spices
Charles H. Baldwin & Sons
413-232-7785
www.baldwinextracts.com
Pure extracts from anise to peppermint.

Penzeys Spices
262-785-7676
800-741-7787 (U.S. only)
www.penzeys.com
Family-owned and -operated premium spice company. Catalog is full of great facts. Retail stores in 29 states.

The Spice House
1512 North Wells St.
Chicago, IL 60610
312-274-0378 (Ships to Canada)
www.thespicehouse.com
One of the best spice companies. Patty Erd's folks started Penzeys Spices. She carries many different hard-to-find items such as matcha tea powder, maple sugar and flavored flower sugar.

Index

(v) = variation

A

All Spiced-Up Bites, 158
Almonds
    Almond Apricot Donuts, 92
    Cranberry Almond Donut
        Bites, 162
    Cranberry Orange Donuts, 140
Anjou Pear Fritters, 24
Apples
    Apple Cream Donuts, 93
    Applesauce Donuts, 62
    Apple Spice Donuts, 20
    Caramel Apple–Filled Bars, 68
    Caramel Apple Fritters, 176
    Crisp Apple Filling, 212
Apricots
    Almond Apricot Donuts, 92
Autumn Spiced Sugar, 204
    All Spiced-Up Bites, 158
    Anjou Pear Fritters, 24
    Applesauce Donuts, 62
    Buttermilk Donuts, 65
    Cake Sticks, 66
    Caramel Apple Fritters, 176
    Churro Bites, 186
    Cinnamon Honey Donuts (v),
        38
    Holiday Eggnog Donuts, 134
    Mini Pumpkin Donuts, 164
    Orange Honey Donuts, 108
    Pumpkin Bars, 84
    Pumpkin Nutmeg Spice
        Donuts, 83
    Rum Raisin Donuts, 88
    Simple Spice Donuts, 111
    Spicy Donuts Balls, 157
Aztec Donut Bites, 142

B

Bacon
    Maple Bacon Bars, 184
Baked donuts, making, 21
    All Spiced-Up Bites, 158
    Almond Apricot Donuts, 92
    Apple Cream Donuts, 93
    Apple Spice Donuts, 20

Baked Maple Mini Donuts,
    159
Baked Whole Wheat Pecan
    Donuts, 118
Banana Bran Donuts, 94
Banana Pecan Donuts, 95
Blueberry Bites, 160
Blueberry Donuts, 96
Cherry Blossom Donuts, 97
Chocolate Donuts, 98
Chocolate Rum Cream
    Donuts, 99
Citrus Donut Bites, 161
Coconut Marshmallow
    Donuts, 100
Cranberry Almond Donuts,
    162
Cranberry Orange Donuts,
    140
Double Chocolate Raspberry
    Donuts, 101
Elvis Memphis Donuts, 194
Framboise-Glazed Donuts,
    102
Green Tea Bites, 163
Green Tea Donuts, 103
Honey Bran–Glazed Donuts,
    104
Lemon Crème Donuts, 105
Maple Cinnamon Donuts, 106
Mini Pumpkin Donuts, 164
Oat Berry Mini Donuts, 165
Orange Donuts, 107
Orange Honey Donuts, 108
Pineapple Macadamia Nut
    Donuts, 109
Red Devil Donuts, 110
Roasted Peanut Donuts, 115
Simple Spice Donuts, 111
Sour Cream Blackberry
    Donuts, 112
Strawberry Cream Bites, 166
Strawberry Donuts, 113
Tangerine Donuts, 114
Vanilla Bean Donuts, 116
White Chocolate Crème
    Donuts, 117
White Chocolate Key Lime
    Donuts (v), 117

Banana Cream Filling, 208
    Apple Cream Donuts, 93
    Apple Spice Donuts, 20
    Banana Crème Donuts, 168
Bananas
    Banana Bran Donuts, 94
    Banana Cream Filling, 208
    Banana Crème Donuts, 168
    Banana Pecan Donuts, 95
    Elvis Memphis Donuts, 194
Bavarian Cream Custard, 209
    Apple Cream Donuts, 93
    Apple Spice Donuts, 20
    Bavarian Crème Bites, 144
    Boston Cream Donuts, 170
    Red Velvet Chip Donut Bars,
        86
Belgian Chocolate Ganache
    Glaze, 197
    Blackout Donuts, 64
    Chocolate Cake Donuts, 70
    Chocolate Donut Holes, 154
    Chocolate Donuts, 98
    Chocolate Rum Cream
        Donuts, 99
    Dark Devil's Food Donuts, 90
    Delicate Dainty Donut Bites,
        148
    French Bites, 150
    Fresh Vanilla Bean Donuts, 42
    Peppermint Chocolate
        Squares, 136
    Red Devil Donuts, 110
    Red Valentine Heart Donuts,
        135
    Triple Chocolate Bites, 152
Berries
    Oat Berry Mini Donuts, 165
Bittersweet Chocolate Glaze, 197
    Aztec Donut Bites, 142
    Blackout Donuts, 64
    Boston Cream Donuts, 170
    Chocolate Cake Donuts, 70
    Chocolate Donut Holes, 154
    Chocolate Donuts, 98
    Chocolate Rum Cream
        Donuts, 99
    Coffee Bites, 155
    Dark Devil's Food Donuts, 90

Espresso Buttermilk Bars, 82
Mocha Raised Donuts, 50
Peanut Chocolate Cake
  Donuts, 80
Perfect Chocolate–Glazed
  Donuts (v), 52
Red Devil Donuts, 110
Red Valentine Heart Donuts,
  135
Red Velvet Chip Donut Bars,
  86
Roasted Peanut Donuts, 115
Vanilla Bean Donuts, 116
Blackberries
  Blackberry Bites, 146
  Sour Cream Blackberry
    Donuts, 112
Black Forest Donut Bars, 34
Blackout Donuts, 64
Blood Orange Filling (v), 211
  Orange Honey Donuts, 108
Blueberries
  Blueberry Bites, 160
  Blueberry Donuts, 96
  Blueberry Filling, 212
  Blueberry Raised Donuts, 36
Boston Cream Donuts, 170
Boules de Berlin Donuts, 172
Bow ties, making, 29
  Honey-Glazed Bow Ties, 28
Brown Butter Glaze, 198
  Baked Maple Mini Donuts,
    159
  Caramel Apple–Filled Bars, 68
Butter, 9
Buttermilk
  Buttermilk Donuts, 65
  Cake Sticks, 66
  Chocolate Donut Holes, 154
  Coffee Bites, 155
  Espresso Buttermilk Bars, 82
  Oat Berry Mini Donuts, 165
  Peanut Chocolate Cake
    Donuts, 80
  Pineapple Macadamia Nut
    Donuts, 109
  Pistachio Bites, 156
  Spicy Donuts Balls, 157

C

Cake-based donuts, making, 19
  Applesauce Donuts, 62
  Blackout Donuts, 64
  Buttermilk Donuts, 65

Cake Sticks, 66
Candied Ginger Donut Stars,
  67
Caramel Apple–Filled Bars, 68
Chocolate Cake Donuts, 70
Chocolate Donut Holes, 154
Coconut Donuts, 72
Coffee Bites, 155
Dark Devil's Food Donuts, 90
Espresso Buttermilk Bars, 82
Fresh Peach Pecan Donuts, 75
Fresh Strawberry and Cream
  Donuts, 76
Holiday Eggnog Donuts, 134
Lemon Crème Bars, 78
Lemon Mist Donuts, 18
Peanut Chocolate Cake
  Donuts, 80
Peppermint Chocolate
  Squares, 136
Piña Colada Donuts, 190
Pistachio Bites, 156
Pumpkin Bars, 84
Pumpkin Nutmeg Spice
  Donuts, 83
Red Valentine Heart Donuts,
  135
Red Velvet Chip Donut Bars,
  86
Rum-Glazed Donuts, 192
Rum Raisin Donuts, 88
Spicy Donut Balls, 57
Strawberry Rose Donuts, 138
Whole Wheat Pecan Donuts,
  74
Candied Fruit Donuts, 124
Candied Ginger Donut Stars, 67
Caramel Apple–Filled Bars, 68
Caramel Apple Fritters, 176
Champagne
  New Year's Champagne
    Donuts, 130
Cherries
  Cherry Blossom Donuts, 97
  Cherry Glaze, 198
  Fresh Cherry Donuts, 40
  Fresh Cherry Filling, 211
Chocolate, 12. See also Cocoa
    powder
  Belgian Chocolate Ganache
    Glaze, 197
  Bittersweet Glaze, 197
  Chocolate Cake Donuts, 70
  Chocolate Donut Holes, 154

Chocolate Donuts, 98
Chocolate Fudge Filling, 215
Chocolate Rum Cream
  Donuts, 99
Christmas Swirl Donuts, 120
Double Chocolate Raspberry
  Donuts, 101
Milk Chocolate Glaze, 201
Minty Chocolate Donut Bars,
  126
Mocha Glaze, 202
Red Velvet Chip Donut Bars,
  86
Triple Chocolate Bites, 152
Truffle Fudge Icing, 196
White Chocolate Crème
  Donuts, 117
White Chocolate Macadamia
  Mousse Filling, 216
Christmas Swirl Donuts, 120
Churro Bites, 186
Cinnamon Donut Sticks, 178
Cinnamon Honey Donuts, 38
Citrus Donut Bites, 161
Citrus Sugar, 205
  Buttermilk Donuts, 65
  Cake Sticks, 66
  Citrus Donut Bites, 161
  Lemon Crème Bars, 78
  Lemon Mist Donuts, 18
  Tangerine Donuts, 114
  White Chocolate Key Lime
    Donuts (v), 117
Cocoa powder. See also
    Chocolate
  Aztec Donut Bites, 142
  Black Forest Donut Bars, 34
  Blackout Donuts, 64
  Campfire S'More Donuts, 174
  Chocolate Cake Donuts, 70
  Chocolate Donut Holes, 154
  Chocolate Donuts, 98
  Chocolate Rum Cream
    Donuts, 99
  Dark Devil's Food Donuts, 90
  Double Chocolate Raspberry
    Donuts, 101
  Peanut Chocolate Cake
    Donuts, 80
  Peppermint Chocolate
    Squares, 136
  Perfect Chocolate–Glazed
    Donuts, 52
  Red Devil Donuts, 110
  Triple Chocolate Bites, 152

Coconut
  Coconut Donuts, 72
  Coconut Marshmallow
    Donuts, 100
  Piña Colada Donuts, 190
Coffee Bites, 155
Cranberries
  Cranberry Almond Donut
    Bites, 162
  Cranberry Orange Donuts, 140
Cream, 9
Cream cheese, 9
  Banana Cream Filling, 208
  Cream Cheese Filling, 209
  Peanut Butter Filling, 215
  Pumpkin Bars, 84
  Cream Cheese Filling, 209
Crisp Apple Filling, 212
  Caramel Apple–Filled Bars, 68
Crullers
  French Crullers, 187

D

Dark Devil's Food Donuts, 90
Deep-frying tips, 32
Delicate Dainty Donut Bites, 148
Donut cutters, 8
Donut pans, 6
Double Chocolate Raspberry
  Donuts, 101
Dulce de Leche Glaze, 199
  Aztec Donut Bites, 142
  Caramel Apple–Filled Bars, 68
  Perfect Chocolate–Glazed
    Donuts (v), 52

E

Eggs, 9
Elvis Memphis Donuts, 194
Espresso
  Coffee Bites, 155
  Espresso Buttermilk Bars, 82
  Mocha Glaze, 202
  Mocha Raised Donuts, 50
  Red Velvet Chip Donut Bars,
    86
Evaporated milk, 9
Extracts, 11

F

Father's Day Tie Donuts, 122
Filled donuts, making, 23
  Apple Cream Donuts, 93
  Apple Spice Donuts, 20

Bavarian Crème Bites, 144
Banana Crème Donuts, 168
Black Forest Donut Bars, 34
Blueberry Raised Donuts, 36
Boston Cream Donuts, 170
Boules de Berlin Donuts, 172
Campfire S'More Donuts, 174
Caramel Apple–Filled Bars, 68
Chocolate Cake Donuts, 70
Coconut Marshmallow
  Donuts, 100
Fresh Jelly Donuts, 22
Fresh Strawberry and Cream
  Donuts, 76
Hanukkah Sufganiyot Donuts,
  180
Island Bites, 26
Italian Crème–Filled Donuts,
  182
Lemon Crème Bars, 78
Lemon Mist Donuts, 18
Orange Honey Donuts, 108
Piña Colada Donuts, 190
Potato Flour Donuts, 56
Pumpkin Bars, 84
Red Valentine Heart Donuts,
  135
Red Velvet Chip Donut Bars,
  86
Strawberry Donuts, 113
Tangerine Donuts, 114
Fillings
  Banana Cream Filling, 208
  Bavarian Cream Custard, 209
  Blood Orange Filling (v), 211
  Blueberry Filling, 212
  Chocolate Fudge Filling, 215
  Cream Cheese Filling, 209
  Crisp Apple Filling, 212
  Fresh Cherry Filling, 211
  Italian Crème Filling, 208
  Lemon Cream Custard (v),
    213
  Lemon Zest Filling, 213
  Marshmallow Filling, 210
  Meyer Lemon Cream Custard
    (v), 213
  Meyer Lemon Curd, 213
  Peanut Butter Filling, 215
  Raspberry Filling (v), 214
  Strawberry Filling, 214
  Sunset Orange Filling, 211
  White Chocolate Macadamia
    Mousse Filling, 216

Flour, 10
Food processor, 6
Framboise-Glazed Donuts, 102
French Bites, 150
French Crullers, 187
Fresh Cherry Donuts, 40
Fresh Cherry Filling, 211
  Black Forest Donut Bars, 34
  Boules de Berlin Donuts (v),
    172
  Fresh Jelly Donuts (v), 22
  Potato Flour Donuts, 56
  Red Valentine Heart Donuts,
    135
Fresh Jelly Donuts, 22
Fresh Peach Pecan Donuts, 75
Fresh Strawberry and Cream
  Donuts, 76
Fresh Vanilla Bean Donuts, 42
Fritters, making, 25
  Anjou Pear Fritters, 24
  Caramel Apple Fritters, 176
  Mandarin Orange Donuts, 48
Fryers, 6

G

Glazes. See Icings
Green Tea Bites, 163
Green Tea Donuts, 103
Green Tea Glaze, 199
  Green Tea Bites, 163
  Green Tea Donuts, 103
  Spiced Chai Donuts (v), 111

H

Hand tools, 7
Hanukkah Sufganiyot Donuts,
  180
Holiday donuts, 119–140
Honey Bran–Glazed Donuts, 104
Honey Glaze, 200
  Almond Apricot Donuts, 92
  Anjou Pear Fritters, 24
  Apple Cream Donuts, 93
  Apple Spice Donuts, 20
  Aztec Donut Bites, 142
  Bavarian Crème Bites, 144
  Blackberry Bites, 146
  Black Forest Donut Bars, 34
  Blueberry Raised Donuts, 36
  Boules de Berlin Donuts, 172
  Candied Fruit Donuts, 124
  Caramel Apple Fritters, 176
  Chocolate Donuts, 98

Chocolate Rum Cream
    Donuts, 99
Christmas Swirl Donuts, 120
Cinnamon Donut Sticks, 178
Cinnamon Honey Donuts, 38
Coconut Donuts, 72
Coconut Marshmallow
    Donuts, 100
Cranberry Orange Donuts, 140
Father's Day Tie Donuts, 122
Fresh Cherry Donuts, 40
Fresh Jelly Donuts, 22
Fresh Peach Pecan Donuts, 75
Fresh Strawberry and Cream
    Donuts, 76
Green Tea Bites, 163
Green Tea Donuts, 103
Honey Bran–Glazed Donuts,
    104
Honey-Glazed Bow Ties, 28
Island Bites, 26
Italian Crème–Filled Donuts,
    182
Key Lime Donuts, 44
Lemon Crème Donuts, 105
Lemon Poppy Seed Mini
    Donuts (v), 161
Light-as-Air Glazed Donuts, 46
Mandarin Orange Donuts, 48
Maple Cinnamon Donuts, 106
Mother's Day Crown Donuts,
    128
New Year's Champagne
    Donuts, 130
Orange Honey Donuts, 108
Orange Yeast Donuts, 14
Perfect Chocolate–Glazed
    Donuts (v), 52
Persian Walnut Donuts, 54
Pineapple Macadamia Nut
    Donuts, 109
Potato Flour Donuts, 56
Pretzel Twist Donuts, 58
Sour Cream Blackberry
    Donuts, 112
Spiced Chai Donuts (v), 111
Strawberry Cream Bites, 166
Strawberry Donuts, 113
Strawberry Rose Donuts, 138
Twisted Praline Pecan New
    Orleans Donuts, 30
Vanilla Bean Donuts, 116
White Chocolate Crème
    Donuts, 117

I

Icings. See also Sugar toppings
    Belgian Chocolate Ganache
        Glaze, 197
    Bittersweet Glaze, 197
    Brown Butter Glaze, 198
    Cherry Glaze, 198
    Dulce de Leche Glaze, 199
    Green Tea Glaze, 199
    Honey Glaze, 200
    Lemon Zest Glaze, 200
    Maple Glaze, 201
    Milk Chocolate Glaze, 201
    Mocha Glaze, 202
    Orange Glaze, 202
    Pineapple Topping, 196
    Raspberry Glaze, 203
    Rum Glaze, 203
    Simple Sugar Glaze, 205
    Strawberry Glaze (v), 203
    Sunset Orange Glaze, 204
    Truffle Fudge Icing, 196
Injected donuts. See Filled donuts
Island Bites, 26
Italian Crème Filling, 208
    Italian Crème–Filled Donuts,
        182

K

Key Lime Donuts, 44

L

Lavender Sugar Dust, 206
    Blueberry Bites, 160
    Blueberry Raised Donuts, 36
    Lemon Crème Donuts, 105
    White Chocolate Crème
        Donuts, 117
Lemons
    Citrus Donut Bites, 161
    Citrus Sugar, 205
    Lemon Cream Custard (v),
        213
    Lemon Crème Bars, 78
    Lemon Crème Donuts, 105
    Lemon Mist Donuts, 18
    Lemon Poppy Seed Mini
        Donuts (v), 161
    Lemon Zest Filling, 213
    Lemon Zest Glaze, 200
    Meyer Lemon Cream Custard
        (v), 213
    Meyer Lemon Curd, 213
    Sunset Orange Filling, 211

Lemon Zest Filling, 213
    Boules de Berlin Donuts (v),
        172
    Fresh Jelly Donuts (v), 22
    Lemon Crème Bars, 78
    Lemon Mist Donuts, 18
    Potato Flour Donuts, 56
Lemon Zest Glaze, 200
    Citrus Donut Bites, 161
    Coconut Donuts, 72
    Lemon Crème Bars, 78
    Lemon Poppy Seed Mini
        Donuts (v), 161
    Pistachio Bites, 156
Light-as-Air Glazed Donuts, 46
Limes
    Citrus Sugar, 205
    Key Lime Donuts, 44
    White Chocolate Key Lime
        Donuts (v), 117

M

Macadamia nuts
    Island Bites, 26
    Pineapple Macadamia Nut
        Donuts, 109
    White Chocolate Crème
        Donuts, 117
    White Chocolate Macadamia
        Mousse Filling, 216
Mandarin Orange Donuts, 48
Maple Bacon Bars, 184
Maple Bars, 60
Maple Cinnamon Donuts, 106
Maple Glaze, 201
    Applesauce Donuts, 62
    Baked Maple Mini Donuts,
        159
    Baked Whole Wheat Pecan
        Donuts, 118
    Blackberry Bites, 146
    Delicate Dainty Donut Bites,
        148
    Father's Day Tie Donuts, 122
    French Bites, 150
    Maple Bacon Bars, 184
    Maple Bars, 60
    Maple Cinnamon Donuts,
        106
    Orange Yeast Donuts, 14
    Pumpkin Bars, 84
    Pumpkin Nutmeg Spice
        Donuts, 83
    Rum Raisin Donuts, 88

Maple Glaze (*continued*)
  Thanksgiving Maple Donuts, 132
  Whole Wheat Pecan Donuts, 74
Maple syrup
  Baked Maple Mini Donuts, 159
  Maple Bacon Bars, 184
  Maple Bars, 60
  Maple Cinnamon Donuts, 106
  Maple Glaze, 201
  Thanksgiving Maple Donuts, 132
Marshmallow Filling, 210
  Campfire S'More Donuts, 174
  Coconut Marshmallow Donuts, 100
Meyer Lemon Cream Custard (v), 213
Meyer Lemon Curd, 213
Milk Chocolate Glaze, 201
  Aztec Donut Bites, 142
  Blackberry Bites, 146
  Blackout Donuts, 64
  Chocolate Cake Donuts, 70
  Chocolate Donut Holes, 154
  Chocolate Donuts, 98
  Chocolate Rum Cream Donuts, 99
  Dark Devil's Food Donuts, 90
  Double Chocolate Raspberry Donuts, 101
  Father's Day Tie Donuts, 122
  French Crullers, 187
  Fresh Vanilla Bean Donuts, 42
  Mini Pumpkin Donuts, 164
  Oat Berry Mini Donuts, 165
  Orange Donuts, 107
  Orange Yeast Donuts, 14
  Peanut Chocolate Cake Donuts, 80
  Peppermint Chocolate Squares, 136
  Perfect Chocolate–Glazed Donuts, 52
  Red Devil Donuts, 110
  Red Valentine Heart Donuts, 135
  Triple Chocolate Bites, 152
Milk, 9
Mini Pumpkin Donuts, 164
Minty Chocolate Donut Bars, 126

Mocha Glaze, 202
  Aztec Donut Bites, 142
  Blackout Donuts, 64
  Chocolate Cake Donuts, 70
  Chocolate Donut Holes, 154
  Chocolate Donuts, 98
  Coffee Bites, 155
  Dark Devil's Food Donuts, 90
  Espresso Buttermilk Bars, 82
  Mocha Raised Donuts, 50
  Peanut Chocolate Cake Donuts, 80
  Peppermint Chocolate Squares, 136
  Perfect Chocolate–Glazed Donuts (v), 52
  Red Valentine Heart Donuts, 135
  Triple Chocolate Bites, 152
Mother's Day Crown Donuts, 128

N
New Orleans Beignets, 188
New Year's Champagne Donuts, 130
Nuts, 11. See also individual varieties

O
Oats
  Baked Maple Mini Donuts, 159
  Oat Berry Mini Donuts, 165
  Pineapple Macadamia Nut Donuts, 109
Oils, 10
One-bite donuts
  All Spiced-Up Bites, 158
  Aztec Donut Bites, 142
  Baked Maple Mini Donuts, 159
  Bavarian Crème Bites, 144
  Blackberry Bites, 146
  Blueberry Bites, 160
  Chocolate Donut Holes, 154
  Citrus Donut Bites, 161
  Coffee Bites, 155
  Cranberry Almond Donut Bites, 162
  Delicate Dainty Donut Bites, 148
  French Bites, 150
  Green Tea Bites, 163
  Island Bites, 26

Lemon Poppy Seed Mini Donuts (v), 161
Mini Pumpkin Donuts, 164
Oat Berry Mini Donuts, 165
Pistachio Bites, 156
Spicy Donuts Balls, 157
Strawberry Cream Bites, 166
Triple Chocolate Bites, 152
Oranges
  Blood Orange Filling (v), 211
  Citrus Donut Bites, 161
  Citrus Sugar, 205
  Mandarin Orange Donuts, 48
  Orange Donuts, 107
  Orange Glaze, 202
  Orange Honey Donuts, 108
  Orange Yeast Donuts, 14
  Sunset Orange Filling, 211
  Sunset Orange Glaze, 204

P
Pastry bags, 8
Pastry tips, 8
Peaches
  Fresh Peach Pecan Donuts, 75
Peanut Butter Filling, 215
  Elvis Memphis Donuts, 194
Peanuts
  Chocolate Donuts, 98
  Peanut Chocolate Cake Donuts, 80
  Roasted Peanut Donuts, 115
Pears
  Anjou Pear Fritters, 24
Pecans
  Baked Whole Wheat Pecan Donuts, 118
  Banana Bran Donuts, 94
  Banana Pecan Donuts, 95
  Cinnamon Honey Donuts (v), 38
  Fresh Peach Pecan Donuts, 75
  Pretzel Twist Donuts (v), 58
  Rum-Glazed Donuts, 192
  Twisted Praline Pecan New Orleans Donuts, 30
  Whole Wheat Pecan Donuts, 74
Peppermint Chocolate Squares, 136
Perfect Chocolate–Glazed Donuts, 52
Persian Walnut Donuts, 54
Piña Colada Donuts, 190

Pineapples
  Piña Colada Donuts, 190
  Pineapple Macadamia Nut
    Donuts, 109
  Pineapple Topping, 196
Pistachio Bites, 156
Potato Flour Donuts, 56
Pretzel Twist Donuts, 58
Pumpkin
  Mini Pumpkin Donuts, 164
  Pumpkin Bars, 84
  Pumpkin Nutmeg Spice
    Donuts, 83

R

Raised donuts, making, 16
  Anjou Pear Fritters, 24
  Aztec Donut Bites, 142
  Banana Crème Donuts, 168
  Bavarian Crème Bites, 144
  Blackberry Bites, 146
  Black Forest Donut Bars, 34
  Blueberry Raised Donuts, 36
  Boston Cream Donuts, 170
  Boules de Berlin Donuts, 172
  Campfire S'More Donuts, 174
  Candied Fruit Donuts, 124
  Caramel Apple Fritters, 176
  Christmas Swirl Donuts, 120
  Cinnamon Donut Sticks, 178
  Cinnamon Honey Donuts, 38
  Delicate Dainty Donut Bites,
    148
  Father's Day Tie Donuts, 122
  French Bites, 150
  Fresh Cherry Donuts, 40
  Fresh Jelly Donuts, 22
  Fresh Vanilla Bean Donuts, 42
  Hanukkah Sufganiyot Donuts,
    180
  Honey-Glazed Bow Ties, 28
  Italian Crème–Filled Donuts,
    182
  Key Lime Donuts, 44
  Light-as-Air Glazed Donuts,
    46
  Mandarin Orange Donuts, 48
  Maple Bacon Bars, 184
  Maple Bars, 60
  Minty Chocolate Donut Bars,
    126
  Mocha Raised Donuts, 50
  Mother's Day Crown Donuts,
    128

New Orleans Beignets, 188
New Year's Champagne
  Donuts, 130
Orange Yeast Donuts, 14
Perfect Chocolate–Glazed
  Donuts, 52
Persian Walnut Donuts, 54
Potato Flour Donuts, 56
Pretzel Twist Donuts, 58
Thanksgiving Maple Donuts,
  132
Triple Chocolate Bites, 152
Raspberries
  Double Chocolate Raspberry
    Donuts, 101
  Framboise-Glazed Donuts, 102
  Raspberry Filling (v), 214
  Raspberry Glaze, 203
Raspberry Filling (v), 214
  Boules de Berlin Donuts, 172
  Fresh Jelly Donuts, 22
  Hanukkah Sufganiyot Donuts,
    180
  Potato Flour Donuts, 56
  Red Valentine Heart Donuts,
    135
Raspberry Glaze, 203
  Candied Ginger Donut Stars,
    67
  Delicate Dainty Donut Bites,
    148
  Framboise-Glazed Donuts, 102
  French Bites, 150
Red Devil Donuts, 110
Red Valentine Heart Donuts, 135
Red Velvet Chip Donut Bars, 86
Roasted Peanut Donuts, 115
Rose Petal Dust, 206
  Blackberry Bites, 146
  Blueberry Bites, 160
  Cake Sticks, 66
  Cherry Blossom Donuts, 97
  Fresh Strawberry and Cream
    Donuts, 76
  Lemon Crème Donuts, 105
  Strawberry Cream Bites, 166
  Strawberry Rose Donuts, 138
  White Chocolate Crème
    Donuts, 117
Rum
  Rum Glaze, 203
  Rum-Glazed Donuts, 192
  Rum Raisin Donuts, 88
  Truffle Fudge Icing, 196

Simple Spice Donuts, 111
Simple Sugar Glaze, 205
  Almond Apricot Donuts, 92
  Anjou Pear Fritters, 24
  Apple Cream Donuts, 93
  Apple Spice Donuts, 20
  Baked Maple Mini Donuts,
    159
  Baked Whole Wheat Pecan
    Donuts, 118
  Banana Bran Donuts, 94
  Banana Pecan Donuts, 95
  Bavarian Crème Bites, 144
  Blueberry Bites, 160
  Blueberry Donuts, 96
  Campfire S'More Donuts, 174
  Candied Fruit Donuts, 124
  Candied Ginger Donut Stars,
    67
  Caramel Apple Fritters, 176
  Cherry Blossom Donuts, 97
  Citrus Donut Bites, 161
  Cranberry Almond Donut
    Bites, 162
  Cranberry Orange Donuts,
    140
  Elvis Memphis Donuts, 194
  Framboise-Glazed Donuts,
    102
  French Crullers, 187
  Fresh Cherry Donuts, 40
  Fresh Peach Pecan Donuts, 75
  Green Tea Bites, 163
  Green Tea Donuts, 103
  Hanukkah Sufganiyot Donuts,
    180
  Italian Crème–Filled Donuts,
    182
  Lemon Crème Donuts, 105
  Lemon Poppy Seed Mini
    Donuts (v), 161
  Minty Chocolate Donut Bars,
    126
  Mother's Day Crown Donuts,
    128
  New Year's Champagne
    Donuts, 130
  Persian Walnut Donuts, 54
  Pineapple Macadamia Nut
    Donuts, 109
  Pistachio Bites, 156
  Sour Cream Blackberry
    Donuts, 112
  Spiced Chai Donuts (v), 111

Simple Sugar Glaze (*continued*)
 Strawberry Donuts, 113
 White Chocolate Crème
  Donuts, 117
 White Chocolate Key Lime
  Donuts (v), 117

S
Slotted spatula, 8
Sour Cream Blackberry Donuts,
 112
Specialty donuts, 167–194
Spiced Chai Donuts (v), 111
Spices, 12
Spicy Donuts Balls, 157
Stand mixer, 6
Strawberries
 Fresh Strawberry and Cream
  Donuts, 76
 Strawberry Cream Bites, 166
 Strawberry Donuts, 113
 Strawberry Filling, 214
 Strawberry Glaze (v), 203
 Strawberry Rose Donuts, 138
Strawberry Filling, 214
 Boules de Berlin Donuts (v),
  172
 Fresh Jelly Donuts (v), 22
 Fresh Strawberry and Cream
  Donuts, 76
 Potato Flour Donuts, 56
 Red Valentine Heart Donuts,
  135
 Strawberry Donuts, 113
Strawberry Glaze (v), 203
 Delicate Dainty Donut Bites,
  148
 French Bites, 150
 Fresh Strawberry and Cream
  Donuts, 76

Oat Berry Mini Donuts, 165
Strawberry Cream Bites, 166
Strawberry Donuts, 113
Strawberry Rose Donuts, 138
Vanilla Bean Donuts, 116
Sugars, 10
Sugar toppings
 Autumn Spiced Sugar, 204
 Citrus Sugar, 205
 Lavender Sugar Dust, 206
 Rose Petal Dust, 206
Sunset Orange Filling, 211
 Orange Honey Donuts, 108
 Tangerine Donuts, 114
Sunset Orange Glaze, 204
 Blackberry Bites, 146
 Father's Day Tie Donuts, 122
 Key Lime Donuts, 44
 Light-as-Air Glazed Donuts
  (v), 46
 Mandarin Orange Donuts, 48
 Mother's Day Crown Donuts,
  128
 Orange Honey Donuts, 108
 Orange Yeast Donuts, 14
 Tangerine Donuts, 114
Sweetened condensed milk, 9

T
Tangerine Donuts, 114
Tea
 Green Tea Bites, 163
 Green Tea Donuts, 103
 Green Tea Glaze, 199
 Spiced Chai Donuts (v), 111
Thanksgiving Maple Donuts,
 132
Thermometers, 8
Toppings. See Icings
Triple Chocolate Bites, 152

Truffle Fudge Icing, 196
 Aztec Donut Bites, 142
 Blackout Donuts, 64
 Chocolate Cake Donuts, 70
 Chocolate Donut Holes, 154
 Dark Devil's Food Donuts,
  90
 Double Chocolate Raspberry
  Donuts, 101
 Fresh Vanilla Bean Donuts,
  42
 Peanut Chocolate Cake
  Donuts, 80
 Peppermint Chocolate
  Squares, 136
 Perfect Chocolate–Glazed
  Donuts (v), 52
 Red Valentine Heart Donuts,
  135
Twisted Praline Pecan New
 Orleans Donuts, 30
Twists, making, 31

V
Vanilla Bean Donuts, 116

W
Walnuts
 Persian Walnut Donuts, 54
White Chocolate Crème Donuts,
 117
White Chocolate Key Lime
 Donuts (v), 117
White Chocolate Macadamia
 Mousse Filling, 216
 Island Bites, 26
 Piña Colada Donuts, 190
Whole Wheat Pecan Donuts,
 74
Wooden chopsticks, 8

Geary, George
    150 best donut recipes : fried or baked / George Geary.

Includes index.
ISBN 978-0-7788-0411-6

    1. Doughnuts. 2. Cookbooks. I. Title. II. Title: One hundred fifty best donut recipes.

TX770.D67G43 2012   641.86'53   C2012-902797-9